A STUDY OF
HOUSEHOLD
SPIRITS
of Eastern Europe

RONESA AVEELA

BENDIDEIA
PUBLISHING

Cover Design by Nelinda, www.nelindaart.com.
Cover Art by Anna Błaszczyk (Evelinea Erato). © Bendideia Publishing.
Interior layout design by Nicole Lavoie, www.JustSayingDezigns.com.
Vecna font is used in the book's title. It is available for commercial use from Pixel Sagas at www.pixelsagas.com.

Contents

Foreword

This series about spirits and creatures from Eastern Europe developed from an idea about a future book in the *Dragon Village* series. In the first story, "Unborn Hero," a character possesses a book called *Lamia's Bible*, which holds the secrets of all the mythical creatures in Zmeykovo (Dragon Village). I wondered what those secrets might be. If I owned a magical book, I'd want to know the weak spots in my adversary's character. How could I defeat each creature? How could I control them? I began my research with Kikimora and discovered a wealth of information—too much to include in a magical tome, but too much to discard as well. Thus, this book about household spirits begged to be written.

My original intent was for the book to contain beings that appear only in Bulgarian folklore—whether from Thracian, Slavic, or Proto-Bulgarian origins—since the focus of my work to date has dealt with Bulgaria. But again, as I extended my research beyond Kikimora, many of the Slavic spirits I came across were not popular in Bulgaria, but they add so much color to the world of Eastern Europe that to exclude them would have been a loss to the reader.

The stories and other information from across Eastern Europe vary from country to country, and even from region to region. I have compiled that information into a composite whole to paint a picture of each spirit. There are so many more spirits, too many to include in this book. What I have included are some of the most popular, plus a few that may be obscure.

Many, if not all, of the beliefs and rituals about these spirits originate from pagan times. When Christianity dominated the region, "double-belief" became popular—a mixture of Christian-orthodox and pagan belief systems. The old gods may have vanished or become insignificant, often being replaced with the saints. However, the lesser divinities, including the spirits, remained. Christianity did not "replace" the old beliefs; it merely added to them. Peasants viewed the new religious beliefs relevant for their life after death, but to survive in this life, they believed they needed the protection of the spirits who lurked everywhere.

This book is meant to be fun, to inform you about these fascinating spirits, to give you a glimpse into a culture you may be unfamiliar with. You'll "experience" the spirits through more than words. Where I could, I've included various artistic interpretations of the spirits: in art, music, and video, as well as in literature, both old and new. I've also included additional material to enhance your understanding of the people and their culture.

As you read this book, imagine you live in a rural area, filled with the unknown. You make your living from the land, where nature is sacred. She can be harsh or she can provide you with plenty. Understand that all of these beliefs and rituals have not completely faded from existence. You can still find places where these spirits are a part of people's lives. Who's to say they're wrong? I certainly won't.

Whether you believe or not, it's an enlightening journey discovering these spirits who have existed at least on the pages of stories and have spread from one generation to the next by word of mouth. I hope it will be a journey you'll enjoy and remember.

Kikimora. Illustration by Anna Błaszczyk (Evelinea Erato). © Bendideia Publishing.

Kikimora (Кикимора)

From a Kikimora don't expect a shirt.

Kikimora (singular); **Kikimori** or **Kikimory** (plural)

Other names: kikamora, kikimara, shishimora, shishimara, mara, suceka, gizmo, shishiga,[1] domnitza,[2] domania, domovikha,[3] domikha, domavikha, domavichka.[4]

Slang: Refers to an ugly, ill-tempered woman who wears shabby clothing. She's forever grumbling and making her husband's life (and that of other men) unbearable.[5] Other women stamped with a negative connotation of this name:
- Those with funny, ridiculous, sloppy, or untidy appearances.
- The unsociable or wicked.
- Cheaters and deceivers.
- Those who are homely.
- Beggars.

Being called a Kikimora can also be positive, as women who diligently work with yarn are seen as the industrious Kikimora who never slows down.

Do you hear creaking, scratching sounds coming from the walls and floors, or the clatter of pots at night? Are objects not where you placed them the day before? Has yarn become tangled and a garment's stitches pulled out? All these may be signs a Kikimora lives in your house. This female spirit causes havoc from dusk until dawn. As daylight approaches, she slips away—afraid of the light—and becomes invisible, hiding in crevices behind a hearth or stove, or in the cellar or attic, or perhaps even under floorboards.

The Kikimora prefers to live in an occupied residence, although she also has been known to dwell in abandoned buildings, taverns, bathhouses, threshing floors, hen houses, and stables. You're certain to find her inhabiting "unclean" or "cursed" places such as a building set by a crossroads or fork or near a cemetery, in a house that has burned, or one where a person committed suicide.

Stand back, Superman. A Kikimora has some super powers of her own: she can become invisible, run fast, and see long distances. She's restless, constantly on the move and jumping around making noises. You'll find that she's most active spinning during times people are forbidden to spin: midnight, Fridays, Christmas Eve, and other special occasions.

Variations of the Spirit

In olden days, the Kikimora predominantly occupied homes, and this chapter will concentrate on her in this capacity. Variations of the Kikimora living in fields, forests (Leschikha), or swamps (Bolotnik) are more prevalent today, and they deserve a brief mention here.

Etymology

Various sources suggest different possible origins for the word Kikimora:

- It may have come from an old Finnish word *kikke mörkö* (F., Lucia) or a Finn-Urgic word *kikka-murt* ("scarecrow"; literally "bag-made person") (Wikipedia, "Kikimora").
- It could come from a phrase meaning "malicious spirit of Mara" (Slavic Folklore and World Dreaming).
- *Mora* has been connected to the *mare* part of nightmare (Wikipedia, "Kikimora"). Many sources, however, say that Mora is a different creature, that the Kikimora is not the one who causes nightmares. (See more about this topic later in this chapter.)
- *Mora* is also a Slavic word connected with the souls of the dead (Georgievtrifon).
- *Mora* has a connection with morgue and moribund, and the spirit has a relationship with other creatures that personify disease or death (Ivanichka, 208).
- Others have suggested the word may have originated from the French word *cauchemar* for "nightmare" (Georgievtrifon). This may be derived from *Shishimora*, an alternate Russian word for a Kikimora, where *shish* is a demon (Ralston, 133).
- Another suggestion is that the word is from the Balto-Slavic *kik* (*kyk*, *kuk*) for "crookedness" or "hunchback," and the Slavic *mor* for "death" (Planeta.by).
- Kikimora may come from an Old Ruthenian (term used in Western Europe for the ancestors of modern Eastern Slavic people) word, *kykati*, which means "howl" (Kamoń).
- Similarly, another source says a Kikimora could be "a *mara* who cries (*kikaet*, *kichet*, *kychet*)"—an onomatopoeic word that describes the call of a bird—thus making the name related to the sound she makes, rather than her appearance (Secunda, 353).
- The Kikimora entry on the Russian Wikipedia lists several other variations of the name and sources of origin (Russian Wikipedia, "Кикимора").

Stories advise you to avoid walking in a pea field in the summer or you may meet a Kikimora carrying a pan large enough to fry you on—because that is her intent if she catches you. You should skirt the woods as well. It's there that the Kikimora Leschikha, along with her partner-in-crime Leshy, carries unsuspecting or lost people off into the forest—never to be seen again. And if you happen to stroll along a marshy area, beware of the Kikimora often called a Bolotnik, a creature who frightens passersby and kidnaps children. This spirit wraps herself in moss like a fur coat and weaves forest grass through her hair instead of ribbons. If she happens to feel lonely and enters your home, she'll leave a trail of wet footprints wherever she's wandered during the night.

The Kikimora has been associated with the witch Baba Yaga, who also has a link to chickens. In addition, she's been credited with being the mother or sister of a Rusalka (mermaid), the "hostess" for a Vodyanoy or Vodnik (water creatures), and having a connection with marsh witches, werewolf shifters, spirits causing hysteria and fever, and the personification of various diseases. She travels from one place to another in folklore, much more than other spirits and creatures who stay in their designated area.

Origins

A Kikimora can be created in some rather gruesome ways.

- The death of an "unholy" child: a stillborn, miscarried, or aborted infant, or one who dies shortly after birth before it has been baptized.
- A child who's suffered a "wrongful" death, such as one who was murdered.
- After the death of a child with some sort of abnormality, such as no arms or legs.
- When a dead child has been buried beneath a home's foundation (which was a common practice).
- At the gravesite of a person who committed suicide.
- A child is cursed by his/her parents. This allows evil spirits to snatch the child from the home. This can occur even when the child is within its mother's womb. Be advised not to utter the words, "The old devil fetch thee!" to your children, for that master of deceit will come immediately and take your offspring away and raise them as his own. When these children become adults, they are invisible—neither human nor devils, but they fear the cross and holy water.
- A child kidnapped by a Kikimora can become one herself. When the spirit steals a child, she leaves something in return: the Kikimora's own offspring, an enchanted object, or even a mossy log.

Kikimora in the Swamp.
By Денисов, Василий Иванович [Public domain], via Wikimedia Commons.
Published in the U.S. before 1923 and public domain in the U.S.

- A woman who dies suddenly, especially if it occurs during labor.
- An elderly female ancestor whose soul has not left this world.
- A doll created by a sorcerer and hidden somewhere in the house can turn into a Kikimora. (See another explanation of this doll later in this chapter.)
- If a black cat jumps over the grave of someone recently deceased, the person will turn into a Kikimora or vampire.
- The child of a human and serpent-like evil spirit.

In some stories, the sire of a Kikimora flies through the air, emitting sparks on the roof, then enters the house through the chimney. He appears to a grieving woman as the illusion of her lost love.

In other stories, he leaves enchanted gifts—such as combs, ribbons, and jewelry—along the road for girls who have lost their innocence before marriage. Once they bring the objects into their home, the evil spirit has free entry. In the morning, after the woman's treacherous lover has left, the "gifts" turn to sand, ash, or manure.

If the girl doesn't die from the encounter with the evil spirit, her pregnancy can last up to three years. Any child that survives birth is born black, has hoofs, is hunchbacked and hairy, and has pointed features and small eyes. It becomes a blessing to the mother when the evil spirit sprints his offspring away to become a new Kikimora.

In other situations, parents may fear that if their child behaves differently, people may call him a child of a Kikimora as is the case in the example below:

Did you know?

A Kikimora sings with her daughter, a Rusalka (mermaid), their magical music luring solitary travelers into a watery death (Russian Wikipedia, "Кикимора").

Nor ever think, I earnestly entreat,
Of burdening childhood's years with bookish lore.
Already do our neighbours think Ivan
A startling prodigy of infant-wit;
But were he seen with manuscript in hand,
With one accord they would pronounce the boy
Addicted to the necromantic art,
Or view him else as kikimora wild.[6]

As the above story continued, the parents decided to avoid having their child learn to read at such a young age.

Appearance

Descriptions of a Kikimora have run the gamut—from tall to short, young to old, female to male or even animal—although mostly she's an ugly, hunchbacked hag with straggly, long hair covered by a kerchief—a tradition among married Slavic women. The Kikimora's face may be somewhat human, but deformed.

On occasion she appears as a beautiful, young temptress with a long braid, or even with her hair flowing freely and uncovered in the way of unmarried women. She might be barefoot and naked or dressed in a simple white, red, or black shirt, without the usual embroidered embellishments of the Slavic people.

Depending on how the house spirit came into existence, she may also resemble a family member's ancestor: mother, grandmother, or great-grandmother.

The most common description, however, portrays her as a petite—verging on scrawny—unkempt woman wearing dirty, ragged clothing. Her body is covered with sparse, short feathers or wool. She is so thin she fears going outside in bad weather, in case the wind blows her away. She has a thimble-sized head; goat horns and a tail; bright, bulging eyes; a long, thin nose or a beak; clawed or crooked hairy hands with bony fingers; long arms; and short legs ending in chicken feet.

LURKING IN THE DARK

Think back to your childhood days. You're asleep in bed, but a noise downstairs wakes you. What could it be? Your parents have told you about creatures that come out at night to cause mischief—and even to steal children. Are they real? You creep out of bed and peek through a crack in the floor. There. Something moved in the darkness. Two creatures: Domovoi and Kikimora! The terrifying female looks up and catches your eye.

Hide, close your eyes, sleep!

If you can't see her, then she can't see you. You slip beneath the covers. Unknown to you, a hand reaches out…

Add spooky music and animated characters and you get "Domovoi and Kikimora," a short animation directed by Lily Goodchild and Nicola Everill, produced at Staffordshire University.

Watch the clip and feel the terror: https://vimeo.com/66619155.

Domovoi and Kikimora video.
https://vimeo.com/66619155. (Photo and video used with permission of the creators.)

Inspired by Slavic mythology. A film about scavenger spirits and the child who spies on them. Video and image copyright Lily Goodchild and Nicola Everill, Directors, "Domovoi and Kikimora," produced at Staffordshire University, May 21, 2013.

Getting to Know the Kikimora

While you sleep, the Kikimora slinks out of her hiding place with the intent to do mischief. She loves to sit at a spinning wheel all night. She may also occupy her time with weaving, needlework, or mending a shirt. Granted, if she attempts to work on any project you haven't hidden from her, you're likely to find the yarn lumpy and tangled, and the shirt stitches uneven. But on the bright side, despite her nightlong efforts, she normally makes little to no progress. To help prevent this disaster, Slavic women recite protection prayers when they've finished their domestic activities for the day.

Did you know?

Writing a curse on birch bark makes it stick to the first victim who passes a crossroad (Dynda, 70).

You'll have a better chance the spirit won't cause quite as much damage, however, if you keep a tidy house. She favors women who live traditional lives—cooking, child-rearing, household activities—and those who perform their work skillfully and graciously.

Your house spirit may even finish your chores (baking bread or washing dishes), take care of the children (rocking a sleeping infant or sending a child good dreams), and tend to your animals (feeding and grooming them). At times, the Kikimora will act as a guardian and save your family's home during a fire by driving away the flames with a handkerchief—and most likely a little magic. But she'll do these tasks only if you've left your home in a way that meets her approval.

An Unhappy Spirit

If your house is untidy, be forewarned, she's adverse to living in a messy home and is certain to let you know of her disapproval after you've tucked yourself under the sheets. You'll hear her moaning, whistling, or whining—the noises often sounding like the spinning wheel she loves so much. She'll stamp her feet, clang pots and pans, break dishes, and turn your food sour. Doors will open and slam shut as she runs from one room to the next, her feet sounding like scuttling cockroaches or mice. She'll turn tables and chairs upside down and scrape furniture across the floor, making the pieces bounce as if dancing—all in her pursuit to keep you from sleeping. If you smell smoke, she probably has set your kitchen towels on fire.

That's not all. If she can make it into the bedrooms, she'll mess up your sheets, tug on your earlobes, and pull out your hair while you're off in dreamland. Her preferred method to torture your children is tickling them until they scream. If you happen to be awake when she emerges from her

Did you know?

When a marsh Kikimora brews beer, fog rises over the river (Russian Wikipedia, "Кикимора").

hidey hole, she's likely to throw things at you: anything from shoes to bricks to coals.

Her antics when she's upset are not confined to the home. If you have animals, she gets pleasure out of tormenting them as well: she'll pluck a chicken's feathers and scare the fowl so they don't lay eggs; she'll shear a sheep's wool, ride horses to make them stampede, and cause the milk from goats and cows to go dry.

When you leave your bedroom in the morning, don't be surprised if you discover no mess at all. On the other hand, even if you see swarming spiders, scuttling rats, and hordes of bats, and your home appears filthier than you left it, these may be illusions she's created, tricks to make you leave her gifts so she'll set things right the next evening.

Kikimora. Illustration © Andy Paciorek. Used with permission of the artist.

Bearer of News

Besides being a prankster, a Kikimora acts as a guardian, using her psychic abilities to warn her family of impending disaster—not in word, but by her appearance, action, and behavior. If you see her sitting by the front entrance, someone from the household will be certain to receive unhappy news or suffer misfortune. Her crying and moaning may foreshadow the death of a family member.

Witnessing or hearing a Kikimora spinning is another sign someone is about to die. The wheel creaks and groans—quite like how her name spoken aloud sounds. Some people compare her to the Fates, who spin to control a person's destiny. It's no wonder, then, that spinning occupies her time, since from ancient times, the spinning wheel has been an instrument symbolic of fate. People say this is how the Kikimora creates magic she can use for evil purposes.

If you want to extract details about any misfortune from her, you have to wait until you hear her child crying. Throw a cloth on the floor, stove, or wherever the noise is coming from. The spirit will go crazy because she won't be able to find and comfort her child. She'll answer any question you ask, hoping you'll remove the cloth and let her go to her child.

Modes of Entry

Once the Kikimora is inside your home, she roams about at will. Your neighbors may even get a visit from her—although probably not on a windy day. Since she's so scrawny, she'll blow away.

Kikimora. Tale N. Manaseinoy. With drawings by T. Hippius. "As daughters, or as sisters, take me, good people."

By Гиппиус Татьяна Николаевна (1877-1957) (Журнал «Тропинка». 1909, №20) [Public domain], via Wikimedia Commons.

As described earlier, one of the ways a Kikimora can take up residence in your home is through the death of an infant or her mother. If your house happens to have been built upon a location that was considered "unclean"—such as near where a person who committed suicide has been buried—you may also find the spirit lurking in your residence.

Other ways exist as well for a Kikimora to enter your home. For one, you may unwittingly invite her in. She's a master of deceit, who pretends to be someone in need, such as a lost child. What compassionate person would turn away such a waif? She can also appear as animals, plants, or objects that you pick up and bring home.

Revenge also plays a role in how a Kikimora ends up in newly built homes or other buildings. If you're unhappy with the cost or quality of the work from the carpenters or the stove-maker you've hired,[7] think twice before you complain to them. They may take offense and have a sorcerer capture the spirit of a Kikimora and place it inside a *chudinka*,[8] a wooden or rag ceremonial doll that's sometimes soaked in blood. The builders will then hide the doll in a hard-to-find place—oftentimes under the ceiling beam, between logs at the front corner of the house, in the roof rafters or basement, beneath the stove, or in a woodpile. This type of Kikimora is usually quite aggressive toward people.

On the Dark Side

A Kikimora can cause suffocation, sleep paralysis, or nightmares—to the point where your affliction makes you ill and die, or gives you thoughts about suicide.

Most references attribute this nightmare stalking to a different creature called a Mora, Mara, or the goddess Marena. She is said to be the soul of a living person who leaves her body at night, or she can pass from a witch's lips in the form of a butterfly. You can tell it's her because she appears as a wisp of straw or hair, or even as a moth. She manifests in nightmares as a spirit who covers your eyes with mist, distorts your sense of reality, and pushes you toward dangerous places. Perhaps over time and across cultures, one creature evolved into two: Mara and Kikimora.

Jan Máchal describes her as follows:

Kikimora. Tale N. Manaseinoy. With drawings by T. Hippius. "Kikimora is running, she is running very thin, little and black."

By Гиппиус Татьяна Николаевна (1877-1957) (Журнал «Тропинка». 1909. №20) [Public domain], via Wikimedia Commons.

It is a general Slavic belief that souls may pass into a Mora, a living being, either man or woman, whose soul goes out of the body at night-time, leaving it as if dead. Sometimes two souls are believed to be in such a body, one of which leaves it when asleep; and a man may be a Mora from his birth, in which case he has bushy, black eyebrows, growing together above his nose. The Mora, assuming various shapes, approaches the dwellings of men at night and tries to suffocate them; she is either a piece of straw, or a white shadow, or a leather bag, or a white mouse, a cat, a snake, a white horse, etc. First she sends refreshing slumber to men and then, when they are asleep, she frightens them with terrible dreams, chokes them, and sucks their blood. For the most part she torments children, though she also throws herself upon animals, especially horses and cows, and even injures and withers trees, so that various means are employed to get rid of her.[9]

This invisible being brings you nightmares by sitting on your chest while you sleep, the weight crushing the air from your lungs, causing you to scream in your dreams. You may even experience a sensation of something sucking on your body like a vampire.

Upon waking from a nightmare, you may find a blue spot on your body where the spirit sat upon you. In the ways of the Slavic people, you can curse the creature who disrupted your sleep by saying, "The mora pressed me."

The household spirit appears to both sleeping men and women as a beautiful, young female. In the dreams of a man, she enflames his desire for her. While for a woman, she stirs up jealousies and suspicions of unfaithfulness. Both nightmares cause havoc in a couple's relationship.

The following tale about a Mora tells how she can shape-shift into an animal or a tuft of hair with the intent of tormenting her victim.

> Once a Mora so tormented a man that he left his home, took his white horse and rode away. But wherever he wandered the Mora followed after him. At last he stopped to pass the night in a certain house, the master of which heard him groaning terribly in his sleep, so he went to look at him. Then he saw that his guest was being suffocated by a long tuft of white hair which lay over his mouth. So he cut it in two with a pair of scissors. Next morning the white horse was found dead. The horse, the tuft of hair, and the nightmare, were all one.[10]

No More Nightmares

You have several options to protect yourself—and your children—from nightmares brought on by the spirit:

- Block the keyholes to bedroom doors by keeping a key in the opening or stuffing it with paper.
- If you suspect the spirit is already in your bedroom, avoid eye contact at all costs. The Kikimora may catch you unaware, so don't look at anything that has a keyhole: doors, dressers, chests, wardrobes, or cabinets. She may be lurking inside. Look out the window or turn your pillow toward where you think she is and make the sign of the cross on it.

MARA: DEATH AND REBIRTH

Mara has been associated with a seasonal rite of death in winter and rebirth in spring called "Mara and Lisanka," in which people seek blessings of fertility and protection from disease and hail. She was fashioned as a doll dressed in a local costume, or even dressed as a scarecrow. Her body is twisted, showing its connection with the old Slavic *lih* (bad spirit), as well as *liho* (trouble), represented in tales as a cross-eyed woman who brought misfortune and death.

The ritual called "Mara and Lisanka" is performed on a sunny Wednesday after Easter. As part of the ceremony, people take one yellow and one red slipper from three recent brides and wear the footwear around their head like a bridal wreath. They sing as they circle the village. At the end, they bathe Mara, the doll, in the river and wash their own faces. Boys grab the doll, which symbolizes a lazy girl, and toss it into the river while they sing:

> "Maro and Lisanko,
> will you come soon?"
> "Soon next year,
> on the empty Sunday" (Ivanichka, 209).

- Leave a broom upside down behind your bedroom door.
- Place a belt on top of your bedsheets.
- Recite a prayer or poem before you get into bed.
- Make the sign of the cross and pray over objects in your home so the Kikimora won't touch them.
- Wear a protection amulet made of Purple Loosestrife around your neck or wrist. Legends say this plant grew from the tears the Virgin Mary shed at the crucifixion of Christ. It's best if you gather the plant on the Russian holiday of Ivan Kupala, celebrated on June 24 (July 7 in the Julian calendar). Or you could try charms made with white onions or black beads.
- Carry a Bible with you.
- If you feel the spirit sitting on you at night, try moving the big toe of your right leg to free yourself of her weight.

Preventive Maintenance

If a Kikimora hasn't already invaded your home, the surest way to prevent her from taking up residence is to keep keys or paper in the keyholes of any doors coming into the house in the same manner that you keep her out of your bedroom. Another option is to bury a silver object near entryways or sprinkle salt around the outside of the doorway. You can also make crosses with chalk, paint, or coal in each corner of your house, by faucets, and by the well to keep her out.

Remember, she's a spirit: she's able to sneak through the smallest gaps and windows, so even these tactics may not be enough. But don't worry, even though she'll be difficult to get rid of, it's not impossible. More complex rituals exist that you can try.

Getting Rid of a Kikimora

You can't kill the spirit since she already belongs to someone who died, although some people claim if you throw a cross on her, she'll cease to exist. Another method to try to get rid of her is by attaching camel wool onto the arch of the kitchen stove using a type of resin.

If the spirit originates from a cursed child, you can cut a cross on the top of her head. This will turn her back into a human—albeit one who now has a disability: muteness, stammering, poor memory, or dementia. That's a terrible thing to do to a child you only *think* is a Kikimora.

If none of those methods work, it's likely going to take someone knowledgeable in how to expel demons to remove the Kikimora—especially if an enemy left a *chudinka* doll in your house. You'll have to go back to the sorcerer who created the doll

Kikimora. Figure by Ivan Bilibin, 1934.
[Public domain], via Wikimedia Commons.

11

to help you find it. If that fails, locating the offending doll requires ripping apart your house. The owner must hack away at the bottommost boards and say, "Here's to you, and that's for that."[11] After you've found the doll, you'll have to burn it to rid your home of the spirit.

Good luck with any of those options.

A better way—if you can wait—is to attempt this yourself on Gerasim Grachevnik, March 17 (or March 4 in the Julian calendar). Although ordering the Kikimora out of your home won't work most days, it will on this holiday since the spirit is more complacent and obedient.

What better day to attempt to remove evil influences than on a saint's day? It's a good occasion to literally sweep her out of your house—just in time for spring cleaning. Get your broom and swish away at the hearth, the corners of all rooms, the basement, the attic—anywhere the spirit may be hiding. Removing the dirt is not enough; you must also recite:

> Get out of here, Kikimora. Get away quickly from my home, or I will chase you with iron bars; I will set you on fire with fiery fire; I will pour black pitch on you. My words are strong and cast from now up to a century![12]

When you've finished, take the dirt and debris far from your home and burn it.

If you successfully remove the Kikimora, she'll be unable to return as long as rooks have settled in your yard—at least until autumn when the birds migrate. Why rooks? Because they're associated with the Russian holiday Gerasim Grachevnik, which, much like the Bulgarian holiday Blagovets (March 25), is a day to welcome spring. While in Bulgaria, people look for the return of the cuckoo, in Russia, it's the rook appearing on this day (*grak* is the Russian word for "rook"). Not only does the bird eat insects in your yard, it also keeps out evil spirits from both inside and outside of your home.

Appeasing the Kikimora

If you can't get rid of her, you can try to keep her happy—and hope she doesn't behave too badly. The following approaches may make this house spirit less confrontational:

- The easiest way to get along with a Kikimora has already been mentioned: keep your house clean and tidy! Nothing infuriates her more than mess and clutter. To rephrase a popular saying, "If Kikimora ain't happy, ain't nobody happy."
- The Kikimora is fond of ferns. If you wash your dishes, pots, and pans with water in which you've boiled ferns, she'll no longer damage the kitchenware.

You'll also want to try a few methods to protect your farm animals, if you have any.

- While a Kikimora likes ferns, juniper scares her. If you have chickens, hang juniper twigs above their coop. This will prevent the Kikimora from stealing eggs and tormenting the fowl.

KIKIMORA IN SONG

To get a taste of the creepiness of the Kikimora, listen to this modern music by KCHÖRTOO (links below). You'll feel yourself walking through the forest at night. The breeze chills you. Or is it the sound of a Kikimora spinning, spinning, spinning?

In his own words, Stephan Friedman talks about this recording.

> This album is dedicated to the lore of the Ural Mountains where I was born and raised. Mythology and folk tales play a large part in the life of this region. Ever since childhood I've been fascinated and greatly influenced by various tales and oddities. What drew me to Kikimora as a subject for the song is the mystery and complexity of the character of this creature. It is sorrowful, malevolent and fleeting. I wanted the song to sound both scary and melancholy. I used kantele, a traditional Finnish string instrument, to create the enchanting, fairytale quality of the melody.

Имра имра-и	Imra Imra-ee
Имра имра-у	Imra Imra-oo
Семеро ребят, семеро козлят	Seven little kids, seven little goats
Выжидают ночь	Waiting out the night
Семеро волчат по углам скучат	Seven little wolfs griping at the corners
Да подруга-дочь	And a homegirl-daughter
Кто-то стелется, селится под окном	Someone is creeping, settling under the window
Вьется, ужится, кружится веретеном	Winding, snaking, spinning like a spindle
Имра имра-и	Imra Imra-ee
Имра имра-у	Imra Imra-oo
Волк луну сожрал, черт в углу насрал	The wolf devoured the moon, the devil shat in the corner
Свиньи – вороны	Pigs – ravens
Козья шерсть кругом, бес под потолком	Goat wool all around, demon under the ceiling
Стоны – стороны	Moans – sides
Кто-то стелется, селится под окном	Someone is creeping, settling under the window
Вьется, вертится, сердится веретеном	Winding, fidgeting, sulking like a spindle
В проливной глуши хоть колом теши	In the teeming backwoods even if you're pigheaded
Не накрестишься	Crossing yourself won't help
Не видать души, все вокруг шиши	Can't see a soul, fiends are all around
Челобесища	Human-demon-ity

Used with permission of the copyright owner. Music and lyrics by Stephan Samokhin.
© 2018 Valkoinen Pöllö Studios / ℗ 2010 - 2018 Valkoinen Pöllö Studios / All rights reserved.

Available from: **Bandcamp**: https://kchortoo.bandcamp.com/track/kikimora
Soundcloud: https://soundcloud.com/kchortoo/kikimora
YouTube: https://youtu.be/nH0wypOoh5Q
iTunes: https://itunes.apple.com/album/id1434843510
Spotify: https://open.spotify.com/album/5v4bpxngJfcWAPjFG43qdb
Deezer: https://www.deezer.com/us/album/72029182

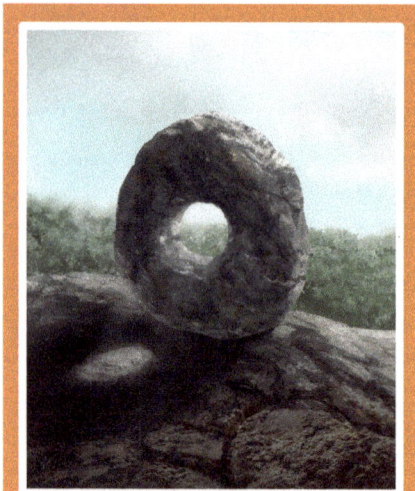

Kurinyi Bog or Chicken God.
Illustration by Dmitry Yakhovsky.
© Bendideia Publishing.

- If juniper isn't available, you can tie the neck of a broken jar over the place where the chickens roost or on barn doors.
- You can also call on the protection of the Kurinyi Bog or "chicken god," a spirit living inside a special stone. To do this, hang a black adder (a stone that has a natural hole bored all the way through it) by a string inside the chicken coop. This amulet has also been called "a one-eyed kikimora."[13] For best results, do this on January 1 (January 14 in the Julian calendar), which is Silvestrov Day, or Sylvester's Day. While cleaning out the coop, it's a good idea to also clear out any other lurking evil spirits with incense or the smoke from burning embers.

Fact or Fiction?

This may all sound like the workings of a fanciful mind, but people in the past and still today believe that strange happenings are the result of spirits. A few stories follow.

Early Accounts

The first historical mention of a Kikimora was in 1635 where she was described as an "unclean spirit who 'made many dirty tricks' in the house, destroyed horses and frightened away the cow herd." Another reference occurs in old Russian literature around the 1640s to 1650s:

> While we were coming from this city [Kostroma], the road that goes to Moscow, suddenly we met a certain demon in a woman's appearance, simply hairless and without a belt. Its tail was sticking up to the sky, turning like a big circle, and all sorts of demonic dreams were cast.[14]

Earlier in this chapter, you learned that due to her spinning, the Kikimora is similar to the Fates of Greek mythology, but she may have links to an even older deity. Her association with spinning, wool, and protection of women and the home indicates she may have a connection with Mokosh, Slavic goddess of spinning, weaving, mothers, and unmarried girls.

Beware Stray Objects

The Kikimora has appeared in the news in more recent times as well. In 1977, a group of researchers visited a Russian village and recorded stories about a poltergeist type of being causing havoc.[15] The residents claimed it was a devil or Kikimora, whom one man's wife had unintentionally brought into her home. While down at the bathhouse, she found a lovely handkerchief, which she picked up and carried into her house. From that point onward, strange things happened in the village:

- People saw a young girl (or sometimes a woman) who wasn't from the village sitting in a shed and a bathhouse, combing her long, yellow, silky hair. No one, however, could recall specifics about her appearance.
- The spirit hurled items at people: felt boots, a stove door (which cut one man's forehead), a knife, mittens, and an axe (flat side aimed toward the man, not seriously harming him).

14

- People found items in places other than where they had left them: in particular, someone (the spirit presumably) had moved a barrel of frozen water from a house to a shed.
- Strange footsteps in households sometimes sounded like a bird, other times like boots.
- Villagers attempted to rid themselves of the spirit, first by calling on a priest. An "unnatural force" tossed the holy man's prayer books from the house. The police, too, found their possessions hidden after they pitched a tent near the house the Kikimora occupied.

For up to six years, strange phenomena occurred until one day, the owner's home was engulfed in a blue flame—only it wasn't on fire. When this "cold fire," as they called it, disappeared, so did the Kikimora.

The appearance of a blue flame has occurred among the Finno-Ugric people as well. Called the *ort*, or doppelganger soul, it's associated with the prediction of a person's impending death. A blue flame is said to flare up after the appearance of the *ort*.

Harmless Pranks

In another village, similar incidents occurred. They called the mischief-maker a *bubula*. The pranks it played were harmless:

- Moving furniture.
- Throwing dishes.
- Making a samovar filled with tea jump on the table.
- Causing rifles standing upright in a corner to "dance" by themselves.
- Tossing items on a stove onto the floor in an empty house.

A Kind Soul

Today, various groups of people take offense at bad reports circulating about the Kikimora. They say the creature is benevolent—and no more harmful than the Domovoi, the male house spirit whom many people encourage to inhabit their homes. In fact, they say the Kikimora assists those who dwell in the home she occupies, and shows them how to escape harm. She will even help you get rid of spirits that are even more bothersome than she is. They refute the belief that a person seeing the Kikimora spinning will die.

Kikimora in Literature

Kikimora is a popular subject in literature. The following are a couple works—one old and one new—where you can discover her.

- *Kikimora* ballet by Léonide Massine, first produced in 1916.
- An excerpt from the novel *Kikimora* by Emma Woodcock, published in 2015.

Kikimora in Ballet

The opening scenes of a Russian ballet by Léonide Massine (1896 – 1979) are about the Kikimora and her cat. Born in Moscow as Leonid Fyodorovich Myasin, the composer grew up in a musical family and later became a choreographer and ballet dancer.

His first ballet was *Soleil de Nuit* (*Midnight Sun*) in 1915. *Kikimora*, his second, was first presented in 1916. The original production contained only the story of Kikimora. Commentary about this ballet says, "Massine's love for the humorous and the grotesque is so well-known that there is no surprise in finding the second of his ballets devoted to the theme of children's tales" (Beaumont, 5). After its success, he added stories to the ballet (not included here): the Swan Princess, a dragon fight and funeral, and Baba Yaga. In 1919, Massine added two comedic interludes as well.

Léonide Massine

I have combined two published versions of his ballet: one is a retelling by Cyril W. Beaumont in *Children's Tales* (6 – 8), and the other comes from Edith Sitwell's *Children's Tales from the Russian Ballet, Retold* (29 – 39). The following rendition lacks the stage directions of the original text, and I present it in more of a story-like format, with my own perceptions of the story.

Kikimora sits bolt upright in her wooden cradle that's decorated with gigantic flowers. Sunlight streams through the tattered curtains fluttering on the solitary attic window. Its deep-red frame is no match for the sun's glaring red and white rays, which dance around the three wooden beams that support the roof. Spots of light tickle the bright-orange walls before they find a green-enameled stove, a low table, and two square stools. A white cat, with an orange handkerchief tied around its neck, lies curled on a stool, dozing from its previous night's activities. Dust motes glitter across the emptiness of the rest of the vast attic where the spirit resides.

Her cradle rocks, creaking like the spinning wheels she loves so much. *Crick. Crick. Crick.* Back and forth. Back and forth.

She runs her fingers through the thorny blue wilderness of her hair.

What has awoken her so early? Nighttime is when the half-witch, half-fairy is usually up and about.

She stops her cradle and cocks her head to the side. Faint at first, the sound rises toward her abode.

Him again! The street vendor has come to manipulate her life with his strings and wooden toys. She knows his routine by heart.

Drums and tambourines beat below to the tune of a simple folk song. Kikimora imagines the man dancing in his red boots to his own melody, snapping his whip through the air. His quick, sliding steps move across the cobblestones. The smile encased within his red-bearded face will widen as crowds gather. *It always does*, she muses. He'll tug on his white-and-crimson costume, delaying, delaying, waiting for his audience to quiet.

She counts to ten. Now. Silence reaches her ears.

Her body jerks as the street vendor holds at arm's length the wooden puppet that represents her—"the embodiment of wickedness" as he calls her. He has disfigured the puppet's cheeks with a broad, black stripe, and encircled its eyes with black rings. On the top of its head, he has bunched the dark, tangled hair into a pile that bobs every time he moves its wooden arms and legs. *Hideous*, she thinks.

In his other hand, she knows he shows the audience the second puppet—her cat, which he calls "her protector, the symbol of human malice." The real feline has been her faithful companion and nurse since Kikimora's childhood.

Soon the play will begin. The street vendor shakes each puppet in turn, and she groans. Curtain time. Kikimora dreams of the day she'll break free of his command and perform her own misdeeds.

Music from below begins again, and the crowd cheers.

The real cat's ears perk up, and the feline yawns. It stretches and leaps to the floor to begin its morning bath. Lift one hind leg; wash stomach. Lift other leg; wash stomach some more, smoothing down its fur.

Kikimora snaps her teeth and clenches her fists, the sharp nails on her fingers clawing through the air. Is this her own action or that of the street vendor manipulating her? She shrieks and curses. When will she ever break free?

Her faithful protector bounds to her side, nuzzling the cradle so it rocks again. Purring, it stretches out its paws, gently kneading her belly until she nestles into her cradle, calmer. The music from below becomes a lullaby.

The feline ceases rocking the cradle to resume its bath, wetting its paws and washing behind its ears. Once satisfied with its cleanliness, it curls into a ball and naps at the front of the cradle.

Crick. Crick. Crick. The cradle rocks, but Kikimora grows restless again. The music doesn't lull her to sleep. Why hasn't the cat continued to comfort her?

She sits up and uncovers knitting needles from the side of her cradle. *Click, clickety-click.* She occupies her time for a short spell, knitting invisible threads into the air. It's not working. She remains restless.

The lullaby from the street grows heavier, more monotonous. Finally, in a fit of temper, Kikimora throws aside her blanket and clambers from the cradle. Her blue skirt hitches upward, revealing natty red stockings. She crumples the bottom of her tattered pink blouse. Her sharp claws tear more holes through the brown, grease-coated patches.

Crick-crick-crick. Crick-crick-crick. Crick-crick-crick. Her wooden bed shakes as if in fear of her fury.

It's not the bed that needs to worry.

The cat blinks as it stares up at its fuming mistress, who curses the feline while she gnashes her teeth and bites her thumb. In a frenzy of rage, Kikimora stamps her feet on her way to the stove. She shakes her fists at every object in the attic, as if to terrify them. None respond.

She snatches a pair of sticks connected by a straw rope. Too late, the cat has missed the warning signs. The infuriated spirit dashes back and lashes the creature with the weapon. The touch of straw against skin, or in this case fur, forebodes great evil. All will not end well for the unfortunate feline.

Has the street vendor meant for his play to have gone this far? Or has Kikimora broken free of his control?

It takes a moment for fear to overtake the cat's astonishment. The feline leaps to its feet, dashing from side to side to avoid its mistress's lashes. Still it tries to soothe her by rubbing against her legs.

She'll have none of that. Malice and spite fill her. The cat shouldn't have stopped comforting her earlier. Shouting her curses, she claws at the creature when it's too close for her sticks to do their damage. The cat dodges her blows, and Kikimora kicks over one of the stools—first with one foot, then with the other. The pain increases her anger, and she stomps the floor like a pouting child.

Mewling, the cat leaps onto the other stool. It paws the air, trying to reach her.

Kikimora ceases kicking her stool and lunges at the cat. It hisses from fright and now waves its paws in defense. A swipe from the maddened spirit's claws swishes past the feline's ear, and the cat rockets upward out of reach.

Enraged at the cat's escape, Kikimora rushes to her cradle. Her pet and protector won't get away from her again. She fumbles beneath the blankets, searching for a more terrifying weapon. There! Her fingers touch the splintered wood. She tugs out an axe, which slices her bed coverings. Her own eyes glow red in the reflection of the rusty axe head.

The cat has failed her one time too many.

A sinister laugh escapes her as she turns around with slow, determined movements. Where has her protector and friend hidden? She gazes around the room and stops her search at the far corner. The cat crouches, its fur bristled and its ears laid back.

Kikimora dashes toward the creature and grabs it by the throat. No more will it feign comfort, brought on by the street vendor's play-acting. She pounds the cat's skull with the axe—once, twice, thrice!

A primordial screech erupts from the feline's throat as it struggles to escape. But Kikimora doesn't stop her brutal attack, fueled on by her pent-up frustration.

With one last weak mewl and sad eyes gazing at its mistress, the cat goes limp. Kikimora releases her grip, and the creature thuds to the floor. Its legs stick out straight. In vain, it paws at the floor, trying to stand. It heaves one last breath, then rolls to its side. Dead!

Kikimora dances with glee. She leaps into the air on an invisible broomstick and zooms out of a hole in the roof. Her hair is like a wisp of blue flame as she soars above the man who has tormented her for years. No more will the street vendor rule her life. She can now cast her own evil spells upon the world!

Her evil laughter bubbles from her lips as the man gazes from his puppets to her. His pasted-on grin for his audience fades, and horror fills his eyes. He drops the puppets and dashes up the stairs.

Kikimora stares in the window, anticipating his reaction when he reaches the attic.

The door slams open, and the street vendor stares, horrified, at the cat lying bloodied and broken on the floor. He snaps his whip across the cat's back. The creature jerks like a monster being born and scrambles to its feet. Its eyes wide, it scampers out of the room.

How can that be? Kikimora wonders. It was dead. It had to be. Or … is this still somehow all part of the street vendor's play? Has he altered his routine only to play her a fool?

A Modern Kikimora Tale Influenced by Music

In 1909, Anatoly Lyadov (1855 – 1914) composed a tone poem called *Kikimora, Op. 63* (you can listen to it here: https://youtu.be/4mli4z0Fuvg). He was born into a family of eminent Russian musicians. Described as writing compositions with great precision and fine attention to details, he demanded as much effort from the music students he taught as he did from himself.

Anatoly Lyadov

The program notes for his *Kikimora* composition state:

She grows up with a magician in the mountains. From dawn to sunset the magician's cat regales Kikimora with fantastic tales of ancient times and faraway places, as Kikimora rocks in a cradle made of crystal. It takes her seven years to reach maturity, by which time her head is no larger than a thimble and her body no wider than a strand of straw. Kikimora spins flax from dusk to dawn, with evil intentions for the world (Beggerow).

The music starts out slow and mysterious, reflecting Kikimora's magical upbringing. From there, the notes speed up to a climax, with Kikimora performing some malicious deed. It finally quiets as Kikimora slinks away from the household she's invaded (Beggerow).

The music has been described as follows:

> Lyadov … embodies the tale in orchestral poesy. The craggy wastes, the drowsy accompaniment of Kikimora's cradle-song are with inexpressibly delicate humour blended with the music of the venomous purring of the sapient Cat: all three, though each complete in itself, are here joined in an Introduction which is a work of genius, and which, for its expressiveness and striking picturesqueness, could hardly be surpassed.
>
> Beginning restrainedly, the Introduction gradually works up into a presto. Kikimora, awakening, rubs her crafty eyes, and surveys the neighbourhood in company with her yellow-orbed companion; the 'Cat' motive in varying forms runs through the whole tale. The blended themes are gradually broadened out … and after a powerful climax a big, descending chromatic passage leads into the real exposition: shrieks and clamour, whistling and hissing—one has to keep one's ears alert so that no details of the wonders concealed in this music, no feature of the straw-slender witch and none of her evil intentions are lost to the listener. But the most wonderful thing in this fairy-tale picture is its creator: his artistic sense unfailingly keeps the composer in bounds; without it the illusion would be shattered … Lyadov was incapable of pandering to the instincts of the mob … In this picture his work attains perfection (Montague-Nathan, 418).

At least one modern story has been inspired by Lyadov's notes. Emma Woodcock published *Kikimora* in the latter part of 2015. In her blog, she writes:

> As soon as I heard those words it was a story I wanted to read. It conjures so much that is familiar from the kind of stories I loved when I was growing up, from fairy tales and folk tales.
>
> Kikimora grows up with a magician – like so many iconic protagonists. Like the *Sorcerer's Apprentice*, like *The Once and Future King*, like many of Diana Wynne Jones' books: *Howl's Moving Castle*, *Charmed Life*, *The Lives of Christopher Chant*.
>
> The magician's cat can speak – like the Cheshire Cat in *Alice in Wonderland*. Like Aslan. And, again, there are many examples in Diana Wynne Jones' books.
>
> The cat tells endless stories – like Sherazade in 1001 nights.

Kikimora's head is no larger than a thimble – bringing to mind classic fairy tales, like Thumbelina or Tom Thumb.

And like Rumpelstiltskin, she spins flax.

With just a few words Lyadov has summoned a storm of associations and memories – treasured memories from childhood, of the magical, fantastical stories I loved best, and that transported me to other lands and other lives.

But then right at the end, he gives it a twist: she has evil intentions for the world. So is she the heroine of this story, or is she the villain? (Woodcock)

To find the answer Woodcock came up with, you'll have to read her book. Here's an excerpt found on her blog to whet your appetite for more.

Kikimora gathered up her embroidery to finish in the pantry. It was cold in there, but that had never troubled her. She was a creature of the cold, and though she enjoyed the comfort of a crackling fire, her resilience to Korsakov's bitter winters was remarkable. She had never owned a pair of shoes, nor felt their lack.

She was almost at the door, when the North Wind said, "Wait. How old are you now, girl?"

"Almost seven."

Anatoly's long fingers fumbled as he filled the glasses, which all clinked and rattled against one another.

"Has it been so long?" asked the North Wind in some surprise. "Surely it is time?"

Anatoly swallowed his vodka at a gulp. "There is still much I would teach her. Her reading is sorely neglected. She has not yet begun The Art of War—"

The North Wind snorted his disdain. "She might have completed all the reading even you could wish for years ago if you didn't have her working as your skivvy all the day long! I heard your banshee wail," he told Kikimora. "It wasn't too bad. What else can you do? Can you sour the milk with an evil thought?"

Kikimora nodded.

"Can you hide from human eyes? Creep past men silent and unnoticed?" Two more nods.

"Can you send bad dreams to trouble the sleep of man, woman or child?"

She hesitated.

"Well?"

"I have no one on which to practice such a skill."

The North Wind frowned and harrumphed. "What of that cat I've seen around the place? Surely you could disturb its sleep?"

Kikimora's eyes grew wide at this suggestion, and Anatoly muttered that it was more than any of their lives were worth to interfere with the cat.

Leshy took a bite of cake, and exclaimed at its sweetness. Washing it down with a mouthful of vodka, he added that he'd never tasted finer spirit. Kikimora knew he was trying to cheer her up, and she summoned a smile to show she appreciated it.

"Congratulations," the North Wind said sourly. "Your monster is a fine cook and house-keeper. How those men will tremble in their boots" (Woodcock, reprinted with permission of the author).

***

You've learned about the terrible things Kikimora can do, so men are certain to tremble when Kikimora is set loose on the world.

Domownik. Illustration by Anna Błaszczyk (Evelinea Erato). © Bendideia Publishing.

Domovoi (Домовой)

In an old stove the devil warms.

Domovoi or **Domovoy** (singular);
Domovye or **Domoviye** (plural)

Other names: domovik (Slovak), domownik, domowik (Polish), damavik (Belarusian), domovyk (Ukranian), dědek (Czech), domaći (Serbian[16] & Croatian), domovoj (Slovanian),[17] plus many other variations.

Names of respect: Most often, people don't call the house spirit "Domovoi"—when speaking *to* him or *about* him. When addressing him directly, they use affectionate and respectful euphemisms for "grandfather," such as *dedushka*, *dedko*, *dedo*, or *chelovek* (fellow). If he's particularly irritating, they may call him by the derogatory name of *barabashka* (pounder or knocker).[18] When speaking *about* him, they refer to him as "master," "well-wisher," "the other half," "he," "himself," and "that one."[19]

The heavens blacken and a tumultuous clamor resounds from their depths, shaking the very foundation of the land below. Mankind trembles. All eyes focus upward. What terrible beast roars amidst the realm of the gods?

Fire rips apart the fabric of the sky. Humans cower from the blinding light. One moment. Two. Three. The cacophony of sounds dwindles to a murmur. Now, only a flutter of wings stirs the breeze.

The day brightens, and people shade their eyes with their hands as they look heavenward again. Dark shapes scatter in the wind.

What manner of evil now befalls mankind?

Unclean spirits, the people say, have been exiled by Svarog, the Slavic god of celestial fire and blacksmithing.[20] This corps of *domovye* tumble to the ground and scatter near and far to every part of the land: the depths of the earth, forests, waters, air, backyards, and even down chimneys and into stoves. Those who fall into the home are the most benevolent toward their hosts. The ones who land outside, close to the home, guard their new residences but are wary of humans. All the rest who plunge into wild places away from the home remain malevolent toward humans.

At first, the spirits all retain the same characteristics. But as ages pass, those that have merged with the creatures of the land become dwarves, fauns and satyrs, water spirits, masters of whirlwinds and storms, and various others that inhabit the fields, yard, and outbuildings. Those spirits who occupy the home retain the name of *domovye*.

Had you been a witness to the revolt when the universe was created—what we now call the Fall from Grace—you might have experienced the above expulsion of angels-turned-demons. But since neither you nor I were privy to those events, we'll trust the matter to those who have passed on the story from generation to generation.

Etymology

Domovoi comes from the Russian word *doma*, for "house," and the word translates to "[he] from the house." The name in other languages means "home" or "owner."

Although rural peasants call the creatures who fell from the heavens "demons," they more accurately represent the elements: earth, water, air, and fire—all important for the survival of mankind. These spiritual inhabitants fill every aspect of the peasant's life, with fire, in particular in the home, being the most sacred. It's by the hearth, you'll learn, that the Domovoi finds his abode, for he's symbolic of this warmth, which sustains life.

Origins

People past and present speak lovingly about their Domovoi and treat him with respect—as the name Dedushka Domovoi (Grandfather Houselord) implies. At the beginning of this chapter, you read a legend describing the *domovye* (and other spirits) as being demons tossed from heaven. This may have been the way the household spirit initially made his way into our world. However, over time, he has been more commonly connected to ancestor worship. Perhaps, as the other fallen ones merged with the creatures in their designated areas, the Domovoi also became one with the spirits of the departed who resided in the home. This, in part, could explain why the Domovoi at times takes on the appearance of a family's ancestor—because, in fact, he was considered to actually be the spirit of the former head of household or even the family's founding ancestor.

Slavic people believe (at least in the past) that "the souls of fathers watched over their children and their children's children, and that therefore departed spirits, and especially those of ancestors, ought always to be regarded with pious veneration, and sometimes solaced or conciliated by prayer and sacrifice."[21]

Sometimes many spirits reside in a single home; other times, only one. The difference appears to be that the spirit designated as the Domovoi is a special guardian angel. Ceremonies performed for the Domovoi often mimic those associated with worship and adoration of the spirits of their ancestors, or *rodiyelui*.[22] These actions center around the stove, the hearth, and the threshold, as well as the practice of leaving gifts of food for the spirit. You'll discover more about each of these practices in sections below as you become familiar with the Domovoi himself.

Did you know?

One Domovoi was so much a part of his family that a peasant woman petitioned the government to provide him food rations along with the other household members (Zavalishin, 345).

When people make promises to the gods or spirits, they keep them "because they believe that in keeping their promises their life is protected."[23] And life for peasants is always hard: tilling the sometimes-unresponsive soil, struggling to keep warm during bitter cold winters, surviving numerous wolf attacks. So, spirits abide not only in the home, but swarm in every aspect of their lives—the forests, the fields, the waters. Even the weather and disease are personified as demons—all things that are threats to a peasant's survival. Each spirit has to be appeased with sacrifices. The household spirits are the most benign, but the farther away from the homestead the spirits roam, the more fearsome they become.

Under the influence of the Orthodox Church—especially toward the end of the nineteenth century— the pagan Slavic gods became demoted or cast as demons. The Domovoi and his wife (who goes by various names) are likely to have been transformations of Rod (god who represented the "general power of birth or reproduction" and Rozhanitsy (goddess who was the "special mistress of individual birth and individual destiny"). Even in this aspect, a connection to ancestors exists: *rod* means "kin," and *rozhenitsy* means "one who gives birth."[24]

The kindly ancestral spirits did not escape the Church's scrutiny, though, and they were demonized as being "unclean dead" or "cursed by God." Peasants have not perceived these demons as pure evil, however, as hard as the Church has tried to represent them that way. Instead, people look at them as a mixture of good and evil, with some, like the Domovoi, being more mischievous than bad.

In the early 1900s, a researcher asked a peasant about the Domovoi's state of grace:

"What, in your opinion, is the *domovoi*—the devil?"

The peasant, quite offended, answered: "Why should he be the devil? He does no harm."

"Then is he an angel?"

"God forbid! How can he be an angel seeing that he's hairy?"[25]

No, the Domovoi is just the *Domovoi* to them. He doesn't have to be classified by labels.

Appearance

It's a good thing the Domovoi is a spirit so he'll be invisible—at least most of the time. Otherwise, you might be frightened upon seeing him. Literature and word of mouth have described him as a goblin, a gnome, a dwarf, a brownie, a demon, an elf, a banshee, and even a leprechaun—all terms familiar to the western world, as scholars try to fit Slavic creatures into known categories.

Domovoi. Figure by Ivan Bilibin, 1934.
[Public domain], via Wikimedia Commons.

Those who have seen him say he's petite, around the size of a five-year-old boy. But his appearance is not youthful; he's like an old man, with a wrinkled face, yellowish-gray hair, and a white beard. Not only that, but he's hairy as the peasant above stated—not like the old men you're used to with long strands sticking out of their nose or ears. Instead, he's been called an "animated haystack."[26] The household spirit sports a long beard and is almost completely covered with hair or silky fur—leaving only the area around his eyes and pointed nose exposed. Even his palms and the soles of his feet are shaggy, as those who have seen his footprints left in the snow can attest.

During an interview, a man once described a boyhood encounter he had with a household spirit:

> One time we were lying with Mother on the floor, sleeping. Father was sleeping on the trunk, drunk. I wake up, someone is shaking me by my big toe. I open my eyes, some kind of small, black, wooly-headed little man is standing at my feet and looking. As soon as I doze off, he's pulling my toe again. I open my eyes—he's standing there. We keep looking at each other; he didn't even turn away. Then he left and went into the other room. I fell asleep as soon as he was out of my sight. I fell asleep and didn't say a thing to Father or Mother.[27]

The Domovoi sometimes appears with piercing eyes, horns, and a tail—a reminder of his demonic nature introduced when the Slavs became Christianized. Gentler descriptions refer to him as a beautiful boy dressed in white.

Upon occasion, he shape-shifts into a dog, cat, or bear. The animal's fur is always the same color as the hair of the master of the house. That's because the Domovoi likes to imitate the homeowner (or in some instances another respected, older person of the household, whether living or dead)—in hair color, attire, attitude, voice, and mannerisms. He often appears as the person, toiling away at his tasks, while the true owner is likely sleeping, hungover from a vodka-drinking binge. Why vodka, you ask? Because during the time of serfdom of the Russian peasants (*moujik*), that was their drink of choice.

In various stories told about the Domovoi, the clothing he wears while impersonating the homeowner reflects the attire of the district in which the man lives. Sometimes the spirit sports a red shirt with a blue belt, at other times a blue cloak with a rose-colored belt.

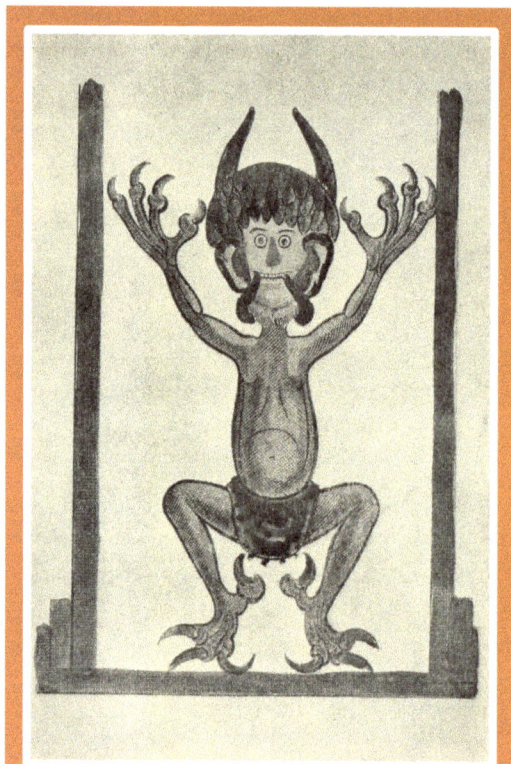

Šetek or Skřítek, a Bohemian version of Domovoy (the Slavic god of the household, deified progenitor of the kin) in his Christianized representation as a hellish hobgoblin, 1918. From Máchal ("Slavic"). By Jan Máchal [Public domain], via Wikimedia Commons.

Getting to Know the Domovoi

The nature of the Domovoi has transformed over the centuries—from fallen angel to protective ancestral spirit and back to somewhat benevolent demon—but always, he remains a cherished occupant of many homes. It was common for peasants in rural Russia to discuss the doings of their Domovoi in all aspects of their life: work, leisure, shopping, partying.

> "What will the Domovoi do to-day?" is the Russian peasant's first thought.
> "What can he do?" we may ask. Much![28]

Much indeed. Like a petulant child, the Domovoi throws tantrums on occasion, so be careful not to upset your household spirit.

- Don't fight.
- Don't mention his name after twilight.
- Don't sleep where he walks: near the threshold, by the stove, or in the middle of the floor.
- Don't sleep on your backs because that may suffocate the spirit.
- Don't make loud noises or swear at noon because you'll wake him from a deep sleep.
- Don't whistle or you could frighten the Domovoi and drive him from your home.
- If you're a woman, don't wear your hair loose. Keep the tradition of braiding or covering your tresses.

Seeing your hair blow in the wind irritates him. If he catches you, he'll do to you what he intended to do to the woman in the story below:

> A certain woman chanced to go out of the house into the passageway at night. The night was bright, the moon was shining, and it was as light as day outside. The woman went out onto the porch and, forgetting that she did not have her head covered, she stood and admired the starry sky. Suddenly she recollected herself and quickly headed back to the passageway, but there the *domovoi* was waiting for her. He seized her by the braid and pulled her up to the attic. She managed to utter, "And God has risen," and the *domovoi* hid in the attic. If she hadn't said these words, something bad would have happened to her.[29]

When situations like the above are not to his liking, he's fond of playing tricks on people. He'll call your name, but you won't see anyone around. That should warn you it's the Domovoi. You can protect yourself from him by saying, "Mary, daughter of Herod, come yesterday."[30] Yes, it's quite a strange chant, but those who have uttered the words swear it works.

"THE DOMOVOI" MUSIC – BY WANDERWELLE

Listen to "The Domovoi" by Wanderwelle from the Lost In A Sea Of Trees album, released July 31, 2017. Feel the wind whistle through your hair as you walk through the woods. Can you feel the Domovoi with you, always protecting you?

Track available for purchase from Silent Season: http://shop.silentseason.com/track/the-domovoi.

Those who don't repeat the words in time suffer from his pranks. He's likely to trip girls to make them stumble; hide the master's boots so he can't go out drinking; smash a flirt's mirror (he hates mirrors); splash hot soup onto a glutton's face; and toss furniture, dishes, and other household items around the room. In fact, people accuse the Domovoi of doing anything that no one else lays claim to having done. (In a family I know, the blame was passed down from the eldest to the youngest. Having no other person to blame, the youngest boy said the dog did it. What luck it would have been if they had heard about the Domovoi. Perhaps, unknown to them, the dog was a household spirit in disguise. He was hairy, after all.)

You wouldn't think anyone would actually *encourage* such a spirit to live with them, but that's the case with the Domovoi. People past and present feel lost and vulnerable without their Domovoi—unlike his spouse, the Kikimora, whom you've already learned they try (mostly unsuccessfully) to get rid of. To ensure that the Domovoi remains in the house at all times, a wife often covers the mouth of the stove so their household spirit won't sneak out when her husband leaves the house—as the Domovoi is particularly fond of the head of household.

You may say, "Why the difference in attitude toward the Domovoi and the Kikimora? They both cause trouble in the house, don't they?"

Considering how long the two spirits must have lived together (they are hundreds of years old, after all), it's not surprising that they behave similarly. Both spirits are apt to play pranks on their host family—especially if the home is untidy or the occupants are quarrelsome. But beyond that, their personalities differ.

Domovoi. By Раев А. (архив.худ.школы) [CC By 3.0 (https://creativecommons.org/licenses/by/3.0)], via Wikimedia Commons.

Whereas the Kikimora is constantly on the move (and accomplishing little), the Domovoi is more laid back. He has no desire to tidy up the house, although from time to time, as mentioned earlier, he performs chores while he's playing the homeowner's double. After all, it can't be the owner himself doing these things! That's so out of character for him since he's left them unattended for so long.

The Domovoi's main function is to protect the home and its occupants: he won't let you starve; he'll find a good suitor for your daughter; he'll protect you from other spirits and their mischief and any other misfortune. Without a Domovoi's protection, the family has a greater chance of becoming ill and dying before their time. You'll want to make sure you keep him happy so he stays.

A Moody Spirit

In order to get your Domovoi to be agreeable to his duties and protection, you must treat him right by leaving him small gifts. He's not greedy; no need to give him your first swarm of bees, sacrifice horses or cows to him, or give him a good portion of your harvest the way some of the others who fell from heaven with him demand. No, all he requires is food and drink. The way to this spirit man's heart is definitely through his stomach as you can see in the following snippet:

[T]he Russian peasant women invoke the aid of the Domovoi, and I have frequently seen her endeavour to propitiate the spirit in favour of her sinning husband, who is out late at night on a drinking bout, by placing outside the outer door provisions, such as bread and a bottle of kvass, in order that the Domovoi may eat and imbibe, and guide her husband's footsteps safely home.[31]

You may recall from the video in the Kikimora chapter that the Domovoi heads straight for the table and chows down on the presents left for him. (You *did* watch the video, didn't you? If not, you have another chance now. Go to the link in the endnote[32] and see what mischief the Domovoi and Kikimora get into when the lights go out. Even if you watched it before, view it again, now that you know more about the Domovoi.)

So, heed this warning: don't forget his nightly snack!

You're also likely to get on his bad side if you try to see him. He's a rather shy spirit, and he doesn't like to be seen or disturbed. He's likely to punish you if you're too curious. Most people are reluctant to do so. Anyone who has happened to see him, therefore, is looked at with awe.

If you really feel the urge to see the spirit, do so in a safe way: wear a harrow or horse collar that has straps. Since these implements form a cross, they'll protect you.

You'll have an even better chance to see him on Easter or Holy Week. On those days, try a different approach: wear new clothes and shoes to church. You'll also have to smear your head with butter. It can't be any butter. It has to have come from seven cows that were milked for the first time. When you're in church, turn around during the liturgy, and he'll be there. Of course, this offends him, so as a result, you'll become ill and remain that way for six weeks. If it's worth that much to you to have bragging rights, go right ahead and do it.

> ## Did you know?
> Before you pour out hot water, you should warn your Domovoi so he doesn't get scalded (Ralston, 123).

When he's in your house, he comes out only at night, after everyone's in bed, so you don't have to always be looking over your shoulder as you take care to avoid him. During the day, his favorite hiding spot is behind the stove in any niche or crack he can find. Sometimes you can also hear him prowling about the threshold, below the porch, or in the attic. He may even visit your bedroom.

If he's in a good mood, he'll braid a woman's hair or a man's beard. You may also feel him pinching you. If it doesn't hurt, your friendly spirit is letting you know he's up and about, keeping you safe. If, however, his actions make you yelp, and you wake up with bruises, he's trying to force you out of the house.

The following excerpt from a journal article, talks about his "pinching":

The morning after our arrival in the country the cook came to pay her respects to her mistress and to offer her opinion on the *datcha* [country house]. The Russian peasantry are extraordinarily superstitious, and our domestics were not different from the rest of their kind. One of the ideas which is received by them almost as an article of belief is, that every house is inhabited by a *domovoy* or spirit, who expresses his approval or otherwise of the inmates soon after they come into occupation. The cook, then, having examined her person, and having found no traces of pinching or other violence on the part of the presiding genius of the place, gave it as her opinion that we should pass a very pleasant time.[33]

Another tactic to get you to leave is to bang on everything in the house—walls, furniture, kitchen items—until you can't stand it and pack up. You must have done too many items on the "don't" list, and he's had enough. Worse yet, if you have trouble sleeping and feel as if something is pressing down on your chest, it could be the Domovoi sitting there, showing his displeasure at how you've treated him. You'd better figure out what you've done and make amends.

The following is a comment made on a forum about an event where the Domovoi showed his displeasure:

> I'm from Russia. My mom once said that the Domovoy once attempted to strangle her in her sleep. She couldn't scream or breathe. It felt like the Domovoy was touching the blanket and tucking it in. She couldn't move her limbs as well. But as soon as she started chanting the prayer in her mind the Domovoy let go of her and she felt relieved.[34]

In addition to the naughty actions described earlier, he'll make all kinds of ungodly noises with his raspy voice to make his displeasure known. The Domovoi may display childish behavior when he's upset, but he doesn't adhere to the adage that a child should be seen and not heard. The opposite is true: you rarely see him, but you can definitely hear creaking and groaning as he putters around your home.

Role as an Oracle

Not all the Domovoi's moaning is due to his displeasure. Sometimes, he's trying to warn you about a disaster that's on its way. If you ignore him and don't prepare yourself, he'll come into your bedroom—not

Domovoy, the Slavic god of the household, deified progenitor of the kin. They are represented as statuettes which were kept in niches near the house's door, and later over the ovens. Here is a statuette from Silesia, photographed in the early 20th century, 1918. From Máchal ("Slavic"). By Jan Máchal [Public domain], via Wikimedia Commons.

to pinch you this time. Instead, he'll run his hairy hand over your face. That's rather creepy, but he's attempting to tell you whether you'll have good or bad luck in the coming days. A warm hand means something pleasant is about to happen, and his touch will help you sleep more soundly. If he passes a cold, bristly hand over your face, you're in for trouble as the story below illustrates, and you'll suffer nightmares about your fate.

> My very own father told me the following shortly before his death: "I don't believe in devils and all sorts of demonic creatures and I don't stand in fear of them. However, my dear son, I shall soon die. Last night just before I lay down but before I fell asleep, someone came up to me. I heard his steps clearly, and suddenly 'he' placed his cold hand to my lips, and I also clearly felt the touch of the hand of the unknown person who had come in." Indeed, somewhat later my father died from a blow.[35]

Bitter sobbing and wailing may indicate that someone in the house is going to die. If it's the head of the household, the Domovoi will also excessively sigh (you know that kind of person), weep, or sit somewhere in the house with his cap pulled over his eyes. If the sounds are more like sorrowful moaning, the Domovoi is trying to tell you plague, war, fire, or another disaster is imminent. This forthcoming disaster may even be enough for the Domovoi to make his way outside and wail in the meadows. Just imagine what that would sound like if the Domovoi from every household joined forces. A chorus of cats yowling on fences couldn't compare.

If the threat is immediate, such as a fire in your house, he'll do his best to wake the head of the household. How's that for a smoke detector? No batteries needed.

Sometimes he makes his presence known by moving around the house—still invisibly—when the family is seated for supper. This informs the family that the Domovoi has something important to tell them. The head of household asks whether the news is good or bad. The Domovoi may knock on the walls in answer, or he may mutter sounds: "Hu" (from the Russian word *hudo* for "bad") or "D…D…D…D" (for *dobro*, the Russian word for "good").[36]

Other actions of the Domovoi are subtler, such as:

- Tugging a woman's hair to warn her about an abusive man.
- Materializing as a sign the person who saw him is going to die. (Another good reason not to try to catch a glimpse of the house spirit.)
- Blowing out candles to indicate misfortune for the family.
- Strumming a comb to tell you someone is going to get married in the near future.
- Dancing and laughing to let you know good times are coming.

The Domovoi is also fond of giving advice to his family through dreams. But you may be better off ignoring him—if you can live with the pranks he'll play on you afterwards because of his displeasure.

What does he tell people to do? Steal from their neighbors or even the land owner. It's not that the house spirit is immoral. He's frugal, and it's his way of taking care of his family, seeing that they have everything they need without them having to exert a lot of effort on their own.

You can see how this could lead to bad relationships, not only with your neighbors, but also with their household spirit, whose goal is to protect and provide for *his* family. Don't worry; you have ways to deal with your neighbor's Domovoi when he gets out of hand, as well as methods to make your own spirit behave.

Remedies for Removing a Stranger Domovoi

Has your Domovoi acted like an alley cat and been in a brawl with another Domovoi over stolen goods? It doesn't matter if your spirit was stealing from the neighbor, or the neighbor's spirit was robbing you. The damage has been done. If the neighbor's Domovoi has won the battle, he's now settled into your house—his victory prize. However, you have a problem. Only your Domovoi is friendly to you; the neighbor's spirit—when not in his own home—is vindictive and dangerous. If he sits on your chest at night, it's not to scold you; it's to suffocate you. You can't appease him with food and drink—although he'll still scoff them down.

The following story recorded in the Urals tells about two *domovye* residing in the same household and the disastrous result.

> A certain woman moved from her old household and invited the domovoi to come live with her. However, the new house already had a domovoi! When night came, the two *domovye* clawed and fought for control of the household. The woman's husband told her, "We can't have two masters. We must get rid of yours." At night, the husband beat the wall with a broom and shouted, "Depart from here, intruder!" The woman's domovoi fled out the window. From then on, there was quiet in the house. Later, the husband saw his wife's banished domovoi in the forest, and the creature tore out his throat.[37]

You'll most definitely want to get rid of that other, malicious spirit, and be on the lookout for him afterwards. But, how can you do that?

The most common method is to beat the walls with brooms while you yell, "Stranger Domovoi, go away home!" as the story above indicates.

If that attempt fails, you can try a more drastic method. You can also perform this and the other actions that follow on your own Domovoi if his quirks become too excessive.

- You'll need a horse, so borrow one if you don't own one. Get a shovel that you use for the stove fire. Once on the horse, ride around the yard waving the shovel, while you chant, calling on "the bright gods" to rid you of "the terrible devil and the stranger Domovoi."[38]
- Another method—if you don't have one of those enormous Russian stoves—is to dip a shovel into tar. While you wave the shovel around the yard (still riding on horseback), the implement will rub against the Domovoi's head, disgusting him. With all that hair, it's no wonder. He'll leave your home and most likely spend much time trying to rid his hair of the sticky mess.
- A more extreme way to get a Domovoi in line is to place the head or skull of a goat under your home's threshold. The Domovoi hates goats, and this will drive him crazy, but may calm him down as well.

Luring Back Your Runaway Domovoi

One problem solved. Now you have to entice your Domovoi back into your home. He's likely feeling sad and lonely, and will need cheering up and reassurance that you want him since he's failed to keep you safe.

Dress up in festive clothes and go outside. You won't know exactly where he's hiding, but walk around, encouraging him to return by saying, "Grandfather Domovoi (Dedushka Domovoi)! Come home to us—to make habitable the house and tend the cattle!"

He'll be so pleased that you've shown him the greatest respect by calling him by the title of Dedushka, and be relieved you still want him, that he'll return at once.

Now that your Domovoi is safely back in your home, he's likely to be on edge. It was as harrowing an experience for him to be separated from you as it was for you to be without him. Don't be surprised if he acts badly for a while. If you have a cat, he may mistreat her as he did another family's cat by holding the feline in the air by the tail, then flinging her on the floor. (My cousin Marisa did that once. I wonder if she was a Domovoi in disguise.)

A stern scolding is what he needs, like any child who'd do that to a pet. Be firm in your tone and say, "Why'd you do that? You ought to be ashamed of yourself! The cat's part of the family, too. Treat her right, and don't do that again."

He should calm down, but if his exile caused him a lot of turmoil, you may have to perform other rituals to get him to behave.

Soothing Your Upset Domovoi

First try to make him happy by salting a piece of bread. He loves his carbs! Wrap it in a white cloth and put it in the hallway where the Domovoi likes to wander. You and all your family members will have to bow toward the four corners of your house, while begging the Domovoi to stop being angry.

If that doesn't work, go to your church and get holy water. Sprinkle all the rooms with it. You should be prank-free right away. Of course, your Domovoi won't be happy with you.

That failing, if you know someone practiced in magic, call him in. Otherwise, you'll have to do the ritual yourself. Kill a rooster at midnight and drain the blood into a bowl. Dip a bath whisk into it and sprinkle its blood into all the corners of the house, both inside and outside, while reciting spells. This is guaranteed to work.

However, if you loathe to kill the rooster, you, as the head of your household, can color an egg red. (This has multiple meanings. For one, it's the pagan symbol of rebirth. Eggs also hold curative powers when used as parts of spells.) Bring it outside at midnight, face the moon, and say, "Master, stand before me as the leaf before the grass, neither black nor green, but just like me! I have brought thee a red egg."[39] Be prepared! You'll actually get to glimpse the Domovoi in human form as he materializes before you. Once he takes the egg from you, he'll quiet down and behave.

A note of warning. If you go this route, you can *never* mention the event to anyone. Remember that the Domovoi doesn't like to be seen or to have you force him to appear. If you spread it around that he did, he could set your house on fire or even harass you so much you commit suicide!

Keeping Your Domovoi Content

Once your Domovoi is back to a normal routine, you must do things to ensure he stays that way. Earlier, you learned that he expects food and drink. If you make him the food he loves the most, he'll be happy and content. He enjoys little cakes baked especially for him. You can leave them on the stove. Or you can place a pot of stewed grain on the hearth in front of the stove and surround it with hot embers to keep it warm. You can put vodka or *krass* (a drink made from rye bread) on the windowsill as well. You can also placate him with porridge, tobacco, incense, juniper, and bread and salt. Just don't put salt in the porridge you give him. The story that follows shows what happens when you change his routine.

> From olden times the household of a certain merchant observed the ancestral custom of placing a pot of *kasha* [porridge] in the attic for the *domovoi* each Saturday night. This *kasha* was always cooked without salt. Once, on leaving the house, the merchant instructed his cook to prepare unsalted *kasha* on Saturday and place it in the attic in the evening. Whether the cook was dissatisfied with her master or whether she forgot, in any case she salted the *kasha* for the *domovoi*. On returning from his journey, the master didn't even manage to enter the passageway when from the attic a pot of *kasha* came flying at his head.[40]

Did you know?

Domovye don't always fight each other. Sometimes they hold loud winter parties together (The Pagan Files).

It's always acceptable to set aside part of your supper for him. You can even encourage him to join you while you eat. Put a white cloth in the hallway near the room he likes to be in the most. This is an invitation to dine with the family. To be even more respectful, you can say, "Oh Dedushka Domovoi, with our little children, we beg your favor to feast with us." Before eating, it's also proper to bow to the ikons and cross yourself three times. Repeat the ritual after the meal, but also say, "Thank you" to both the saints and the master of the house, the Domovoi.

If you hear "He! He! He! Ho! Ho! Ho!," you'll know that you've succeeded. That's the sound the Domovoi makes when he's excited or happy.

Moving into a Different House

What if, after you've finally managed to get your Domovoi settled in your home after his bad experience, you decide to move? Your family is eager to have him join you in your new residence. You think it should be easy to get the house spirit to come with you. All you have to do is ask him. After all, he's attached to your family. If he comes with you, he can forget the battle he lost with the neighbor's Domovoi and create new memories.

> ### Did you know?
>
> If your entire family is going on vacation, after everything is packed, you should sit silently. This is a way to say a temporary goodbye and is a sign of respect to your Domovoi (Wood).

It may not be as straightforward as you think. Your (mostly) friendly spirit doesn't like to move; some people even say he doesn't ever venture outside on his own.[41] A Domovoi may be so attached to the stove that he won't leave, not even if the house burns down or everyone in the family has died. In fact, if your old home falls into ruins or burns down, this is a sure sign your Domovoi never left. He won't seek out a new family, preferring to remain with his beloved stove.

The story below tells of one Domovoi, whose one concern was about how newcomers treated his stove.

> There was a hut in which no one would live, for the children of every one who had inhabited it had died, and so it remained empty. But at last there came a man who was very poor, and he entered the hut, and said, "Good day to whomsoever is in this house!"
> "What dost thou want?" cried out the Old One.
> "I am poor; I have neither roof nor courtyard," sadly said the new comer.
> "Live here," said the Old One, "only tell thy wife to grease the stove every week, and look after thy children that they mayn't lie down upon it."[42]
> So the poor man settled in that hut, and lived in it peacefully with all his family. And one evening, when the poor man had been complaining about his poverty, the Old One took a whole potful of money out of the stove and gave it to him.[43]

If your Domovoi loves his stove as much as the spirit from this story, how can you get him to move?

First, you have to speak to him with reverence as you perform the following ceremonies. Respect and food are the two things he requires. If you fail to give him either, he'll be offended and stay with his stove. This can cause all kinds of troubles with the next family who moves there and brings their own household spirit. The two will fight, and the new family will try to drive out your Domovoi. You'll have to return later to get him, and you know how disappointed he'll be in you. It's best for everyone that you make sure you take him with you the first time.

He's a spirit so how are you supposed to bring him with you? Simple. Cart him along with the embers in the stove. (Or he will attach himself to the hearth implements if you have too far to travel to carry embers.)

But before you can do that, the night prior to your move, you must perform ceremonies with the family's ikons of the saints. The female homeowner places a cloth on a table and puts bread and salt on it. She lights a candle in front of the ikons, and everyone prays to God. Her husband removes the ikons, covering them with the front of his clothes. He opens the cellar door, bows, and says, "Dedushka, let us go to the new home. As we have lived in the old home well and happily, so let us live also in the new one. Be kind to my cattle and family!"

The next morning, once everything's packed and ready to go, the oldest woman in the house lights a fire in the stove. When the wood is blazing, she moves it with the fire shovel into a niche in the stove (*pechurka*). At precisely noon, she rakes the embers into a clean jar and covers them with a white cloth, being careful not to let any fall through the grate. To do so would cause the ancestors to fall into Hell.[44]

She carries the jar to the front door, throws it open, then looks toward the "back corner" where the stove is, and says, "Welcome, dedushka (grandfather), to our new home!" In this way, she invites him to come with her. She, or another member of the family, may also say:

> I bow before thee, my host and father, and beseech thee to enter our new dwelling; there shalt thou find a warm place, and a morsel of provender which has been prepared for thee.[45]

In addition to taking the element of fire, you might also want to bring a clod of earth, especially if you're moving far. As a saying goes:

INTERACTIVE FICTION: THE DOMOVOI

A Domovoi has only a spider to talk with. Is that creature his friend or foe? Its web grows larger the longer the two converse. Is it to trap the spirit or merely to build its home?

> In an old, simple place far from a good railroad, where the soil was too poor for the tractor's plow, the month of March encased a hut with thick ice fences. The weather had sealed the wooden shutters on the windows—all except one, where an unskilled cut had left a one-inch breach that exposed the glass panes underneath. It had been this one inch the spider used to enter the hut, and so, inside this old, simple place, the Domovoi negotiated with the spider (Dyer, "The Domovoi").

This is how the interactive game begins. Marshall Dyer narrates the game, giving his listener two choices for how the story should proceed. The response sets the scene for the next event. This perspective of a Domovoi differs in some ways from what you've learned, but you'll see similarities as well.

You can listen to the narrated version here: https://www.youtube.com/watch?v=liCVF8noVdA, or download the free game yourself at https://bravemule.itch.io/domovoi (story by Kevin Snow, published November 29, 2014, available in English and Russian).

Warning:* The Domovoi *contains depictions of violence and is not suitable for children.

Such earth is useful for the health. You go to another strange little country: there the climates are other, there even the water for our brother can do great harm. But strew your own little earth on the water, and then no land can do aught.[46]

Off you all go to your new home, with ikons, embers, and soil in tow. You'll also have to bring along a rooster and hen, and let them loose inside the house. You can't enter until the rooster crows. Evil spirits can't endure the sound and will scatter, making the house safe for you to enter. The noise won't bother your Domovoi, though, indicating he's no longer the demon who fell from heaven. If the rooster doesn't crow, you're in for trouble. You can't enter the house. It could mean evil spirits are still there, and you'll have to perform additional ceremonies to remove them.

If the rooster does crow, the next step is to introduce the house spirit to the new homestead. The elder woman brings the jar of embers to the gates of the courtyard, where the homeowners have gathered to greet the Domovoi with bread and salt.

The old woman hits the gate posts, saying, "Are the visitors welcome?"

To which the homeowners reply, "Welcome, dedushka, to the new spot!"

The old woman follows the homeowner into the house. She places the jar on the new stove, removes the cloth, which she shakes toward each corner of the house. After that, she pours the embers into a niche in the new stove. She breaks the jar and buries the pieces at night under the "front corner" of the house.

Inside an Izba. Illustration by Dmitry Yakhovsky. © Bendideia Publishing.

IZBA: A PEASANT'S HOME
UPPER CORNER, IKONS, AND STOVE

Peasant houses, as a rule, were built using clay mixed with straw to construct the walls, while the floors remained dirt. This would account for why families were able to bury stillborn babies and sacrificed animals beneath the threshold after the house was completed.

Even before the house was finished, the community would bring bread and wine, and lay them on a table in the eastern corner toward the rising sun, the far right as you enter the house (often called the "upper," "great," "beautiful," or "front" corner). They also tossed wheat for prosperity into this corner and coins for luck—the more money thrown, the better the future.

It was here, too, that the family placed bread and small saucers of food for the ancestors—or meals on the supper table or on a shelf holding the ikons of the saints, also located in the "upper corner." It was improper to sit with your back to the ikons, and so the table often was flush against the wall, making it look as if the ikons were attending the meal.

In ancient times, it was believed that after a family member was buried, his soul resided in the wall behind the sacred pictures (where formerly it held images of their gods). If you heard knocking on the wall behind the ikons, it meant the ancestors were summoning someone in the family to join them.

Opposite the upper corner was a massive stove made of brick and mortar, which occupied the central part of the house. When the smoke subsided, the peasant could close the chimney valve. This not only prevented cold air from coming down the flue, it also enabled the stove to remain warm for a long time after it was heated.

While the upper corner was the center of the peasant's spiritual life, the stove was the center of his material life, providing warmth and food. It also was a place for the elders or children of the family to sleep on top of hemp bast mats, while the adults slept on planks forming a ledge above the stove.

Reverence for the Domovoi and his connection to the stove are all that are left of some ancient form of fire worship related to the worship of the dead. Among these included cremation of the deceased, which the ancient Slavs performed to assist their family's journey into the land of the dead. Fire, to them, cleansed the soul and released it from the body, because it was through fire that the Sun God chose to reveal himself to mankind. In this way, fire came to symbolize the souls of the ancestors.

Fire was so sacred, housewives loathed to lend it to their neighbors, fearing that with the removal of the embers, they would also lose their luck.

Which brings us back to spirits. You could find a spirit anywhere the peasant built fires: the Domovoi inside the home, the Bannik in the bathhouse, and the Ovinnik in the threshing house (more about them later in this book). The Domovoi, however, seemed to be the overlord of them all. Perhaps at one time, they may all have been considered the same, but in today's world, they are unique beings.

In the meantime, the husband places the ikons where they belong, opens the cellar door, and says, "Enter, dedushka!" Everyone prays. When finished, the woman places the cloth on a table again, lights the fire in the stove, and manages the kitchen tasks.

One final thing you can do in order to make sure no evil Domovoi inhabits the homestead is to hang a bear's head, dead hawk, or magpie in the stable. If an evil spirit is around, he won't be able to fight with your own good Domovoi.

Your new home is now ready and acceptable for you and your spirit protector.

You may be wondering what happens if you move far away and forget to properly invite your Domovoi to move with you. Vicki Boykis blogged about her experience with just such an ordeal.

> When I was growing up, we had a domovoi. Every Russian household does. In your head, he looks kind of like a shorter Peter Jackson. But of course, you don't know for sure since you've never seen him. …
>
> Our house doesn't feel homey yet, and I think it's because we don't have a domovoi. We didn't lure him over the right way. …
>
> I am all about keeping Russian pagan traditions going and trying to make our house feel more like a home, especially since it's new construction, so I try to invite the domovoi into our house from time to time. I tell him we have FiOS and free HBO until August. I also try to bring him up in conversation so he knows he's needed. It hasn't worked yet, but there have been a couple of occasions where I've seen hopeful signs.
>
> For example. Mr. B's main job in the kitchen is to do the dishes. One evening last week, he was doing them and found a bowl of cherry pits in the sink that hadn't been dumped in the trash before the bowl was washed. As a result, all the pits and stems spilled over into the sink and Mr. B had to pick them up one by one before he washed the rest of the dishes, because they can clog the garbage disposal.
>
> "Why did you do this," he asked me, frustrated.
>
> "I didn't do it. I don't remember eating cherries this week," I said, getting excited. "Maybe it was the domovoi!"
>
> Mr. B gave me a look. "Are you kidding me?"
>
> "No! He probably wanted some cherries."
>
> "No one in this household eats cherries except for you."
>
> "Be quiet, you're going to make him angry" (although I wasn't sure if the domovoi speaks English).
>
> "I think you need to see a psychiatric professional. You're blaming your laziness on an invisible man that may or MAY NOT live with us."
>
> After this conversation, I became kind of scared. Because when you say the domovoi doesn't exist, all kinds of bad things can happen.
>
> Like, maybe your laundry goes missing for a while. Or the domovoi eats all of your vanilla ice cream. Or maybe the domovoi creeps up on you one night while you're sleeping and creepily whispers in your ear, "I think YOU need to see a psychiatric professional, because I am totally real."[47]

Building a House

Let that be a lesson to you. Don't forget your Domovoi when you move.

If you plan to build a house, you'll face additional problems.

First, where do you keep your Domovoi until the house is completed? One place he likes to hide is inside an old boot or an old bast shoe (type of slipper woven from the inner bark of a birch or linden tree) from peasant times—especially one that's been near the stove, so it's warm and cozy.

Second, an unlived in (in this case, new) house is considered "unclean." Ensuring that the first items you place in your home are your ikons is a good start; they act as a protective talisman. But, you won't find happiness or fortune there until the death of the head of the family, or the oldest member of the family, who will then become your guardian spirit. Because of this belief, the eldest usually enters the house before anyone else since the first one to cross the threshold after the house has been finished will die soon afterward. True, your elder will pass from this world some day and take his rightful place as guardian of the family, but you'll want to keep him around for as long as you can. So, having him cross the threshold first is not a good prospective.

But what else can you do?

- You can kill an animal (maybe the rooster that didn't crow when you moved the last time) and bury its head under the corner of the house where you'll place the ikons, as this is the holiest place in the house.
- When those building the house first begin, they can call out the name of some bird or animal from the forest. This creature will soon die and take the place of any person who would have crossed into the house first. You can bet the homeowners treat the builders well, to make sure none of them mention the name of any family member, instead of that of a forest creature. You might want to stay away from the construction site at the beginning so you don't tempt any builder to mention your name.

Now that that's settled, it's time to get a Domovoi to dwell in your house if you don't have one. If the building's constructed of wood, you may be fortunate, and one already dwells inside. Tree spirits are known to enter buildings through the planks made from tree trunks. So, if any of the trees still had spirits within them, you're all set. Now go about making him happy.

If no spirits lived in the trees used, and this is your first home, you'll have to lure in a guardian spirit. Put a piece of bread on the floor where the stove will go. Of course, you'll have to plan that before you have your stove built.

Or you can try this: Make bread for your first supper in the house. Cut it while you're eating and place the first slice in the right-hand corner of your attic, while you say, "Our supporter, come into the new house to eat bread and to obey your new master."

Birchbark shoes.
By Anne-Lise Reinfelt/Norsk Folkemuseum (https://digitaltmuseum.no/011023156873/sko) [CC BY-SA 4.0 (https://creativecommons.org/licenses/by-sa/4.0)], via Wikimedia Commons.

Family Births and Deaths

It's time to learn a little about how your Domovoi interacts with your family. He's sympathetic to all your joys and sorrows, especially births, deaths, and marriages. For all of these events, the family provides food for their spirit so he can participate with them. They say, "There for thee, Grandfather Domovoi; may your deeds be well for us, and mayst thou aid us with thy kind assistance that our actions may prosper, our children grow up, and our hens and pigs multiply."[48]

You've already learned how distraught he becomes when someone in your family dies. For many days, he wails and moans behind the stove incessantly. Besides the stove, the Domovoi has an association with the threshold, and rituals associated with children. For example:

- Under the threshold is the final resting place of stillborn children, where they become part of the ancestors (*rodiyelui*).
- Families seek his protection for a recently baptized child by holding the infant over the threshold, showing the spirit the new member of the family.
- A mother washes an ill child over the threshold, so the Domovoi will drive that evil from the house.

If a family has lost one infant, they rejoice even more to bring home a healthy one. The following custom is still practiced:

> Returning from church, the godfather laid the newborn on a pillow, with special cloths prepared by the mother-in-law, and placed it on the threshold. The godparents then said: "An unbaptized one was taken from you, but a baptized one has been brought to you."[49]

The family cannot bring the stillborn child into the house because it has not been baptized. The infant has to remain under the threshold, which is a boundary between this world and the world beyond.

Weddings

As upsetting as the death of the stillborn child presents to the Domovoi, weddings are perhaps even more troublesome for him. Although he's happy for the bride as she begins her new life, he's sad as well, because she leaves not only her human family, but also him. He's hurt by her decision to abandon him, and only her acts of contrition will appease him.

Before she becomes a bride, a woman must sever all ties with her own family, including her connection with the family's Domovoi. She can't be tied to two of them; once she marries, she'll take on her husband's Domovoi as her own. This is a sad and even terrifying event as her Domovoi has protected her all her life, and now she must trust a strange one.

She sits by the hearth while her father discusses her marriage with the future groom's representatives. Stretching out her hand toward where her Domovoi resides, she indicates her desire to remain under his protection. She begs the spirit to lessen his anger that she's leaving their home to go take care of her husband's Domovoi.

Did you know?

Uranus has its own Domovoy. It's the second-largest crater on the fourth-largest moon. Perhaps the house spirit of that name also lives there.

Receiving the spirit's forgiveness, she is free to go to her husband's house after she's married. The fire of the new spirit's hearth can purify her of any misdeeds (or perceived misdeeds). If she fears that her husband or his family will mistreat her, she can appeal to the Domovoi's protection by confessing her misconduct, repenting, and promising to be a good and faithful wife.

Here's one final note about the Domovoi and marriage customs. The excerpt from the poem below is about two men taunting each other before a fight for the hand of the lovely Natalia in marriage.

> "…This former conquest in our rivalship,
> Shall spirit me to venture fresh attack;
> While thou, who hast not gained Natalia's heart,
> Shalt not prevail to purchase now her hand.
> This day secures her mine; and soon as e'er
> We enter Kieff, I'll bid her ready make
> The brightened pewter and its scarlet thread."[50]

"The brightened pewter and its scarlet thread" describes a wedding tradition in which the bride prepares a pewter pitcher especially for the Domovoi to reside in. She knots a colored string and passes it through a hole at the top of the container onto which she attaches lead, making it shiny. Next, she wraps the pitcher in a clean cloth and birch bark, and then ties it onto a twig on a fruit tree. Every year she replaces the string.

So there you have it, what the Domovoi is all about.

On the Dark Side

As you've learned, the Domovoi is often good, sometimes bad—but always there to protect his family. He may misbehave for any reason, but on certain nights, he is more likely to show his darker side, and you're advised to make sure he's mollified—or sometimes stay completely out of his way.

- **New Year's Eve**: In some places, the Domovoi shape-shifts into a hag with tusks, a white sheep, or some other creature. He's not really causing trouble, but what a sight he presents. Fortunately, only a sorceress can see this transformation.[51]
- **Eve of Epiphany** (January 6, or January 19 in the Julian calendar): On this night, the Domovoi expects you to make him little cakes, baked especially for him, not something left over from your supper or a celebration.[52] To forget to do so will make him misbehave.
- **Feast of St. Ephraem the Syrian** (January 28): Set a pot of mush or stewed millet on the table before you go to bed. This will keep the Domovoi's tantrums in check and avoid having him sit on your chest, temporarily stopping your breathing, and giving you nightmares.[53]
- **March 25**: It seems some *domovye* hibernate, perhaps the ones in the extremely cold climates. In those places, this is the night he awakes from his winter hibernation. He'll wait only three days for an offering before he causes trouble. Villagers slaughter a black pig and cut it into enough pieces so each resident receives one. They return home and bury their portion under the threshold at the entrance. In other locations, villagers bury eggs instead.[54]
- **March 30**: On this day, you're advised to avoid all contact with your Domovoi. He's out causing trouble from dawn until midnight, and he doesn't care if you're his family or some stranger attempting to rob your home. Leave him plenty of food and drink offerings and cower in your room until his tantrum is over. Two suggestions for his maliciousness are either he's shedding off all that hair as spring arrives, or a mania has taken over his senses, and he has an urge to marry a witch.[55]
- **April 1**: Some regions say the beginning of April is when the Domovoi wakes from hibernation. You may be able to get away with pulling pranks on him while he's still groggy.[56] Be careful, though, that it doesn't backfire, and he plays an even bigger joke on you.
- **Easter Eve**: This is a day people are able to see the Domovoi.[57] But do you really want to? Remember, he doesn't like to be seen, and he's likely to be extra sensitive that people can catch a glimpse of him. You don't know what kind of trouble he'll cause you on the following day.
- **Ivana Kupala** (July 7, or June 25 in the Julian calendar): People feast and celebrate. They clean the house, set food on the table, then they all go outside so the Domovoi can have the place to himself.[58] The previous night was a time for human mischief-making, so perhaps this gives the Domovoi a night where he can perform his own pranks.
- **July 30-31**: Anyone born on the night between these days is exempt from the ministrations of the Domovoi as he causes mischief on March 30.[59]

March 30 has a connection to a famous so-called "ritual murder" in 1911 that was blamed on the Jews. Criminals murdered 13-year-old Andrei Yushchinsky because they believed he had turned them in to the police. Prior to his death, the boy had assisted the gang. They gave him the nickname "Domovoi" because "he was a quick-witted, daring boy, not afraid to go into the lowest slums of the city even at night."[60]

Domovoi. Illustration © Andy Paciorek. Used with permission of the artist.

Perhaps after his death, he took his namesake of Domovoi to heart because one of the gang members insisted his spirit haunted her.

> The body of the boy lay in a shallow grave in the cellar until the evening of March 30, when Vera Cheberiak declared that it must be taken away. She was haunted every night, she said, by the boy's ghost, which came and stood silently beside her bed, with white face, closed eyes, and blood-dabbled hair.[61]

Is it a coincidence that this happened on March 30, a day when *domovye* are especially malicious? You be the judge.

Fact or Fiction?

The Domovoi is as popular among Russians and other Slavic people as the Samodiva (woodland nymph, which you may know better as a Veela) is among the Bulgarians. Loved, revered, and sometimes feared, even today, the guardian spirit makes his presence known in households.

> Houses troubled with banging spirits, rapping ghosts and haunting apparitions have a long history in Russia. Russian folklore most frequently attributed strange noises, groans and knockings in the peasant hut to the domovoi, the spirit of the house. In the late nineteenth century, however, belief in traditional and folkloric spirits was in decline and this is mirrored in newspaper reports about haunted houses. In urban centres, spiritualism became the fashionable and appropriate framework within which haunted houses were interpreted, while reference to the domovoi became regarded as a sign for rural backwardness.[62]

The following excerpt from an article in *The London Daily News* in 1875 shows how belief in the spirit has gone in and out of popularity:

> Now, the hard thing is that when Russian society was in the stage of enlightenment a year or two ago, and when professors did not agree with Voltaire that 'error has its charms,' they preached quite a crusade against the bogies. The domovoy was clearly shown to be a tricky servant-girl, or if he was not that, he was the rats, or the wind, or he was all imagination. This sort of useful knowledge was proclaimed aloud, we learn, in manuals, and instructive little books. What was the result? Before the peasant had learned his lesson, St. Petersburg was found to be greatly preoccupied with spirits no better than the domovoy, and the European Messenger was circulating M. Wagner's ideas about the supernatural in connection with the legs of tables.[63]

An Incident with Madame Blavatsky

When talking about the legs of tables, the author of the above article may have been speaking about Madame Blavatsky or one of her contemporaries. This famed medium had a special affinity with spirits—having been born on the night between July 30 and 31, which you learned earlier exempted her from the pranks of the Domovoi. He, in fact, as well as other spirits, was as real to her as her own family and "had the affections of the child from the first."[64]

An excerpt from a book about her life cites an example of her "ability" to render a table as light as a feather or so heavy it appeared to be screwed to the floor. What's interesting about this is her comment that there could have been two possible reasons for the phenomenon that follows: Either from "the exercise of her own will directing the magnetic currents so that the pressure on the table became such that no physical force could move it" or "through the action of those beings with whom she was in constant communication, and who, although unseen, were able to hold the table against all opposition."[65]

The drawing-room of the Yahontoffs was full of visitors. Some were occupied with music, others with cards, but most of us, as usual, with phenomena. Leonide de Hahn did not concern himself with anything in particular, but was leisurely walking about, watching everybody and everything. He was a strong, muscular youth, saturated with the Latin and German wisdom of the University, and believed, so far, in no one and nothing. He stopped behind the back of his sister's chair, and was listening to her narratives of how some persons, who called themselves mediums, made light objects become so heavy that it was impossible to lift them; and others which were naturally heavy became again remarkably light.

"And you mean to say that you can do it?" ironically asked the young man of his sister.

"Mediums can, and I have done it occasionally; though I cannot always answer for its success," coolly replied Mme. Blavatsky.

"But would you try?" asked somebody in the room; and immediately all joined in requesting her to do so.

"I will try," she said, "but I beg of you to remember that I promise nothing. I will simply fix this chess-table and try. ... He who wants to make the experiment, let him lift it now, and then try *again after I shall have fixed it*."

"After you shall have fixed it?" said a voice, "and what then? Do you mean to say that you will not touch the table at all?"

"Why should I touch it?" answered Mme. Blavatsky, with a quiet smile.

Upon hearing the extraordinary assertion, one of the young men went determinedly to the small chess-table, and lifted it up as though it were a feather.

"All right," she said. "Now kindly leave it alone, and stand back!" The order was at once obeyed, and a great silence fell upon the company. All, holding their breath, anxiously watched for what Mme. Blavatsky would do next. She apparently, however, did nothing at all. She merely fixed her large blue eyes upon the chess-table, and kept looking at it with an intense gaze. Then, without removing her gaze, she silently, with a motion of her hand, invited the same young man to remove it. He approached, and grasped the table by its leg with great assurance. The table *could not be moved*!

He then seized it with both his hands. The table stood as though screwed to the floor.

Then the young man, crouching down, took hold of it with both hands, exerting all his strength to lift it by the additional means of his broad shoulders. He grew red with the effort, but all in vain! The table seemed rooted to the carpet, and would not be moved. There was a loud burst of applause. The young man, looking very much confused, abandoned his task *en désespoir de cause*, and stood aside.

Folding his arms in quite a Napoleonic way, he only slowly said, "Well, this is a good joke!"

"Indeed, it is a good one!" echoed Leonide.

A suspicion had crossed his mind that the young visitor was acting in secret confederacy with his sister and was fooling them.

"May I also try?" he suddenly asked her.

"Please do, my dear," was the laughing response.

Her brother upon this approached, smiling, and seized, in his turn, the diminutive table by its leg with his strong muscular arm. But the smile instantly vanished, to give place to an expression of mute amazement. He stepped back a little and examined again very carefully the, to him, well-known chess-table. Then he gave it a tremendous kick, but the little table did not even budge.

Suddenly applying to its surface his powerful chest he enclosed it within his arms, trying to shake it. The wood cracked, but would yield to no effort. Its three feet seemed screwed to the floor. Then Leonide Hahn lost all hope, and abandoning the ungrateful task, stepped aside, and frowning, exclaimed but these two words, "How strange!" his eyes turning meanwhile with a wild expression of astonishment from the table to his sister.

We all agreed that this exclamation was not too strong.

The loud debate had meanwhile drawn the attention of several visitors, and they came pouring in from the drawing-room into the large apartment where we were. Many of them, old and young, tried to lift up, or even to impart some slight motion to, the obstinate little chess-table. They failed, like the rest of us.

Upon seeing her brother's astonishment, and perchance desiring finally to destroy his doubts, Mme. Blavatsky, addressing him with her usual careless laugh, said, "Try to lift the table now, once more!"

Leonide H. approached the little thing very irresolutely, grasped it again by the leg, and, pulling it upwards, came very near to dislocating his arm owing to the useless effort: the table was lifted like a feather this time![66]

Potato Bombardment

The following excerpt describes an event *Volzhskii vestnik* (*The Volga Herald*) reported as being "true facts," which occurred on December 13 and 14, 1884.

Mr. Florentsov was just about to go to bed, when a loud rap on his apartment's ceiling was heard, which caused worry even to the neighbours. At about the same time, potatoes and bricks began to fly out of the oven pipe and smashed the kitchen window. On the 14th the 'phenomena' continued all day long and were accompanied by many comical episodes. About 10 well-known officers came to Mr. Florentsov's apartment. They put a heavy pole against the oven-door, but the shaft was not strong enough and it soon flew to one side. [After this] potatoes rolled out beneath the furniture, fell from the walls, rained down from the ceiling; sometimes a brick appeared at the scene of action. One officer was hit by a potato on his head, another one on his nose, some were hit by the bullets of this invisible foe at their backs, shoulders and so on. The aide of the district police officer showed up at the battlefield; the flat was thoroughly searched but no explanation could be found. […] The potato bombardment continued and one of the rank and file received such a severe blow, that he was beaten off his feet by fear. However, the soldiers endured the potato fire and calmly collected the shells eating some of them on the battlefield, thus making the most of the fact that many of them were cooked. […] On the 15th many Kazaners visited Florentsov's apartment, quite a few of them spiritualist amateurs or simply fascinated by some kind of devilry or other.[67]

The author of the news article goes on to explain that the phenomenon had to do with some ability of a maid who worked at the building. Perhaps, like Madame Blavatsky, spirits were in tune to her.

Flying Logs

If potatoes falling from the ceiling aren't enough to make you wonder about the existence of spirits, perhaps a story about logs flying around a courtyard will. It was recorded in a journal devoted to psychic research by Michael Petrovo-Solovovo, in reference to an interview with an elderly man, which was published in *Rebus* in 1892. Although ready to accept the possibility that such strange phenomena existed among those deemed fraud and delusion, Petrovo-Solovovo said, "I confess there still remains a good deal of skepticism in my mind."[68]

I am at present in my 61st year. The inexplicable phenomenon, which I witnessed, took place 45 years ago in October, 1846. My father, a controller of the Tver Court of Exchequer, lived in the merchant Nazaroff's house at the corner of Semionovskaia-street, in Tver. This house was built of stone, and had two floors, the upper part being occupied by the Nazaroff family, whilst my father and family lived in the lower; there were no other inhabitants in the house. ...

Our family consisted of my father, mother, two sisters of my father, one of whom was a widow, and the other an old maid, and myself, a boy 15 years old, who was then in the 5th class of the Tver Gymnasium. In the Nazaroffs' service were a cook, a maid, and a coachman, who had also charge of the court-yard (*dvornik*); and we had a cook and a maid, who were both our serfs.

As the Nazaroff family led a very modest and patriarchal life, we had the habit, as soon as my father had left the house, after 6 p.m., to attend to his official duties, of having the gate (leading into the yard) locked and the key given to the *dvornik*; his room was connected with the gate by a wire and bell, and he used to open the gate when the bell had been rung. ...

My father was in the habit of purchasing every year, in January and February, firewood for the whole year, part of which, with our landlord's permission, was placed under the *porte cochère* and close to the wall of the granary. There must have been some three or four *sajènes* [1 *sajène* = 7 feet] of them. These logs were rather large, probably weighing not less than 7 pounds each.

I shall now describe the phenomenon itself; it is very vividly impressed on my memory, though nearly half a century old. In the first half of October, I think, my father had as usual gone at 7 p.m. to the Court of Exchequer, to attend to his official duties, where he stayed as late as 11 and sometimes 12 o'clock; my mother and aunts sat down to work, and I began to prepare my lessons for next day.

About 10 p.m. our maid Martha entered the bedroom where my aunts were sitting and said: "What is taking place in our yard? Someone is stealing the wood, I have heard several logs falling."

I was rather an audacious boy, and felt tired of sitting and working, so I availed myself of this opportunity and began to ask Martha to bring in a candle, as the night was dark, and it was still darker under the *porte cochère*; my mother and aunts also followed us.

When in the yard, I heard a log falling down from the pile, and, about two minutes later, another one. I tried to come nearer with a candle, but my mother laid hold of me and would not let me go. Someone was sent to wake up Nicholas, the *dvornik*; he came in, lit a lantern and even began to make the sign of the cross when he heard the noise made by the logs falling. I have forgotten to add that the yard at the Nazaroffs' was paved with stone. ...

The *dvornik* asserted that he had locked the gate immediately after my father had gone out and showed the key; the back-door, leading into the garden, also proved to be locked; consequently a man would have been unable to enter the yard.

The Nazaroffs heard us talking in the yard and came out also, so that we were twelve in number; three candles and a lantern were brought in and threw sufficient light both over the logs of wood and all the space under the *porte cochère*, and this is what we all saw: out of the middle of the pile (not from the top of it, but out of the middle) a log would fly forth and fall down on the floor three *arschin* off.

All the persons present were greatly frightened and pressed close to each other. I proved to be the most courageous of all and persuaded the *dvornik* to come with me nearer the logs of wood; he carrying a lantern and myself a candle. I thought that perhaps a cat had got in between the wall and the logs, and tried to put my hand [there], but could not do it, as the logs were quite close to the wall.

Meanwhile the logs would fly out with short intervals. This bombardment with logs lasted for about 40 minutes, 27 in all being thrown out; and another remarkable thing was that the empty space, which remained after a log had flown out was not filled up with other logs and that we noticed no movement due to the upper logs coming down, and yet in the morning the pile proved to be quite compact and without any holes. The *dvornik* picked up the logs which had been thrown out and placed them close to another wall. The logs had not flown out of one place only but out of several; but always from the middle of the pile, not from the top of it or from the sides.

In the morning, when going to my *gymnasium* I met the *dvornik* and asked him to try and pull a log out of the middle of the pile. Nicholas, a robust man of about 30, in spite of all his efforts was unable to pull out of the middle of the pile a single log. Of course, all my relatives, as well as the proprietors of the house, put down the whole thing to the *domovoi* (house-spirit) and his tricks.

None of the other witnesses of this phenomenon are alive at present; even a person younger than myself—Nathalie, a daughter of the widow of Nazaroff's son—died in the seventies.

I would have absolutely no reason to invent such a story; and it seems to me that I can be trusted, seeing that I am 60 years old and have served three Emperors in the Ministry of Public Instruction for 40 years.

Ivan Koupreyanoff,

Late Inspector of the Tver District School, belonging to the nobility of Tver.[69]

What Do You Think?

The purpose of this book is to give testimony to what people believe and for you, as a reader, to become familiar with the Domovoi and other spirits. If you don't believe in the supernatural, these events won't be enough to convince you. If you're a believer—whether from Russia or anywhere else in the world—these stories are a few more to add to your collection.

Whether you want to call it "spiritualism," a poltergeist, or the actions of a Domovoi, strange things happen in homes that can't always be explained. Belief in spirits is up to you.

Domovoi in Literature

The Domovoi, like the Kikimora, is a popular subject in literature. The following examples give you not only a sense of the spirit, but also give you a glimpse into Russian and Slavic lifestyles.

- "The Miser" from *Krilof and His Fables*, translated by William Ralston and published in 1883.
- An excerpt from *A Sportsman's Sketches* by Ivan Sergeevich Turgenev, published in 1852.
- An excerpt from *The Mask* by John Cournos, published in 1919.

"The Miser" from *Krilof and His Fables*

Earlier you read a tale about a Domovoi who shared his wealth with the family who came to live with him. The goblin of the following fable (whom Ralston calls a Domovoi), however, has quite the different take about sharing his wealth.

Andreyevich Krylov

Ivan Andreyevich Krylov (1769 – 1844) wrote many tales loosely based off Aesop's Fables and those by La Fontaine, while other, more original works, were of a satirical nature.

William Ralston translated many of these works and published them in *Krilof and His Fables* in 1883. He says of the tales:

> It should be borne in mind that Krilof's fables were seldom mere literary bubbles, blown to create an instant's amusement or admiration, but not intended to serve any useful end, or to suggest any serious idea. Each of them, as a general rule, conveyed either a valuable warning or a wholesome reprimand (Ralston, *Krilof and His Fables*, x).

And Krylov directed many of those reprimands toward the oppression and corruption of the Russian nobility. The stories show not only the harshness of Russian peasant life, but also the customs and mannerisms of the people, and they hold "shrewd insight into the thoughts and motives of the human heart" (Ralston, *Krilof and His Fables*, viii).

A certain goblin used to keep watch over a rich treasure buried underground. Suddenly, he was ordered by the ruler of the demons to fly away for many years to the other side of the world. His service was of such a nature, that he was obliged to do as he was bid, whether he liked it or not. Our Goblin fell into a terrible perplexity, wondering how he should preserve his treasure in his absence—who there was to take charge of it. To build a treasure-house, and hire a guardian—that would cost much money. To leave it to itself—that way it might be lost. Impossible to answer for it for a day. Some one might dig it up, and steal it: people are quick at scenting out money.

He worried himself; he pondered over it; and at last an idea came into his head. The master of the house to which he was attached was a terrible Miser. The Goblin, having dug up the treasure, appeared to the Miser, and said,

"Dear master, they have ordered me to go away from your house to a distant land. But I have always been well disposed towards you, so don't refuse to accept this treasure of mine, as a parting token of affection. Eat, drink, and be merry, and spend it without fear; only, when you die, I am to be your sole heir. That is my single stipulation. As for the rest, may destiny grant you health and long life."

He spoke, and was off.

Ten—twenty years went by. Having completed his service, the Goblin flies home to his native land. What does he see? O rapturous sight! The Miser, dead from starvation, lies stretched on the strong box, its key in his hand; and the ducats are all there intact. So the Goblin gets his treasure back again, and rejoices greatly to think that it has had a guardian who did not cost him a single farthing (Ralston, *Krilof and His Fables*, 24-25).

Moral: When a miser has money, and yet grudges to pay for food and drink, is he not treasuring up his ducats for a goblin?

A Sportsman's Sketches by Ivan Sergeevich Turgenev

Ivan Sergeevich Turgenev's (1818 – 1883) *A Sportsman's Sketches* was his first major publication, a short story collection written in 1852. It's been called "artistic" and the "most delightful" of his novels, and he has been described as "the impersonation of the Slav temperament, of its melancholy—that melancholy which, intensified by the unhappy circumstances of his private life, is the keynote of almost all his novels" (Woolmer, 41).

Ivan Turgenev

He was said to be "happiest in his descriptions of that part of the empire where the 'black-earth zone' begins, where the oak is displacing the birch, and there is a breath of the south in the air through a good part of the year" (Woolmer, 40). And that his "intense love of country and of all thereto belonging breathes in his every page" (Woolmer, 42).

A Sportsman's Sketches is a collection of tales that bring you "so thoroughly into the heart of things that after you have read it, though only in a translation, you fancy you have lived for years with these people and among these surroundings" (Woolmer, 42-43).

The passage that follows has been described thus: "[O]ne of the prettiest pictures in the Tales is where the writer and his comrade lie in the long grass through the short summer-night listening unseen while the horse-boys, who are watching the colts, tell fairy tales" (Woolmer, 40). Turgenev's artistic prose, although not relevant to the telling of the Domovoi story, helps set the scene for the reader, creating atmosphere, as it were, in the telling of a ghost story.

T he hill on which I found myself terminated abruptly in an almost overhanging precipice, whose gigantic profile stood out black against the dark-blue waste of sky, and directly below me, in the corner formed by this precipice and the plain near the river, which was there a dark, motionless mirror, under the lee of the hill, two fires side by side were smoking and throwing up red flames. People were stirring round them, shadows hovered, and sometimes the front of a little curly head was lighted up by the glow.

I found out at last where I had got to. This plain was well known in our parts under the name of Byezhin Prairie. . . . But there was no possibility of returning home, especially at night; my legs were sinking under me from weariness. I decided to get down to the fires and to wait for the dawn in the company of these men, whom I took for drovers. I got down successfully, but I had hardly let go of the last branch I had grasped, when suddenly two large shaggy white dogs rushed angrily barking upon me. The sound of ringing boyish voices came from round the fires; two or three boys quickly got up from the ground. I called back in response to their shouts of inquiry. They ran up to me, and at once called off the dogs, who were specially struck by the appearance of my Dianka. I came down to them.

I had been mistaken in taking the figures sitting round the fires for drovers. They were simply peasant boys from a neighbouring village, who were in charge of a drove of horses. In hot summer weather with us they drive the horses out at night to graze in the open country: the flies and gnats would give them no peace in the daytime; they drive out the drove towards evening, and drive them back in the early morning: it's a great treat for the peasant boys. Bare-headed, in old fur-capes, they bestride the most spirited nags, and scurry along with merry cries and hooting and ringing laughter, swinging their arms and legs, and leaping into the air. The fine dust is stirred up in yellow clouds and moves along the road; the tramp of hoofs in unison resounds afar; the horses race along, pricking up their ears; in front of all, with his tail in the air and thistles in his tangled mane, prances some shaggy chestnut, constantly shifting his paces as he goes.

I told the boys I had lost my way, and sat down with them. They asked me where I came from, and then were silent for a little and turned away. Then we talked a little again.

I lay down under a bush, whose shoots had been nibbled off, and began to look round. It was a marvellous picture; about the fire a red ring of light quivered and seemed to swoon away in the embrace of a background of darkness; the flame flaring up from time to time cast swift flashes of light beyond the boundary of this circle; a fine tongue of light licked the dry twigs and died away at once; long thin shadows, in their turn breaking in for an instant, danced right up to the very fires; darkness was struggling with light.

Sometimes, when the fire burnt low and the circle of light shrank together, suddenly out of the encroaching darkness a horse's head was thrust in, bay, with striped markings or all white, stared with intent blank eyes upon us, nipped hastily the long grass, and drawing back again, vanished instantly. One could only hear it still munching and snorting.

From the circle of light it was hard to make out what was going on in the darkness; everything close at hand seemed shut off by an almost black curtain; but farther away hills and forests were dimly visible in long blurs upon the horizon.

The dark unclouded sky stood, inconceivably immense, triumphant, above us in all its mysterious majesty. One felt a sweet oppression at one's heart, breathing in that peculiar, overpowering, yet fresh fragrance—the fragrance of a summer night in Russia. Scarcely a sound was to be heard around. . . . Only at times, in the river near, the sudden splash of a big fish leaping, and the faint rustle of a reed on the bank, swaying lightly as the ripples reached it . . . the fires alone kept up a subdued crackling.

The boys sat round them: there too sat the two dogs, who had been so eager to devour me. They could not for long after reconcile themselves to my presence, and, drowsily blinking and staring into the fire, they growled now and then with an unwonted sense of their own dignity; first they growled, and then whined a little, as though deploring the impossibility of carrying out their desires. There were altogether five boys: Fedya, Pavlusha, Ilyusha, Kostya and Vanya. (From their talk I learnt their names, and I intend now to introduce them to the reader.)

The first and eldest of all, Fedya, one would take to be about fourteen. He was a well-made boy, with good-looking, delicate, rather small features, curly fair hair, bright eyes, and a perpetual half-merry, half-careless smile. He belonged, by all appearances, to a well-to-do family, and had ridden out to the prairie, not through necessity, but for amusement. He wore a gay print shirt, with a yellow border; a short new overcoat slung round his neck was almost slipping off his narrow shoulders; a comb hung from his blue belt. His boots, coming a little way up the leg, were certainly his own—not his father's.

The second boy, Pavlusha, had tangled black hair, grey eyes, broad cheek-bones, a pale face pitted with small-pox, a large but well-cut mouth; his head altogether was large—'a beer-barrel head,' as they say—and his figure was square and clumsy. He was not a good-looking boy—there's no denying it!—and yet I liked him; he looked very sensible and straightforward, and there was a vigorous ring in his voice. He had nothing to boast of in his attire; it consisted simply of a homespun shirt and patched trousers.

The face of the third, Ilyusha, was rather uninteresting; it was a long face, with short-sighted eyes and a hook nose; it expressed a kind of dull, fretful uneasiness; his tightly-drawn lips seemed rigid; his contracted brow never relaxed; he seemed continually blinking from the firelight. His flaxen—almost white—hair hung out in thin wisps under his low felt hat, which he kept pulling down with both hands over his ears. He had on new bast-shoes and leggings; a thick string, wound three times round his figure, carefully held together his neat black smock. Neither he nor Pavlusha looked more than twelve years old.

The fourth, Kostya, a boy of ten, aroused my curiosity by his thoughtful and sorrowful look. His whole face was small, thin, freckled, pointed at the chin like a squirrel's; his lips were barely perceptible; but his great black eyes, that shone with liquid brilliance, produced a strange impression; they seemed trying to express something for which the tongue—his tongue, at least—had no words. He was undersized and weakly, and dressed rather poorly.

The remaining boy, Vanya, I had not noticed at first; he was lying on the ground, peacefully curled up under a square rug, and only occasionally thrust his curly brown head out from under it: this boy was seven years old at the most.

So I lay under the bush at one side and looked at the boys. A small pot was hanging over one of the fires; in it potatoes were cooking. Pavlusha was looking after them, and on his knees he was trying them by poking a splinter of wood into the boiling water. Fedya was lying leaning on his elbow, and smoothing out the skirts of his coat. Ilyusha was sitting beside Kostya, and still kept blinking constrainedly. Kostya's head drooped despondently, and he looked away into the distance. Vanya did not stir under his rug. I pretended to be asleep. Little by little, the boys began talking again.

At first they gossiped of one thing and another, the work of to-morrow, the horses; but suddenly Fedya turned to Ilyusha, and, as though taking up again an interrupted conversation, asked him:

'Come then, so you've seen the domovoy?'

'No, I didn't see him, and no one ever can see him,' answered Ilyusha, in a weak hoarse voice, the sound of which was wonderfully in keeping with the expression of his face; 'I heard him. . . . Yes, and not I alone.'

'Where does he live—in your place?' asked Pavlusha.

'In the old paper-mill.'

'Why, do you go to the factory?'

'Of course we do. My brother Avdushka and I, we are paper-glazers.'

'I say—factory-hands!'

'Well, how did you hear it, then?' asked Fedya.

'It was like this. It happened that I and my brother Avdushka, with Fyodor of Mihyevska, and Ivashka the Squint-eyed, and the other Ivashka who comes from the Red Hills, and Ivashka of Suhorukov too—and there were some other boys there as well—there were ten of us boys there altogether—the whole shift, that is—it happened that we spent the night at the paper-mill; that's to say, it didn't happen, but Nazarov, the overseer, kept us.

' "Why," said he, "should you waste time going home, boys; there's a lot of work to-morrow, so don't go home, boys."

'So we stopped, and were all lying down together, and Avdushka had just begun to say, "I say, boys, suppose the domovoy were to come?"

'And before he'd finished saying so, some one suddenly began walking over our heads; we were lying down below, and he began walking upstairs overhead, where the wheel is. We listened: he walked; the boards seemed to be bending under him, they creaked so; then he crossed over, above our heads; all of a sudden the water began to drip and drip over the wheel; the wheel rattled and rattled and again began to turn, though the sluices of the conduit above had been let down.

'We wondered who could have lifted them up so that the water could run; any way, the wheel turned and turned a little, and then stopped. Then he went to the door overhead and began coming down-stairs, and came down like this, not hurrying himself; the stairs seemed to groan under him too. . . Well, he came right down to our door, and waited and waited . . . and all of a sudden the door simply flew open.

'We were in a fright; we looked—there was nothing. . . . Suddenly what if the net on one of the vats didn't begin moving; it got up, and went rising and ducking and moving in the air as though some one were stirring with it, and then it was in its place again. Then, at another vat, a hook came off its nail, and then was on its nail again; and then it seemed as if some one came to the door, and suddenly coughed and choked like a sheep, but so loudly!... We all fell down in a heap and huddled against one another. . . . Just weren't we in a fright that night!' (Turgenev, 138-145)

The Mask by John Cournos

John Cournos (1881 – 1966), born Ivan Grigorievich Korshun, wrote *The Mask* in 1919. Although he was born in Russia, he lived most of his life away from his homeland. His family moved to Philadelphia when he was ten, and later he moved to London in 1912, where he began his career as a poet and author. He eventually emigrated to the U.S., where he lived out the rest of his life.

The opening of *The Mask* tells the reader that the story that follows is "the story of the making of a human mask" (Cournos, 7), one which the character Gombarov (called Vanya as a child) wore.

> This mask of Gombarov's, with its subtle contours of repose and irony, was not created in a day. A mask, it may be assumed, conceals more than it reveals. And in this sense a mask is the measure of art. It may express a titanic struggle in an appearance of tranquillity. And in the degree that its appearance is tranquil, to that extent has a spirit conquered life. The chaos of Gombarov's existence strove toward orderliness, his torments toward peace, his pain toward beauty—all these shaped the mask from below into an appearance of tranquillity (Cournos, 7).

As you read the following excerpt, you should recall what you have learned about the Domovoi. This chapter in particular shows the darker nature of the spirit.

One day Spring appeared, with as yet a shy smile.

And Winter, his heart softened, relaxed his hard, white-bearded face, down which ran large, warm spreading tears, and his eyes grown younger laughed through them at the sight of the soothing sun.

Vanya liked the thaw. The dear rivulets revealed the fresh grass, as yet tender as a babe's skin. Here and there skeleton bushes and young trees and clusters of leafless thorns emerged from the deep snow like symbols of a coming resurrection. Mountains of snow rolled away as it were, and released the earth from her entombment.

The fringe of long icicles, edging the caves of houses like a lace, diminished perceptibly, and its patterns grew softer, less austere. Holes opened up in the hard inert stream like eyes waking from a long sleep, and the clear water blinked out of them with animation. Miniature waterfalls formed themselves in the thinner streams in the meadows and following the course of these streams Vanya saw them wind between banks of snow and disappear under the snow, like endless thin serpents entering their lairs.

The little sledge bells jingled along the roads, and in their jingle there was the joy and sadness of last snows. A delicious smell came from the earth in those spots where the white robe slipped from her.

The young man in the *troika* put his lips blissfully for a moment on the hair of the young girl at his side—where it showed under the little fur cap, and breathed deeply at the same time, while the great sun, smiling, put out his long radiant fingers and undid the perspiring driver's sheepskin.

But in the evening, when the Sun closed his eyes and drew the dark bed-cover over his radiant limbs, there was a change.

The Wind, with a great flowing beard like a besom, leant his giant arms on a black cloud and blew from the north. The *troika* driver, going out in the evening for a drink of "something hot," put up his large fur collar and pulled down the ear-flaps over his ears. Winter, sulking, as if he repented, hardened his face again, his tears froze into icicles, and the stream, like a deep furrow on his forehead, crackled as he knitted his brow.

Vanya felt wretched. He went to his room, and in his lonely misery he tore his hair. Later, finding it cold in bed, he went to the kitchen and climbed up on the oven. Here lay Marta, who was glad of company. She pressed Vanya to her hot body and whispered:

"I am glad you have come, *golubohik*, [darling; literally, little pigeon] a *domovoi* a little while ago had his knee on my chest and his hand on my throat, trying to strangle me."

Vanya shivered.

"Don't be afraid, *golubchik*, he never comes when there are two."

"Why don't you marry then, and then he won't come?"

"Ah, you don't understand, *golubchik*,"—and Marta went on to explain. "You see it's this way, it was on the last Kuzma and Demian night, and I lit a candle and sat before a mirror, watching in it for my chosen one to appear. In a little while I thought I heard a low knock on my window, then the door opened and closed, some one seemed to slip in though I didn't see anyone, then there was a slight stir of air as if some one was coming closer,—'my loved one, my *golubehik* has come,' I was thinking, and I looked all excited into the glass. . . ." At this point Marta gave a little sob and could not go on for a moment.

Byess (demon), 1831.
By Pushkin, Alexander Sergeyevich [Public domain], via Wikimedia Commons.

"What's the matter, Marta, what happened?" asked Vanya, all agitated and afraid, but fascinated in some unaccountable way and wanting to know more.

And as soon as Marta could speak, she said:

". . . I saw *him* . . . in the glass . . . looking over my shoulder. . . ."

"*Him?*" asked Vanya. "You mean . . . " and stopped short.

"Yes, the *byess*. [demon] He was grinning at me, as large as life . . . then I fell into a faint . . . when I came to there was nothing. But ever since then, he's come to me some nights . . . and he puts his knee on my chest and his hands on my throat and tries to choke me. The Lord have mercy on me, a miserable sinner."

There was a pause, and in that pause the windows rattled with the wind, and an unfastened shutter struck the wall somewhere with a bang.

"Oh Lord, have mercy . . ." moaned Marta.

Vanya plucked up courage to speak.

"I say, Marta, do you believe in *him*—the *byess*? Papa says there is no *byess*—and no *vyedma*." [witch]

"Lord bless you, child, and I saw one myself the other evening as I was walking alone along a dark lane—she was flying round up in the air on a broomstick, and she looked at me and showed her teeth . . . and so I quickly crossed myself, and she disappeared all of a sudden. You see they are afraid of the cross, that's why they never come nigh a church spire. And now, Vanya, go to sleep, darling,"—and she laid Vanya's head gently on her high, firm bosom, there where the *byess* had had his knee, and had a feeling that Vanya's head would protect her that night, not only because 'her chosen one' came to her only when she was alone. ...[70]

Marta was right. The *byess* did not come to her again that night.

But if he did not come to her, he came to Vanya, if not the *byess* himself, then at least the *byess's* second cousin.

Vanya dreamt that he was in his own bed, and that a tall thin-legged man with a rooster's head came to him and sat down on the chair by the bed. He smiled at Vanya out of his bright green eyes under his big red comb, then rose and beckoned to Vanya to follow him. Vanya felt horribly afraid, but felt drawn on by a strange, irresistible fascination.

He rose and followed his guide. He walked through corridor after corridor in the dark. He knew that his guide was ahead of him, though he could not hear his footsteps: only a dim glimmer of light coming from he knew not where played upon his guide's red cock's comb; they turned corner after corner, there seemed to be no end. But at last they came to a passage where the corridor appeared to stop.

The guide pulled two curtains aside here, and revealed a little alcove and a little door at the end of it, lit up mysteriously as by a dim image lamp. Vanya thought he heard voices, which as he approached the door seemed in some curious way to change into a kind of cackle as of hens.

Then a terrible fear came upon Vanya, and just as his guide was about to take him by the hand and pull him through the door he gave a violent scream and woke up, sobbing. Marta's face was over him, and she was drawing his face to her bosom. Marta was saying tenderly:

"What's the matter, darling? Don't cry, my darling." (Cournos, 84-87)

***

That's all that's written about the Domovoi in this story. It's enough to give you an idea of the darker side of this mostly benevolent spirit.

Stopan. Illustration by Anna Błaszczyk (Evelinea Erato). © Bendideia Publishing.

Stopan (Стопан)

Sacred is the earth when it comes over a grave.

Stopan (singular); **Stopani** (plural)

Other names: stopanin (the stopan), stihya, namestnik, saybia.[71]

In a moment of darkest despair, you sense a departed loved one nearby, comforting you. Or perhaps it's your guardian angel keeping you safe. Regardless what you believe, many people have experienced contact with the unknown, leaving them terrified, bewildered, or comforted.

These tutelary deity or spirits of the home and family—and many other places and occupations as well—have existed since ancient times. During the Roman and Greek eras, the guardians were called *genii* (*genius*, singular) and followed their assigned people from birth until death. A *juno* spirit was assigned to women.

Propitiating a spirit in the appropriate manner is the means to keeping him content so he'll continue to protect you.

In much the same way, similar spirits exist among the Eastern European nations. You've learned about the most popular Slavic one, the Domovoi. Among the Bulgarians, the attending spirit is the Stopan. He's similar in some ways, but quite different in others as you'll discover throughout this chapter.

Consider now the words of the familiar children's nighttime prayer.

> Now I lay me down to sleep,
> I pray the Lord my soul to keep,
> If I should die before I wake,
> I pray the Lord my soul to take.

Or perhaps you've learned an alternate version:

> Now I lay me down to sleep,
> I pray the Lord my soul to keep,
> thy angels watch me through the night,
> And keep me safe till morning's light.

The next time these words drift upward toward heaven, think about all the different types of comforters who roam the spirit realm, there to take care of you. These angels could be one of the faithfully departed, a grandfather or a relative from long ago, protecting his own.

Etymology

Stopan comes from the Old Bulgarian word *stopanŭ* meaning "master of all possessions" and bears a relationship with the Old Persian word *asta-pāvan* ("home guardian"), which is a derivative of *astra* for "celestial star," giving it the further meaning of "celestial guardian," which today we'd call a guardian angel (Stamenov, [12]). It also bears a relationship to the Romanian *stăpân* and the Megleno-Romanian *stăpǫn* ("master") (Wiktionary, "Стопан"). It may link to an early form of the Albanian word *shtëpi* ("house") or possibly the Greek word σπίτι (*spíti*, "home"). (Wiktionary, "Стопан").

Origins

Like the Russian Domovoi, the Stopan from Bulgarian folklore and beliefs has its roots in ancestor worship, and the spirit guards the home and family. This "ancestor" is not necessarily a family member, nor is the spirit's gender defined, although normally the Stopan is considered a male. The spirit could have been an important person in the community in which he lived—usually someone considered a "hero."

Not everyone knows the name of the ancestor who protects them. And not every spirit who passes from this world becomes a Stopan. To reach this exalted state in death, in life, the person has been known for his exceptional beauty, strength, and valor. Even this bit of information comes with a caveat: without knowing who this "hero" was, no one can tell you why he or she deserves the honor of this elevated position in the world of spirits.

In one case, a man identified the family's Stopan as his great-great-great-grandfather Stamen, who had escaped from Macedonia before Bulgaria was liberated from the Turks in 1878.[72] What's interesting about this and many other stories is that the ancestor is frequently someone who lived prior to Bulgaria's freedom. Perhaps the trying times of foreign dominance bred holy and heroic men.

Oftentimes, musical ability is another aspect of the Stopan. For example, ancestor Stamen mentioned above supposedly led a holy life and was proficient at playing a *kaval* (a wooden flute-like instrument). Although he wasn't wealthy, each year Stamen gave a golden coin to a nearby monastery, which showed how holy and good a person he was.

After the Christianization of the Bulgarians, the worship of ancestors branched out to include saints, and even angels took on the role of home—or village—guardians. As heavenly protectors of their charges, saints fit into this role quite naturally.

One instance where a family chooses a patron saint to be the silent guardian is after the construction of a new home. In such a case, no spirit has yet taken up residence, and so this is a viable option to ensure the home has a Stopan.

Not all guardians of the home have such an honorable beginning. As with the origins of the Domovoi, some people believe the first person to enter a new house will die and become its protector. Through rites you'll see later in this chapter, the builder of the house is also someone who becomes bonded to the home, and after his death, he is thought to become its guardian. (Other construction rites—as you'll learn in the Talasum chapter—create a different kind of spirit that guards a building or other structure.)

Appearance

For the most part, people never see the Stopan—at least not in human-like form. He doesn't appear as the family's pet cat, as the Domovoi does from time to time. More often, if you see the spirit, he takes the form of a non-poisonous snake. The snake as a guardian spirit of the home will be discussed in more detail in the Smok chapter. Many guardian spirits appear in the form of a snake. The name of this spirit varies from region to region and country to country.

Encounters with the Stopan are more frequent through dreams. The example cited above about a man's great-great-great-grandfather Stamen does not indicate whether the man saw the ancestor as an earthly apparition or through a dream. He merely describes the spirit as a young man with dark hair and blue eyes.

Getting to Know the Stopan

A Stopan protects the home and village he worked in during his lifetime. But, people don't treat him like a family member. You shouldn't scold him the way you do a Domovoi. Instead, revere the spirit as someone holy, almost angelic. His purpose is to take care of your family. Brides and home builders in particular perform special rites to appease the Stopan.

Relationship with Brides

In a Bulgarian home, when a bride is on the verge of leaving her home for that of her husband, she walks around the hearth in her father's house three times. She prostrates herself before the household spirit each time, asking for his forgiveness that she must leave him. This is her last opportunity to connect with the Stopan before she quits her family home, abandoning all that she's known. She needs—and desires—his blessing, knowing it hurts him that she's deserting him. Her act of humiliation generally appeases him, so she can leave with a clear conscience.

In her husband's home, she once again performs a ceremony for the new household spirit. She sits close to the hearth—and the Stopan—and tends to the fire, tossing wood onto the flames, thereby establishing her connection with her husband's guardian spirit and ensuring his acceptance and protection of her as part of the family.

Building a New Home

A Bulgarian saying about home building indicates its importance: "On growing wealthy, a Turk takes a wife, and a Bulgarian builds a house."[73] Some of the rites related to spirits are similar to those you learned about with the Domovoi, such as offerings for the laying of the foundation and the belief that the first person to enter the home will die soon afterwards to become its guardian spirit. Other rites, however, differ, such as choosing the site upon which to build the house and starting the first fire in the hearth in the finished home.

The general belief is that not only does every home have its guardian spirit, but every place does as well: springs, old trees, fields, vineyards, boundary lines, and so forth. Some spirits are good; others, bad. These guardians take the form of an animal—oftentimes a snake, but they can appear as other creatures as well.

Unlike the Domovoi, whom the Russians encourage to come with them when they move, Bulgarians don't "take" their guardian spirit with them. The Stopan remains as the protector of a homestead, not a family. The new residents offer the spirit sacrifices of food so he'll accept them.

When those who choose to build a new home first search out a suitable site, they look for a place that's not inhabited by a spirit: some of these may be *samovili* or *youdi*, both types of bad fairies. Or *rusalki*, mermaids, may have control of the location. The spirit of the dragon *zmey* may also reside in the selected spot. Builders avoid sites where other bad spirits (such as those who suffered a violent or unnatural death) congregate: caves, unused wells, and old, neglected graves. They also avoid buildings where a threshing-floor, watermill, or sheepfold once existed, or any place where *samodivi*—wild, treacherous woodland nymphs—might have trod. You can tell where these places are because circles of flowers grow where the nymphs have danced.

To determine what kind of spirit lives at a potential building site, people pour ashes over the area and visit the location the next day. If they find no marks, they're safe to build on the site because it's spirit-free. If, however, a spirit lives there, its animal manifestation—whether bird, beast, or reptile—will have left its tracks in the ashes. This lets the builders know what type of sacrifice is needed to appease the spirit. Like for like: they'll sacrifice the type of animal whose tracks they found. The worse scenario is discovering human footprints. This means someone in the family will die soon after the house is completed if the owners decide to go ahead and build there. Definitely not the option to choose.

In some communities, builders roll a freshly baked loaf of bread across the area; they start digging the foundation where it stops.

Sometimes, you may have no choice and have to build on a location where spirits roam. In this case, when you lay the foundation for the home, you must sacrifice a rooster, black hen, or black lamb or ram as a *kurban* and place the animal's bones under the foundation. This should appease the spirits residing there, and keep any evil spirits and diseases from coming into your home.

Another method of "curing" or purifying the land is to collect "silent water"—which is drawn from a river, spring, or other body of water in ritual silence. Put the water into a brass pot, along with herbs and greenery that you gathered on Eniovden (Midsummer's Day), and cover it with a new white cloth. At night, the oldest woman of the household pours the water onto the foundation. She sings the following spell to send the spirits away from the place:

> Samovili, samovili,
> And you bad youdi
> And you white Rusalki
> And gray colorful zmeys
> If you're sitting here,
> And if that's your yard
> Go back to the woods,
> Go back to the end of the world.[74]

The elderly woman repeats this ritual every time the builders lay down another section of the foundation. When they've finished, she digs a hole in the middle of the foundation and buries the herbs.

In other regions, the woman will sprinkle the ritual water on the capstones that the builders lay in each corner of the foundation. The oldest man of the house sits on each one for a few minutes. This is magic to ensure a long life and happiness for the people who live in the house.

Beneath the place where the hearth will be, the builders lay a flat stone, which prevents bad spirits from entering the home. Once the hearth is built, two young, unmarried women bring fire and ashes from two houses of relatives. The oldest woman of the house sprinkles the flat stone with water and starts the first fire. As she makes the sign of the cross, she says, "Dear God, bring this hearth a lot of pots for weddings, christenings, gatherings. Please, God, fill the hearth with baked bread, fill this house with children, and make sure the flame in the hearth never goes out." The color of the first flame in the fire predicts the fate of the house and family.

After a family finally selects a suitable location, they determine when the building should begin. Preferable days are Monday or Wednesday, or on occasion Thursday. In addition, choosing a day when the moon is in full or new stage is a good time. The builder or the future owner digs the first spadeful at dawn where the eastern corner of the house will be. The homeowner then sacrifices a ram or fowl to appease the location's guardian spirit, and lets the blood run into the foundation. After the family cooks and consumes the slaughtered animal, they bury the bones in the foundation as well.

As you learned earlier, one belief is that the first person to enter the completed house will become the guardian spirit when he or she dies. This often means the eldest in the family enters first. Even if this belief isn't prevalent in an area, the eldest often spend the first night in the house before the other family members move in. The old people light and tend the fire as a way to bring wisdom and experience into the home. Even so, the rest of the family will wait for a new or full moon to spend their first night in the home.

Another belief is that the builder will become the home's guardian when he dies. This relates to the builder's "bond" with the house as you learned in the Origins section of this chapter. Many people believe the master builder has magical powers. It's necessary for him to "bless" the house—first by attaching a cross (made from the wood of a fruit tree, which symbolizes fertility and prosperity) to the highest part of the house. The cross is decorated with flowers and greenery, tied to it with a red thread. When the homeowners present the builder with the gift of a new shirt (a common practice among Bulgarians is to give someone a new shirt for any major life event), he calls out a blessing for God to reward the homeowner as generously as he rewards those who built the house. The more gifts (socks, towels, kerchiefs, and linen items being common) the family and relatives provide to the master builder and his crew, the more blessings the homeowner will receive.

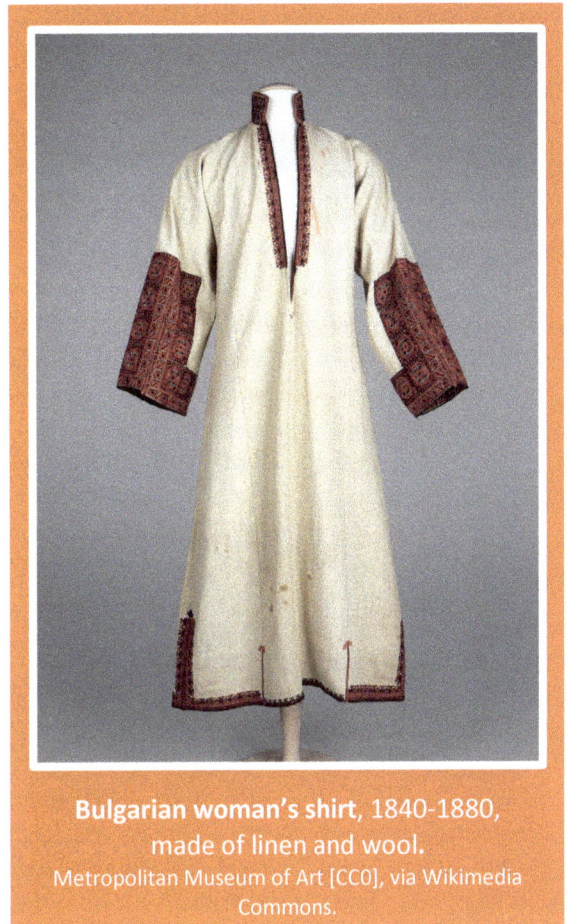

Bulgarian woman's shirt, 1840-1880, made of linen and wool.
Metropolitan Museum of Art [CC0], via Wikimedia Commons.

It's important that the material is linen. You may ask why?

> The fabric of the shirt also contributes to its interpretation as a sacred object. It is made primarily of linen or hemp, materials used for centuries. It is believed that they have protective power, being connected with the sky, with *the upper world*. Their fibers are interpreted as a secure bridge to heaven. The impossibility to count them in the sleeve of the linen shirt is taken as the most solid protection against evil-carrying eyes (*evil eye*).[75]

As a way to encourage more gifts, the master builder says, "May he who gives receive our thanks! May he who does not give be seized with fever by evening!"[76] The gifts are certain to pile up after that implied threat.

The house is now complete. Another way the master builder has a connection to the home is the blessing when he hands over the keys to the homeowner. The owner, in return, pays for the home and also gives the builder money "from the heart"—a sum beyond the agreed-upon price for the home. As the builder gives the owner the keys, he responds with the saying, "May it be your lawful right and property." In this way, he is "forgiving" the homeowner for any non-monetary debt. As MacDermott says, "Mere monetary payment did not give a person the right to appropriate the fruits of another's labour, and the crucial element in a transaction was the granting of 'forgiveness'."[77]

Stopanova Gozba ("The Householder's Festival") for Blessings

The Stopan has a special place in other rituals as well. Whenever you hear noises in the attic or tapping on the ceiling, or if a deceased relative whispers to you in a dream telling you he's hungry, you can perform the *stopanova gozba* (*gozba* means "food") feast for your Stopan. This ceremony was in full power in the 1870s. It's usually celebrated at least once a year on the first Monday after a full moon. Its purpose is to beg the household spirit for prosperity. If you deny him food, he'll inflict diseases or even death on you and your livestock, he'll send hail on your fields and vineyards to destroy your crops, and he'll torture you with terrible dreams.

It's best not to tempt fate and deny him. Be proactive and perform the ceremony.

Even before the feast and ritual begin, you'll want to ensure your entire home is sparkling clean—especially any common rooms. Wash the ash that's accumulated in the fireplace, and dig a small hole on each side, placing a lit candle in each. Dress up your home, too, with flowers; or in the winter use the greenery from a Bulgarian geranium (*zdravetz*).

As it's a special occasion, it calls for you and your family to put on your Sunday best outfits, and even place flowers in your hair. Yes, flowers. Don't worry, boys and men; take a deep breath. You don't have to do a thing, and yet you'll be able to benefit from the Stopan's generosity. This meal, that's held in secret, is performed by women alone.

Widows or women who have been married only once (and not divorced) take part in the celebration since they have a special bond with the home hearth. Therefore, it's the women's "ritual right" to be the ones to call on the guardian spirit for his blessings. These rituals reflect traditions that have survived since the time of the ancient Thracians, but are still practiced today. If women outside of the family participate, no more than three can attend the ritual.

Now, it's time for the ceremony to begin.[78]

First, you'll need water to prepare the meal and bread. It can't be any water, certainly not tap water. The youngest married woman among you has to get it from a river or other water source. It's special "unspoken" or "silent" water—both drawn and carried home in white cauldrons in ritual silence as you learned earlier. And you must not drink from the water; you can use it only for the food preparation. While the young woman is at the river, she could save time by washing the wheat that she'll use for baking; she must cleanse it three times. A note of interest is that in ancient times, women roughly kneaded whole grains into the bread loaves.

Back at home, the woman crushes the grain, then sifts the flour three times before she prepares dough. While it rises, the woman goes to three neighbors and invites one woman from each house to participate in the ceremony. All three women must no longer be able to conceive children. The oldest of the three brings a black hen with her.

After the three women enter the house, they stand by the hearth, where a fire is burning. Lit candles flicker on either side of the hearth. The oldest one starts the ceremony by slaughtering the black hen, making sure all the blood drains into a hole in the hearth that has been specially made for this purpose. She covers the blood with clay. Next, she plucks the sacrificed hen, retaining the feathers for various healing rituals, but burying the intestines in the hole. No part of the hen is thrown out; even its bones remain in the house and are put on shelves after the meal.

While the oldest woman roasts the chicken whole (you can't tear it into pieces), the other two invited women split the dough and bake two pastries: a *banitsa* (made from a whisked egg-and cheese mixture spread over layers of dough) and a *pogacha* (a round puff pastry). They decorate the top of the *pogacha* using a fork. Once the pastries are baking, they carefully watch them to make sure they don't burn.

The food is finally ready, but it's not time to eat yet. The young homeowner retrieves a *sofra* (a low wooden table used for ceremonial meals; it's customary to sit on three-legged wooden chairs around this table). She places the table near the hearth and puts the cooked chicken, *banitsa*, *pogacha*, and a bottle of wine on it. The eldest woman lights incense, spreading the smoke over each item to purify the meal. Next, she sets the table, adding an extra place for the Stopan.

It's time to address the house spirit.

The oldest woman pours wine into the fire while saying, "Be happy, divine householder; be merry house!" She may also add, "It's good to be gathered together at this table. To be wealthy, healthy, strong, and a good host. Dry goes out; wet comes back." The meaning of the latter is that the spirit goes out with nothing, but comes back with a plentiful harvest.

She continues by placing the *pogacha* on her head and breaking it in half, then tearing each piece again. She places the first section on the Stopan's plate and spreads butter and honey over it, while each of the other elder women receives the remaining pieces. The ritual leader then breaks off a piece of *banitsa*, giving it to the household guardian. Next, she tears the left leg from the chicken and places it on the spirit's plate. Finally, she fills three small cups with wine and adds those to the Stopan's meal as well.

His meal is ready, and it's time to bring it to him before the others can eat.

The eldest woman carries the Stopan's plate to the attic, with the other two invited guests following. In one corner, she places the *pogacha* and a cup of wine. The *banitsa* and a second cup of wine go into the next corner, the leg into the third corner, and the last cup of wine into the final corner.

With the guardian's meal laid out for him, she bows and says, "Be happy, divine householder; be merry house!"

The other two women repeat her words. Having "fed" the guardian spirit, the women return to the table to finish the ritual before they eat.

Once again, the eldest woman fills a cup with wine, pouring half into the fire and splattering the other half on the hearth while she recites a prayer to the household spirit:

> Bloom, house; be merry, divine householder!
> Where you go, go, but here you should come back to bring dew.
> If you come from a field, here you should come back—to bring wheat;
> If you come from a vineyard, here you should come back—to bring grapes!

It's finally time for the women to eat. Each time before they drink their wine, they pour a bit onto the hearth and say, "Bloom, house; be merry, divine householder!"

The guardian spirit is certain to get many such blessings during the meal.

At the end of the meal, when one cup of wine remains, the oldest woman again pours half into the fire. While the two other women remain silent, she says:

> Bloom, house; be merry, divine householder,
> Where you go, go,
> but here you should come back to bring in the house:
> to the brood health and long life,
> help the brides to give birth easily;
> protect and guard the sheep, the cattle, the horses, the bees
> and other livestock;
> protect the fields, the vineyards, the sesame, the cotton, the tobacco, the corn
> and all that yields in the field!

Now it's time for the other two women to repeat, "Bloom, house; be merry, divine householder!"

Having completed the ritual and meal, the women clear the table, and the guests leave.

A week later, the women return to see if the Stopan has tasted the food and drink left for him. If he has, it's a great joy to the family, and they shout, "The Stopan ate! The Stopan drank." It's a sign the spirit was pleased with the sacrifice and will bless the family in whose house they performed the ritual.

Feeding the Stopan

The song the oldest woman sings at the conclusion of the meal does more than request prosperity from the Stopan. She sings a sad tale of Boiko and his family, which tells what happens when you ignore the spirit. Like the Domovoi, the Stopan has only two requests of the family he protects: honor him and feed him. He may protect and bless your home, but he also depends on you—especially women—for sustenance. Neglect him by not appreciating his generosity, or by forgetting to feed him, and he'll extract revenge. All that he's given to you will cease. He'll ensure your property suffers damage and your harvests fail; he'll inflict disease on your animals and destroy the fortune of your family. You'll end up worse off than you were before. He could get even more spiteful, and make sure your house burns down.

The story about Boiko tells an even grimmer outcome. The woman's song about the Stopan begins:

> Rejoice, stopan. Be happy house!
> A noise was heard in Boyko's house.
> There was something heard in the attic.
> In a dream saw Boiko's daughter,
> "Make stopan meal; bring fresh wine.
> I'm very hungry. I'm very thirsty."

The girl repeated the request to her father, Boiko, but he ignored her and didn't feed the Stopan.

Angered at the lack of respect, the spirit sent death to visit them. The people died in their beds. The Stopan killed everyone in the house except the daughter. He didn't stop there. He slaughtered the cattle in their stalls, the sheep in their pens, the fowl in their roosts, and all the animals on the farm wherever they stood. He destroyed all the grain that the family had stored in the barn, leaving the Boikovi home desolate and forlorn.

One son happened to have been away, so he survived. A week after the massacre, he returned home. His weeping, distraught sister told him everything that had happened. The boy's grief was overwhelming. How could their guardian have done this terrible thing?

When his sister finished speaking, the young man collapsed onto the ground. He received his answer in a dream. The Stopan told the son that if he performed his duty and did what his father failed to do—that is, feed the spirit and give him something to drink—that the young man would be rewarded with three times as much as the family had before. The house would be three times more beautiful, and his wealth would be three times greater.

After Boiko's son regained consciousness, he set about feeding the Stopan. He asked three women relatives to perform the *stopanova gozban* to appease the spirit.

The next day, even before dawn, a stranger arrived at the house. He took Boiko's son on a long journey. They rode a horse through three villages, finally stopping at a fourth. In this village, the young man found and married the most beautiful and talented maiden, who also happened to be extremely wealthy.

Boiko's son returned to his village with his bride. There, he discovered his yard teeming with sheep, oxen tied to posts, and numerous chickens scurrying about. Not only that, but his barn was filled to the brim with grain, and casks were overflowing with wine and the best *rakiya* (a brandy made from plums or grapes). Inside the home, butter and cheese abounded, as well as golden coins.

How had all this happened? The unknown foreigner was the Stopan himself. True to his word, he multiplied the young man's wealth.

The prosperity didn't end there. As the years went on, the young man's wife gave birth to twins: a son and a daughter. They were the brightest stars. Boiko's son lived out the rest of his days with much wealth and happiness, and never again forsook the Stopan.

A Spiritual Connection

Other folkloric songs about the Stopan follow the same pattern. In them, the spirit tells people what kind of good things he will bring if they respect him and give him a little food. He'll ensure everyone remains healthy, and they all live to an old age; women will give birth easily, and have many children. However, he also reminds them of the unhappiness he'll bring if they don't fulfill his desires.

Another theory of thought doesn't believe that if you neglect the Stopan, he'll ruin you. They say this malicious characteristic attributed to the Stopan is more suitable to a Talasum (whom you'll learn about in the next chapter). Being as honorable in death as in life, the Stopan's only concern is the well-being of the family.

If you neglect the Stopan, you're actually bringing about your own downfall because there's a spiritual connection between humans and immortals.

> [I]n the Thracian-Bulgarian notion of relations between man and heavenly beings it is established that the happiness of the humans and the happiness of the "stopan" is mutually determined. If humans do not "feed" their patrons, the patrons suffer, and the suffering of the patrons sooner or later also causes the suffering of mortal men. This conception of the unity of mortals and immortals is fully in line with the mystical notion reflected in anthroposophy that even the future of the nine spiritual hierarchies depends entirely upon the last, tenth human hierarchy.[79]

The fact that families provide the Stopan with food and drink does not mean he has a corporal body as is often perceived with the Domovoi. As mentioned earlier, the Stopan wasn't "seen" in the physical world. Feeding him is both a sign of respect and "an outward expression of the ancient knowledge that the higher incorruptible beings can communicate with the world of flesh and blood through the faith of the people in them."[80]

Namestnik Ritual for Healing

Another ritual you can perform is a feast for a spirit called a *namestnik*.[81] If you or someone you know becomes seriously ill, in this ritual, friends beg the household guardian to make the evil spirits merciful to help the ill person heal. The name of this healing ceremony possibly comes from the Bulgarian *na myastoto na* (which means "in place of"), with the sacrificial animal (*kurban*) being the substitute for the sick person.

You must petition a man and a woman who aren't married to each other to oversee the ceremony, and it's usually celebrated at least once a year on a Saturday. Why this day? It's one that's dedicated to the deceased. You'll want to choose people you get along with because when the ceremony is finished, they'll become your *pobratim* ("sworn brother") and *posestrima* ("sworn sister"). The terms literally mean "half-brother" and "half-sister" and refer to a relationship where two unrelated people swear everlasting friendship to one another. Each becomes the *pobratim* or *posestrima* to the other. This is a sacred alliance.[82]

At the beginning of the ceremony, the male friend selects a black ram from among the sick person's sheep. (Although it's not common for most people nowadays to have farm animals, in rural places where this ceremony takes place, it's not unusual.) He leads the ram into the house, digs a pit on the right side of the hearth. As you've previously learned, the location of the ritual, the hearth, is where the household spirit resides—a place where, in the past, family members were buried.

There, the man slaughters the animal, draining the blood into the pit. Although he doesn't directly call the household spirit as the women did in the *stopanova gozba* ritual, the rite itself is one that's recorded in Homer's Odyssey (XI), where Odysseus sacrifices a black ram in the underworld to call upon the souls of the deceased.

Next, the man skins and butchers the animal, tossing the inedible parts into the pit. He dips his fingers, a stick, or some other device into the blood and makes crosses on the left side of the hearth. In this way, the earthly (right side of the hearth) and the celestial (left side of the hearth) realms are taken into account—the earthly world through blood in the pit; the celestial one through the blood crosses. In this instance, crosses don't represent the Christian faith; instead, they have a more ancient symbolism: solar signs. Unlike some cultures—like the Romans—where left was considered "sinister" (which comes from the Latin word for "left"), that direction for the ancient Thracians was sacred.

The man's actions taking place from right to left—from lower level of consciousness to a higher one—is standard for blood sacrifice rituals. It's an "expression of prayer through actions," one which enables power to fill the sick person.

After washing the meat and organs, the man will give them to the woman to cook.

She's already been kneading dough to make ten to fifteen sourdough breads. The aroma coming from the kitchen is heavenly, as you can imagine. In addition to the ram that she'll cook, she also makes meat with cabbage, potatoes, rice, grits, *kolivo* (boiled wheat), and an assortment of other traditional foods for the evening dinner. Although the meal is prepared earlier, the fact that it's eaten in the evening once again suggests its connection with nighttime and the afterlife. It's a time when the spirits congregate, enabling people to dine with the divine guardian.

After lunchtime, it's time to invite guests to the ceremony later on in the day. The man and woman pour wine into a *baklitsa*—a small, wooden flask used on special occasions. They hand the flask to a girl from the household, and she goes from house to house in the village, inviting people to the ceremony.

As she hands each one the *baklitsa* to take a drink, she says, "Plenty of health for you; come tonight on a *namestnik*."

Baklitsa.
Illustration by Nelinda.
© Bendideia Publishing.

The guests arrive once night falls. It's time for the ceremony to begin. The man and woman conducting the rites light two candles, placing one at the north side of the room (representing midnight) and the other at the opposite side (representing south, or midday). The candles mark the route for both mankind and the spirits to find their way to each other. With many Christian or even Hellenistic rites, the directions would be east and west, but north and south were sacred directions for the ancient Thracians: north was dedicated to humankind (mortals), while south was reserved for the immortals and the souls of the blessed. In his book, Mishev suggests:

It could be suggested as a rite which includes both spheres of the Cosmos—the space over and under the earth and aims for their unification with a certain idea, which in this case is the healing.[83]

The cooked ram, wine, bread, and other prepared food for the meal now grace the table. One of the two people officiating the ceremony pours wine into a bowl and completely covers the sides and bottom of the bowl with a small bread. Using wool or a woolen cloth, each elder invited to the meal spins the bowl three times spilling a bit of the wine onto the table, making sure their hands touch only the wool and not the bowl, thereby keeping it sacred from human touch. Then the other invited guests and members of the household repeat the process.

Wool is used with making contact with the divinities of the underworld, drawing them closer to humankind. The following describes the beliefs about the power of wool.

> In Bulgarian folk tradition wool belongs to earth, it is to a certain extent connected with evil power and in dreams it is interpreted as *the soul of a dead person*. It has the function of a guarding border between the worlds, which separates and connects them. The woolen thread is used in rituals when one needs help from the other world since it is believed that one can look for prosperity and wealth there.[84]

The man or woman performing the ceremony picks up the bowl of wine using the woolen cloth and places it on a shelf, where it remains until the following week.

Everyone stands by the table while the woman puts a loaf of bread on top of the *kolivo* and passes the plate to each of the guests. Next, the man distributes a plate with the meat and liver to each person until the plate is empty. Their plates full, the guests can now sit at the table and begin the meal. After the guests have eaten and drunk until full, they return home.

The ceremony is finished for the night but resumes the following Saturday when all the guests return. One of the ceremony leaders removes the bowl with the wine from the shelf where it's been sitting for the week. He or she sets aside the old bread and covers the sides and bottom of the bowl with a new loaf of bread. Each person once again holds onto the woolen cloth and spins the bowl three times, spilling a little on the table. They remove the bread, and everyone consumes both loaves.

Did you know?

On Budni Vecher (Christmas Eve) women bring a bit of everything from the evening meal to the graveyard to feed the ancestors.

This concludes the rite. The home's guardian spirit has been duly honored, and in turn will bestow the healing blessing upon the ill person.

Healing Sanctuary

Guardian spirits—especially those appearing as snakes—aren't restricted to houses. According to popular beliefs, a Stopan guards every stream, field, forest, and valley. It's best for you to be respectful of such spirits. The Master Benisa Duono[85] says the following about showing this respect to the spirits:

> Upon arriving in a mountain place, say, "Good and bright beings, keepers of this place, welcome us to you, and let God's blessing be upon you." When leaving, departing the place: "Good and bright beings, guardians of this place, thank you for your hospitality. Stay in peace, and let the blessing of God be upon you."[86]

Once such place exists in the Western Rhodope Mountains. Here, a non-poisonous black female snake guards a sanctuary called "Skrinbina," which the local people call "The Stone." The popular name adequately describes the holy place. A gap or "hole" pierces a stone arch, resembling the "chicken god" you learned about in the Kikimora chapter. This opening, however, is large enough for humans to stand in—and many do just that. The sick come here for healing—those with heart problems, mental illnesses, infertility, repeated nightmares, and so many more disabilities.

Healing Sanctuary. Illustration by Dmitry Yakhovsky. © Bendideia Publishing.

Before healing can happen, both the ill one and the "wise woman" who performs the ceremony must wash their bodies to become ritually clean.[87] This healing practitioner is one who has been chosen by the guardian snake. When the snake decides it no longer wants the current healer to bring the sick to the site, it may bite the woman. Then she passes her role down to a relative—a cousin, a daughter, or another woman from the next generation.

Once ritually clean, the woman leads the sick person to the sanctuary, where she'll begin the ceremony called "riding the stone." As you'll discover, the ceremony has many parallels to ancient Thracian healing cult rituals. Similar to *namestnik*, which you learned about earlier, the rites performed at the rock sanctuary take the ill person from the depths of the underworld to celestial heights as part of his healing process.

The woman leaves her patient at the base of the sanctuary. She approaches the stone and prays toward the south (as you may recall, this is the direction of the immortals). Next, she picks up a rock, knocks on the sacred stone three times, and calls out to the spirit-guardian of the place. A black snake crawls from beneath the stones. The healing ritual can begin with the granting of his permission for everyone to enter the sacred place.

The healer measures the sick person with a red thread as a way to capture the essence of the person through his shadow (you'll learn more about this practice in the Talasum chapter). In this ritual, the thread is used to heal. It creates a "magical double" of the sick person. The healer ties the thread (the sick person's double) to the wooden ladder at the base of the arched rock. This lower location is considered the realm of the underworld. She ascends but doesn't enter the gap in the stone herself. Instead, she climbs to higher ground—the celestial world of divinities—above the arch on the southern side of the stone.

The patient meanwhile climbs behind her and crawls into the gap, like the black guardian snake would crawl into a hole or how it would wiggle to shed its skin. If the rock "squeezes" the ill person—in what is considered a "ritual merger with the sacred rock"—he'll be cured.

The healer holds out her hand to him and draws him back onto the ritual rock beside her. She creates a circle of hemp around him, which she lights on fire. Fire is a mediator between the realms of the gods and mankind, and the flames act as a purifying power of the new body to make it holy. In ancient times, it was a common practice to cremate the deceased, setting their spirits free so they could soar heavenward.

The healer repeats the ritual she's spoken many times. "Be healthy now!" With her next words, she

Stone Circle and Arched Gap.
Illustration by Dmitry Yakhovsky. © Bendideia Publishing.

throws bran onto the ground. "To have for the chickens!"

The ill person tosses money onto the ground, a gift for his restored health.

Like the serpent who sheds his skin and becomes new again (which in mythological and folk traditions is how the snake remains an immortal being), the patient must also cast off his outer skin (the topmost layer of clothing). He then attaches it to a green tree around the sanctuary or stuffs it into a crack in the sacred rock. By abandoning his old garment, he leaves behind his old, ill self and renews his strength.

He passes through a smaller rock arch to the left (the north, which you learned earlier is the location for mortals) at the base of the arch, having thus returned to the underworld.

The healer and the patient repeat the process twice more. At the end, the sick person turns three times to the left. He has now completed the ritual and is free to leave. The red thread, his double, remains in the underworld, tied to the ladder at the base of the arch. In this way, he abandons his old mortal nature.

However, he must exit the sacred place toward the north, and by a different path than the one he entered. He tosses a stone over his head as he departs, never looking back—unlike Orpheus who turned to look back at his wife as he exited the underworld. Having received his blessing from the snake—and not the stone—he no longer needs to look upon the sanctuary.

Decorated Ladder. Illustration by Dmitry Yakhovsky. © Bendideia Publishing.

Fact or Fiction?

The following encounter with an ancestor in the dreamworld provides a more modern look at guardian spirits.[88] While taking a lunchtime nap, in that state where you are between sleep and wakefulness, a man had an encounter with his late grandmother. He did not see her, but only heard her voice, telling him not to be angry with a person who was creating a family problem because he would soon get what he deserved. A month later, her prediction came true.

What is interesting about this is that near the end of this encounter a male spoke to his grandmother—the voice that of a stranger. He told her it was time to leave, that her grandson would remember enough of what she had told him. Many in the past would have assumed that the man was an unknown ancestor. The teller of the story continues by saying before she died, an old man, with a white beard and almost glowing white clothes, visited his grandmother when she was in a semi-awake state. She was unable to identify him with any specific ancestor, although she assumed it could have been one she didn't know about. His presence happened during a time when she suffered mental anxiety due to a family crisis. The events he told her came true over the next few months.

If you scour the internet or books, or talk to people, you're certain to find many more examples of people being contacted by the dead to warn them of troubles ahead. Is it your loved ones who have passed on? Is it an angel revealing himself to you in a way that won't frighten you? Is it some other completely scientific phenomenon? That's up to you to decide.

ANCIENT SNAKE CITY

Many sanctuaries from ancient times are scattered throughout the forests and mountains of Eastern Europe—more than 250 alone across the Rhodope Mountains. Invisible guardians in the form of snake sentries carved into the rocks continue to protect the holy places from prying eyes. The spirits are forever "faithful to their heathen gods," guarding abandoned sanctuaries and their "secrets of a lost civilization."

All protectors have not been successful in hiding their sanctuaries because the human mind is curious. Here is one of these fascinating discoveries.

In June of 2016, three journalists intended to film the Eagle Rocks cult complex in the Rhodope Mountains in southern Bulgaria. This sanctuary, which contains about 90 niches, was used for rituals and burials and dates back to the sixth to fourth centuries BC.

However, the journalists became lost in the forest and instead discovered a "snake city." Using a drone to take pictures from above, they discovered a semi-circle of rock structures. Snake heads had been hewn into the rocks. Also visible were profiles of human bodies with snake heads, niches, and a cave. A staircase winds around, leading to a portal in the rocks.

Archaeologist Prof. Ana Radouncheva is certain they must have been carved into the rocks around the eighth millennium BC. She says the sanctuary creators "belonged to an advanced society, which mysteriously disappeared around the 4th millennium." She provides even more details about the discovery.

"The snake is a multifaceted figure in the spiritual culture of prehistory," the archaeologist explains. "They may play the role of sentries, watching over the bones of the sacrificial animals, or be a "motor of time." Snakes are also seen as the figure mediating between man and the gods in ancient cults, with the worship taking place in the rock sanctuaries, especially at the close of the copper-stone age when the institution of high priests came into being" (Tsankova).

How many more of these sacred places will reveal their secret histories as archaeologists continue their searches? It's an exciting prospect.

Border of "Snake City." Illustration by Dmitry Yakhovsky. © Bendideia Publishing.

Talasum. Illustration by Anna Błaszczyk (Evelinea Erato). © Bendideia Publishing.

Talasum (Таласъм)

Evil is older than the world.

> **Talasum** (singular); **Talasumi** (plural)
>
> **Other names**: talasŭmìn, talasòn, talsòn, sènkya, sènishte, dràkus.[89]

The bridge spans the churning water. With your foot raised to take the first step onto the creaking boards, you hesitate. What's that sound coming from below? The wailing of a grieving mother, or perhaps the skirl of a bagpipe? You lower your foot, resting it against solid ground. Is there another route you can take? Stories claim the builders of old immured a victim within the walls of the bridge.

The sun dips behind a hill, chilling the air. Moaning begins again. You survey your surroundings. No shadowy creatures lurk nearby. Yet still…

Perhaps it's best to put off your trip for another day. You turn around and return home.

Origins

A Talasum has been described as a triple spirit. In some respects, he's similar to the Russian Domovoi or the Bulgarian Stopan, who each protect the home and family from fire, death, evil spirits, and plague. This version of the spirit is called the master of the house and often appears in the form of a snake or hedgehog. He can be good or bad, bringing prosperity or disaster. He is, however, sacred and shouldn't be killed. Depending on the part of Bulgaria you're from, the guardian spirit may be called Talasum, Stopan, or Smok, among other names. You'll read more about snake-related guardians in the Smok chapter.

A second type of Talasum appears in large structures, mills, and deserted buildings. This spirit is evil and does bad things to prevent people from living in a home or building. This type of Talasum is thought to be a wandering soul, who's looking for a place to rest and find shelter. He may also serve a different purpose: not to haunt buildings, but instead to guard buried treasure. To create this type of spirit, the person who buries the treasure must perform a special ritual. And anyone who attempts to retrieve the wealth must perform a ritual as well.

The third, and most popular type of Talasum, is an "artificially created" guardian spirit. In earlier ages, people believed that newly constructed buildings and other places as well—bridges, *chesmas* (drinking fountains), and even monasteries—could be strong only with a sacrifice.

> [A] foundation offering is a magic practice known since antiquity, performed during the construction of new residential buildings, but also of sacred or defensive buildings, roads and bridges. The foundation offering … should ensure the well-being of the users and residents of the building and strengthen the building's durability by giving it the life of a living being.[90]

Etymology

Talasum may come from the Turkish *tílsím* for "spell" or "talisman," or from the Greek *telesma* for "talisman" (Bulgarian Wikipedia, "Таласъм").

You've learned about foundation sacrifices, where an animal's blood is offered to the spirit for his protection in return. Larger buildings, however, require more protection, and so a person's "shadow" is built into a foundation wall. You may think this is odd, but by capturing the shadow (by various means you'll discover later in this chapter), builders believe they can prevent large structures from crumbling. The person whose shadow is built into the wall later becomes the guardian, or Talasum, of the structure.

Appearance

The living don't see the Talasum spirit during the day, but at night the spirit moans, weeps, and shouts. He appears at times as a white-eyed old man with a white beard; at others, a gypsy in a red coat. If the apparition is male, he may be playing the *kaval* (a long, wooden, flutelike instrument) or even a *gaida* (a Bulgarian bagpipe). The spirit of a woman, especially if she had been a bride, often spins or sings. Or she may appear as an unwed woman with loose hair.

In other cases, the Talasum makes its appearance in the shape of an animal—a buffalo, ram, bear, wolf, snake, bird, hen, dog, cat, or goat being popular—and even a goose as the story below shows:

> Our friend Nicolaki one evening saw a white goose on the top of a fountain, which all at once changed itself into a cat, and commenced rubbing itself against his legs in a most friendly way. Nicolaki suspected that there must be something uncanny in the transformation of a goose into a cat, and jumped over a little stream of water which trickled from the fountain, thus placing an insurmountable obstacle between himself and the object of his fear…[91]

The "little stream" mentioned above was enough to protect the man because those who are familiar with Talasumi know that the spirits can't cross water.

Gaida.
Illustration by Nelinda.
© Bendideia Publishing.

Getting to Know the Talasum

If you meet a Talasum, avoid speaking to the demonic spirit, even if he talks to you. Responding could make you become blind or deaf. You should be safe during the day, though, because the spirits hide in basements or attics, but at night they roam the places they guard—whether that's a building, bridge, fountain, or treasure. Even so, do what you can to never encounter one. The story below tells of one "enamored" *cheshma* (fountain) spirit who wouldn't give up her pursuit of a man.

When the Spirits appear as beautiful women they are (perhaps naturally) still more dangerous, the mere sight of them being sometimes sufficient to cause death. Dimitri of Derekuoi was harassed by the persecution of one of these ladies, whom he could never go out of his house without seeing, and after in vain trying to exorcise his tormentor by the aid of the Church, he applied to a Turkish Hodja, who prescribed a remedy which we have been unable to learn, but which was perfectly efficacious. For some weeks Dimitri did not see the Lady of the Fountain, but, rendered careless by fancied security, he neglected to comply with the Hodja's injunctions, and one evening was seized upon by his supernatural inamorata, who imprinted a fervent kiss upon his lips; a week afterwards Dimitri was dead.[92]

Yikes! Talk about the ultimate deadly stalker.

Shadows Built into Walls

A popular belief is that every stone building will collapse if a sheep, rooster, or human shadow is not built into its foundation. Although building shadows (and even people) into walls and foundations to keep structures strong is popular in folklore, the actual practice of interring a live person was thought to have occurred only in these stories. Wenska, in an article about Slavic sacrifices, says: "It is not clear whether or not this custom was actually practiced and it is often the case that folk ballads and fairytales make use of dramatic metaphors."[93]

However, in 2016, archaeologists found the skeleton of a Bulgarian princess buried *within* (not under) the foundation of St. George Church near the town of Trudovets in northwestern Bulgaria. They say she was buried at the end of the Shishman Dynasty, which ruled the Second Bulgarian Empire (1185 – 1396). Along with her bones, they found a monogramed ring and other female adornments. The archaeologists believe the church was used as a "temple-mausoleum for the local Bulgarian aristocracy in the 14th century" because they found five other graves at the site. But only that of the princess was built into the foundation.[94]

Was she buried alive? Or was she enclosed there after her death? Would a burial, rather than an entombment, serve the same purpose in making the building strong?

The stories might be true after all, so you should be leery if someone measures your height with a white string as you pass a construction site. Why? This is one method for "capturing" the essence of a human. Since your shadow is part of you—you can't get rid of it while you're in the light—it offers up the perfect "substitute" for you.

As a note of interest, people use two threads—one white and one black—when measuring the dead for a casket. They bury the black thread with the deceased, but place the white one in a secure location, such as under the eaves. This prevents the deceased from taking the "luck" of the house with him when he's buried.

So, now you know the builder's intent when he takes out a thread: he's measuring you for death. Once he's taken your measurement, he'll put the string into a specially prepared chest, which he'll lay into the foundation. Thus, the countdown to your funeral begins. Within 40 days, you'll become ill and waste away to nothing. After your death, from 8 p.m. until 3 a.m., you're stuck being the Talasum of whatever structure the workers were building. When the rooster crows, you'll disappear, only to stand guard again the next evening, and every evening after that for the rest of eternity.

If you escape before he measures you, the builder may try to capture the shadow of the first animal that passes. He'll have to capture the creature as well and kill it as a *kurban* (sacrificial animal). You'd think he'd do that first, but the spirit of a person makes the structure stronger.

> ## Did you know?
>
> A peasant woman, upon hearing cackling and peeping in her home, declared that masons had built the shadow of a hen and her chicks into her foundation ("Old World Building Customs," 200).

A less violent method used in homes in some regions of Bulgaria is to place one of the following into the foundation: a stone, a thread, an iron rod, or a tree branch. Each must be the height of the owner. This measured item will then become the Talasum. It appears as a harmless mute man or a shadow.

Legends of Immurement

Legends of this sort have accompanied the creation of many such buildings in the past, frequently a bridge or monastery. Quite often, the victim of the tale was the wife or sister of one of the builders. A few anecdotes from some famous stories follow:

- **The bridge of Arta in Greece**.
  The wife of the head builder curses the bridge as her husband and crew bury her alive in the foundation. She desires the bridge to flutter like a leaf, and those who pass it to fall like leaves. When reminded that her absent brother might pass the bridge on his return home, she reverses the curse into a blessing: "As the tall mountains tremble, so shall the bridge tremble, and as the birds of prey fall, so shall passers fall."[95]

- **The monastery of Arges in Romania**.
  Prince Negru Vodă hired workers to build the most beautiful monastery in the country. As in other stories, the workmen must immure someone to keep the walls from crumbling. Part of the song goes:

  > It is time for the ritual
  > It is time to brick the sacrifice
  > And the sacrifice apparently should be someone's wife
  > The one who will come at dawn
  > Carrying food and drink
  > (…)
  > If we want to build the monastery
  > Do not pity the woman[96]

  And pity her they didn't. But, as head builder Manole's pregnant wife Ana approaches the monastery, he grieves. To avert having her built into the building, he prays that God will send a rainstorm, so she'll return home. The rain comes, but his wife doesn't turn back. He has to proceed with the sacrifice.

  The builders pretend it's a game as they build walls around her. When she understands they've tricked her, she begs her husband to let her go. Knowing this is the only way they can complete the monastery, he refuses.

  The men get their deserved punishment, however. When the monastery is complete, the prince asks the men if they could build another building as splendid as this one, and they reply that they could. The prince strands them on the roof until they die so they'll never build anything as spectacular as his monastery again.[97]

- **The castle of Déva in Hungary**.
  This story is a bit more gruesome than the others. The builders believe the way to end the curse of the castle collapsing is to murder the first wife who appears. Once again, it's the master builder's wife who approaches. The men slit her throat, burn her body, and mix her ashes with the whitewash they apply to the building. When the father returns home and tells his son what he and the others did, the boy visits the castle where his mother died. There, he himself dies from grief.[98]

- **The Kadin bridge in Bulgaria**.

Every day the violent waters of the Struma river wash away what the builders erect of the Kadin bridge. The builders agree that the first wife to arrive that day will be built into the foundation. Struma, wife of Manol, arrives first with her infant, and she becomes their sacrifice. Weeping, Manol pushes his wife into a hole in the bridge that they left especially for her. She begs the men to leave a gap so she can nurse her baby. People say they can still hear her crying at night. At one time, mothers unable to nurse took a piece of granite from the bridge, boiled it, and drank the water, believing this would restore their milk.

It's interesting to note the word *Kadin* comes from the Turkish word for "of a bride," and that the river now bears the name of the sacrificed wife.[99] (See a modern retelling of this story at the end of this chapter.)

Kadin Bridge. Illustration by Nelinda. © Bendideia Publishing.

- **The Spring of the White-Legged Woman**.

A Turkish vizier falls in love with a Bulgarian girl who's washing her legs in the village *cheshma* (fountain). He asks her to join his harem. After discussing with him the differences between their two cultures, the girl decides she wants to be a free woman. The vizier doesn't force her to join him. Instead, he orders workers to build a *cheshma* dedicated to her loyalty and courage. They do, but they take matters further and build the girl into the *cheshma* as well.[100]

- **The city of Skadra in Serbia**. (You can read the poem in full at the end of this chapter.)

Symbolism of the Sacrifice

Sacrificing a woman, especially a nursing mother, does more than make the structure strong. According to Romanian historian Mircea Eliade (1907 – 1986), it symbolically represents a Bulgarian myth in which a female body (that of a *Samodiva*—woodland nymph—who has died) not only creates the world, but also maintains its stability. Nature arises out of her dead body. From her eyes, lakes appear; her torso becomes a tree, and her hair turns into clover.[101]

Other folklorists compare the immurement of the mother to women maintaining order in a household.

> Her power to create, hold, and perpetuate emerges from her literal and symbolic role as the "keystone" in a building. As it merges with the foundation, the woman's immured or walled-in body becomes a unifying, binding material.[102]

In much the same way, a woman is the binding force or "building block" keeping the family strong. Her marriage and motherhood are the ways she lays a strong foundation within her new family.[103]

Buried Treasure

From buried people, we'll now turn to buried treasure. You may be familiar with the notion that dragons hoard gold and treasures. In Bulgaria, this dragon is called *zmey*. He lives in a cave where he's accumulated great wealth. When the dragon knows his death is imminent, he buries his treasure and leaves a Talasum behind to guard it. Dragons are not the only ones who hide treasure, though. Many people, invaders and natives alike, have hidden wealth in the ground. The sole purpose of this type of Talasum is to protect the treasure. He won't go out of his way to harm people—unless, of course, they are there to steal the gold.

While no special rites are associated with creating the "walled-in" Talasum you just learned about, a person does perform a rite over treasure he's buried in order to create a spirit to guard it. While sacrificing an animal, the burier proclaims a curse against anyone who tries to dig up what he's hidden. The spirit of the animal he kills becomes the guardian, watching over the hoard at night. Sometimes, the person who's hiding the treasure becomes the guardian when he dies.

If you want to find this treasure, you'll have the most luck on special holidays, such as Christmas (December 25), Survaki (January 1), Epiphany (January 19), Blagovets (March 25), Gergiovden (May 6), and Eniovden (June 24).[104] At midnight, a blue flame dances over the location where the treasure has been buried. (In some countries, it's a red flame.) The flame may flash three times, then disappear, so it may take you several nights to find the exact spot. You can also locate the treasure by lighting straw on fire. Cover it with a large willow basket and walk around the area you suspect treasure has been buried. When the flame turns blue, you've found the location.

Now that you know where the treasure's buried, it's another matter to retrieve the hidden wonders. You can't just dig them up. Don't forget that a Talasum guards them. You have to bribe the spirit with a sacrifice. To determine exactly what type of sacrifice he requires, sprinkle ashes or flour over the ground where you discovered the blue flame—the same way you do when determining what type of spirit inhabits a possible building site. Don't just dump it on the spot; use a sieve to cover the area with an even layer of powder. And, if you're using ash, it can't be the residue from wood burned any day. It has to be scraped up from the hearth during the "dirty days." (This is the time between Ignatius Feast on December 20 and the Epiphany on January 6. During this period, the Virgin Mary went into labor, gave birth to Jesus, and had him baptized.)

The next morning, examine the prints left in the dust. This will tell you what type of spirit-animal the Talasum is. With this information in hand, you should be able to find out what type of sacrifice you'll need to free the spirit. If you're unsure what the animal is, go ask your local *znahar* (wise woman and clairvoyant, who often heals with herbs). Usually you'll sacrifice the same kind of animal as those of the tracks—or a person, if the steps are human. "No way! I'm not murdering someone!" you may say. You're right; if you don't want to go around killing people, it's best to look for treasure elsewhere.

Another option is possible as well. At midnight, when the Talasum appears, you can fight him until dawn, since he'll fade away with the sunlight. No easy feat, so you might want to reconsider if it's worth the effort. Treasure that a Talasum guards is called "cursed money." It's likely to cause you misery rather than provide you with a life of leisure. People often say, "A fat lot of use that money will bring."

If you're not one to heed warnings, then to retrieve the treasure, you'll have to throw a piece of your clothing on the place where the blue flame appeared. The plunder will rise to the surface without you having to exert yourself digging.

You can read about several excursions to extract treasure at the end of this chapter in the "Tales of Treasure Hunting" section.

Getting Rid of a Talasum

Talasumi may live in residential homes. People in some areas consider them good, and the spirits behave the way the Domovoi, Stopan, and Smok do—as protectors of the home. However, more often, abandoned buildings are the stomping ground for evil Talasumi. Perhaps the buildings they previously guarded have crumbled with age, and they now seek a new residence. If you enter one of these abandoned places, be warned: the spirit is likely to choke you. If you're more fortunate, he'll only follow you home.

Don't consider yourself lucky quite yet. He doesn't turn into a benevolent being once he's in your home. If one happens to have made himself comfortable in your abode, he may appear as a dark apparition in your attic. He'll try his best to chase you away by making all kinds of noise and causing mischief. Don't speak to him or scold him the way you would a Domovoi. The Talasum is not friendly. Remember the earlier warning: you could become blind or deaf if you talk to him.

"How do I get rid of him then?" you're bound to ask. No need to worry too much. It's not quite as difficult to drive him away from any place he's taken shelter—be it your home or an abandoned hut—as it is to rid your home of a Kikimora.

First, the spirits—like demons—fear light, fire, prayer, the cross, incense, and a crowing rooster. If none of those devices make him scramble from your house, you'll have to trick him into leaving.

To do this, let him overhear that you're going to a wedding feast. The Talasum will follow you. Instead of proceeding to a wedding party, lead him into the woods to an abandoned hut. Open the door and place a little food inside for the spirit. He'll think it's part of the feast—especially when you remark that you're off to collect the guests for the wedding party. Most importantly, however, toss a ball of tangled yarn into the hut before you leave. As an extra precaution, you can bolt the door from the outside. Then run away as fast as you can.

"How will that work?" you may ask. The spirit can't endure anything that's not finished. He'll spend hours trying to untangle the yarn. By the time he does, you'll be long gone. He'll be stuck in his new home—at least until the next person unwittingly enters the building. At that point, the Talasum can follow his new victim home.

Fact or Fiction?

Stories still abound today about creatures inhabiting deserted places. Some have been seen, while others remain invisible while they wreak their havoc. Call them what you will, but strange occurrences happen—whether they're the result of a vivid imagination or are real is for you to decide. A few of these tales follow:

Ghostly Footprints

A clatter on the ceiling sends a family upstairs to check what the trouble is. Nothing disturbs the room; all is in its place. It could be a Talasum. To discover what kind of spirit-creature haunts the house, they dust the floor with flour. The next morning, they discover that the footprints that dot the residue are ones they're unfamiliar with. What can they do? It's not a *znahar* (village wise woman) they invite to the home to tell them what to do, but a priest to read prayers. Three nights in a row, a different priest comes. Finally, the strange creature ceases to return, and the home is quiet again.[105]

Baking Bread … and More

When you pass the ruins of a deserted mill, keep in mind the following story. Something more dangerous than broken or rotted slats may await you inside.

When a certain mill was in operation, an uncle told his niece a story about a creature that inhabited the building. The man and his father were accustomed to bring wheat to the mill, which was outside the village. The elderly owner showed them how to grind the grain and make bread. As he was putting the dough into the old stove, a small creature appeared. His eyes, the color of fire, shone in the dark.

The creature hopped around, shouting, "Uncle is baking bread. I want to bake something, too." With that, he tossed live frogs into the stove.

Terrified, the man and his father ran outside. The miller forced them back inside to taste the bread. He told them that the Talasum, as he called the creature, caused mischief, but he wouldn't harm them. The creature had lived there ever since the miller's father had bought the building. The two frightened men glanced at the Talasum as it hopped in its corner, making smacking noises with its lips.[106]

I'm sure the men ate the bread in haste and made a quick retreat, looking for a new place to grind their grain in the future.

Shishenci

Eerie voices of men, women, and children after dark set the dogs to barking.[107] Villagers from Shishenci (located in northwestern Bulgaria, near the Serbian border)[108] lock their doors and peer out their windows, but they discover nothing out of the ordinary. Yet still, they don't dare go outside. If they can't see the spirits that roam the night, how can they tell where they are? Only the very old, those who witnessed past events, are not as disturbed by the presence of the spirits—at least not any longer. They've lived through the terror of the Tatars slaughtering their people—once an entire wedding party. Now the spirits of these people haunt the place forever.

The more skeptical claim the sounds are dogs fighting. Even people from other villages mock the believers, but the villagers of Shishenci are not deterred; they know something strange is going on. Then the mayhem spreads beyond the village to the outlying areas as the Talasumi wander.

In an attempt to stop at least one soul from his nightly journeys, the villagers dig up a man's grave and shoot his bones, hoping to prevent him from moving.

One woman tells of a scare she had. While she was preparing food, shouts and eerie laughter came from the street. She tossed away the food and hid, thinking her deceased mother was returning to collect her own husband. Soon after that, the woman's father did die. Every month, it seemed to her, someone in her family died: first her sister-in-law, then her father, and next her husband.

If that's not enough to scare you, consider this. What better proof that a Talasum was terrorizing the place than the story of one man who found gold coins hidden under a tree that had fallen. "Cursed money" is what it was. He had all kinds of trouble since then. Utensils went flying about his house; a cauldron of food overturned itself while it was cooking over the fire; flames burst forth from the hearth when the man hadn't kindled a fire. When the mayor went to see what was going on, an axe slammed into the door behind him.

Freaky, yes! Are there other explanations? You decide.

BRIDGE SONGS

Although this doesn't pertain to Eastern European folklore, you might find the notion that songs about London Bridge and other bridges have a possible connection with the foundation sacrifices you've been reading about.

For example, a song about the "Golden Bridge" seems rather explicit about "mending" the bridge with bones, although it's quite likely this is metaphorical.

Now march along, now march along,
The Golden Bridge we're crossing;
'Tis broken down, 'tis broken down;
With what shall we mend it?

With sticks and stones and little bones,
With one of a kind and two of a kind.
The last one is our prisoner.
("Old World Building Customs," 199, note 1)

The theme of a prisoner being sent to a prison (perhaps entombed in a hole in the bridge made especially for the purpose) appears in five variations of the London Bridge song as well. Alice Bertha Gomme proposed that this referred to foundation sacrifices, although many folklorists disagree, as no archaeological evidence of this existed in the bridge's foundation in the numerous times it has been rebuilt (Wikipedia, "London Bridge Is Falling Down," note 11).

The lyrics to one version of the children's song follow:

London Bridge is broaken down,
Is broaken down, is broaken down,
London Bridge is broaken down,
My fair lady.

Penny loaves will mould away,
Mould away, mould away,
Penny loaves will mould away,
My fair lady.

Build it up with bricks and mortar,
Bricks and mortar, bricks and mortar,
Build it up with bricks and mortar,
My fair lady.

What have this poor prisoner done,
Prisoner done, prisoner done,
What have this poor prisoner done?
My fair lady.

Bricks and mortar will not stay,
Will not stay, will not stay,
Bricks and mortar will not stay,
My fair lady.

Stole my watch and lost my key,
Lost my key, lost my key,
Stole my watch and lost my key,
My fair lady.

Build it up with penny loaves,
Penny loaves, penny loaves,
Build it up with penny loaves,
My fair lady.

Off to prison you must go,
You must go, you must go,
Off to prison you must go,
My fair lady. (Gomme, 335-336)

Highlights of Gomme's claims that this refers to a foundation sacrifice follow:

- The song is describing all the ways the bridge by ordinary means have failed. Then suddenly, a prisoner is mentioned. Is this indicative of a new way to try to fortify the bridge? She says yes. *continues*

BRIDGE SONGS *continued*

- Traditions said that the blood of children was splattered on the bridge's stones.
- The blood of animals was mixed into the mortar with which the bridge was built. So is it too far-fetched to think they could have also used human blood and more?
- Beginning in 1305, after prisoners were executed, their heads were put on the bridge and city gates. And what happened to their bodies?

In addition to the above, she says the way children played the game itself indicates the entombment of prisoners, and how they were "locked" up, as the children locked the players up in their arms.

Two players form the arch, all the others follow in single file. The words of the story are sung while all the players run under or through the arch. The players are all caught in turn in the arch, and then stand aside; their part is finished. In some cases the game begins by all forming a circle, and the verses are sung while the circle dances round. The arch is then formed, and all run through it in single file, and are caught in turn by being imprisoned between the lowered arms. Also, we find the circle-dancing following the arch ceremony. … In stories where a victim is offered as a foundation-sacrifice, the victim, often a prisoner, is sometimes forced to enter a hole or cavity left on purpose in the building, which is then walled or built up, enclosing the victim (Gomme, 501).

NOTE: "London Bridge" has been built and rebuilt many times. The Romans are believed to have created a pontoon, or floating, bridge across the Thames River to aid in the conquest of Britain. In 55 A.D., they replaced this bridge with a timber piled one, which may have been destroyed and rebuilt in 60 A.D. In the early fifth century, the end of Roman rule ended and so did the use of the bridge, which fell into disrepair. Alfred the Great may have rebuilt the bridge in the late ninth century. Or the Saxon king Æthelred the Unready may have done it in the year 990, only to have it destroyed again in 1014. King William I rebuilt the bridge after the Norman conquest of 1066. It was destroyed again in 1091 by a tornado and in 1136 by fire. The final timber version of the bridge was in 1163.

In 1176, construction of the first stone bridge began, which took 33 years to complete. The first head to appear on a spike on the bridge's gates was in 1305. This bridge, in its various states of repair, existed from 1209–1831.

"New" London bridge came into existence after a competition in 1799 to design a better bridge. Thomas Telford's design of a single iron arch was accepted, then dismissed after learning it required demolishing valuable properties. Instead, they chose a design of five stone arches, which opened in 1831. This bridge sank an inch every eight years. By 1924 the east side was three to four inches lower than the west side. In 1968, Robert P. McCulloch bought the bridge and had it shipped stone by stone to the U.S., where he rebuilt it in Arizona.

The current London Bridge opened in 1973. Three spans of prestressed-concrete box girders span the river (Wikipedia, "London Bridge").

Old London Bridge in 1616, with Southwark Cathedral in the foreground.
The spiked heads of executed criminals can be seen above the Southwark gatehouse.
Angr [Public domain], via Wikimedia Commons.

Talasum in Literature

Many of the Talasum stories revolve around the immuring of a person in a wall or foundation. Here are two, one old and one new that demonstrates the art of storytelling handed down from generation to generation. The third story is a collection of tales told to two novelists while they were in Bulgaria.

- "Shadow and Breath," an excerpt from *Light Love Rituals* by Ronesa Aveela, published in 2015.
- Epic poem, "The Building of Skadra," date unknown.
- Excerpts from *Twelve Years' Study of the Eastern Question in Bulgaria* by S.G.B. St. Clair and Charles A. Brophy, published in 1877.

Shadow and Breath" from *Light Love Rituals*

The following excerpt—from my book about rituals and customs in several Bulgarian holidays—occurs when the fictitious Pavol family is visiting the grave of a family member, the grandmother's husband. Baba loves to tell the children stories. This one is about the building of the famous Kadin bridge.

While Maria continues to greet other families, Baba relaxes on a bench, and Rada and Niki sit with her. Baba stretches out her legs. "Let me tell you a story. In 1469, three brothers were building the Kadin Bridge in the southeast. Every time they made progress, they returned the next day to discover the raging waters had destroyed everything, and they had to start over. The eldest said, 'The only way we can make the foundation strong enough is to build someone's shadow into it.'

"They argued about who should sacrifice his life to make the bridge strong. 'All of us are needed to work on the bridge,' the youngest said.

" 'Then it'll have to be one of our wives,' the middle brother decided. 'We'll trap the shadow of the first one who comes to the site tomorrow.'

"The youngest didn't like the idea, but both his brothers convinced him it was the only way. He went away fearing the worst. The two older brothers remained at the site and made plans to discourage their wives from coming the next day, saying they were taking a break from work. At noon the next day, the wife of the youngest brought her husband his meal. Heartbroken, he looked at his brothers, who only shrugged. 'It has to be done,' the eldest said.

" 'Struma,' the man said to his wife, 'I've dropped my wedding ring into a crevice in the wall. Will you find it for me?'

"When she stooped to look, the two older brothers hurried to build a wall around her shadow.

" 'Husband, what have you done?' She backed away from the brothers. 'What will happen to our child with me gone?'

"The youngest brother wept. Soon afterwards, his wife became ill and died. The brothers completed the bridge, and it still stands today against the strong waters of the river that now bears the name of the wife, Struma."

As Baba finishes the story, a butterfly lands on her hand. "My Georgi, you're here," she whispers, and tears fill her eyes (Aveela, 119).

The Building of Skadra

In this version of the tale, a king and his two brothers attempt time and again to build a bridge, failing each time. A Vila (like the Bulgarian Samodiva) tells them how to make it endure—with a human sacrifice. Many of these stories follow the same theme: the structure being built collapses each night; someone—saint, fairy, bird, or otherwise—tells the builders that a person has to be immured into the foundation or walls; the unsuspecting woman comes along. Some are heroic about being entombed; others are not. The end result is the same: no escape.

Brothers three combined to build a fortress,
Brothers three, the brothers Mrljavchēvich,
Kral Vukāshin was the eldest brother;
And the second was Uglēsha-Voivode;
And the third, the youngest brother, Goiko.
Full three years they labour'd at the fortress,
Skadra's fortress on Bojana's river;
Full three years three hundred workmen labour'd.
Vain th' attempt to fix the wall's foundation.
Vainer still to elevate the fortress:
Whatsoe'er at eve had raised the workmen
Did the Vila raze ere dawn of morning.

When the fourth year had begun its labours,
Lo! the Vila from the forest-mountain
Call'd—"Thou King Vukashin! vain thine efforts!—
Vain thine efforts—all thy treasures wasting!
Never, never, wilt thou build the fortress,
If thou find not two same-titled beings,
If thou find not Stojan and Stojana:
And these two—these two young twins so loving,
They must be immured in the foundation.
Thus alone will the foundations serve thee:
Thus alone can ye erect your fortress."

When Vukashin heard the Vila's language,
Soon he call'd to Dēssimir, his servant:
"Listen, Dessimir, my trusty servant!
Thou hast been my trusty servant ever;
Thou shalt be my son from this day onward.
Fasten thou my coursers to my chariot:
Load it with six lasts of golden treasures:
Travel through the whole wide world, and bring me,
Bring me back those two same-titled beings:
Bring me back that pair of twins so loving:

Bring me hither Stojan and Stojana:
Steal them, if with gold thou canst not buy them.
Bring them here to Scadra on Bojana:
We'll inter them in the wall's foundation:
So the wall's foundations will be strengthened:
So we shall build up our Scadra's fortress."

Dessimir obey'd his master's mandate;
Fasten'd, straight, the horses to the chariot;
Fill'd it with six lasts of golden treasures;
Through the whole wide world the trusty servant
Wander'd—asking for these same-named beings—
For the twins—for Stojan and Stojana;
Full three years he sought them,—sought them vainly:
Nowhere could he find these same-named beings:
Nowhere found he Stojan and Stojana.
Then he hasten'd homewards to his master;
Gave the king his horses and his chariot;
Gave him his six lasts of golden treasures:
"Here, my sov'reign, are thy steeds and chariot:
Here thou hast thy lasts of golden treasures:
Nowhere could I find those same-named beings:
Nowhere found I Stojan and Stojana."

When Vukashin had dismiss'd his servant,
Straight he call'd his builder, master Rado.
Rado call'd on his three hundred workmen;
And they built up Scadar on Boyana;
But, at even did the Vila raze it:
Vainly did they raise the wall's foundation;
Vainly seek to build up Scadra's fortress.
And the Vila, from the mountain-forest,
Cried, "Vukashin, listen! listen to me!
Thou dost spill thy wealth, and waste thy labour:
Vainly seek'st to fix the wall's foundations;

Vainly seek'st to elevate the fortress.
Listen now to me! Ye are three brothers:
Each a faithful wife at home possesses:—
Her who comes to-morrow to Bojana,
Her who brings the rations to the workmen—
Her immure in the wall's foundations:—
So shall the foundations fix them firmly:
So shall thou erect Bojana's fortress."

When the king Vukashin heard the Vila,
Both his brothers speedily he summon'd:
"Hear my words, now hear my words, my brothers!
From the forest-hill the Vila told me,
That we should no longer waste our treasures
In the vain attempt to raise the fortress
On a shifting, insecure foundation.
Said the Vila of the forest-mountain,
'Each of you a faithful wife possesses;
Each a faithful bride that keeps your dwellings:
Her who to the fortress comes to-morrow,
Her who brings their rations to the workmen—
Her immure within the wall's foundations;
So will the foundations bear the fortress:
So Bojana's fortress be erected.'
Now then, brothers! in God's holy presence
Let each swear to keep the awful secret;
Leave to chance whose fate 'twill be to-morrow
First to wend her way to Scadar's river."
And each brother swore, in God's high presence,
From his wife to keep the awful secret.

When the night had on the earth descended,
Each one hasten'd to his own white dwelling;
Each one shared the sweet repast of evening;
Each one sought his bed of quiet slumber.

Lo! there happen'd then a wond'rous marvel!
First, Vukashin on his oath he trampled,
Whisp'ring to his wife the awful secret:
"Shelter thee! my faithful wife! be shelter'd!
Go not thou to-morrow to Bojana!
Bring not to the workmen food to-morrow!
Else, my fair! thy early life 'twill cost thee:
And beneath the walls they will immure thee!"

On his oath, too, did Uglesha trample!
And he gave his wife this early warning:
"Be not thou betray'd, sweet love! to danger!
Go not thou to-morrow to Bojana!
Carry not their rations to the workmen!
Else in earliest youth thy friend might lose thee!
Thou might be immured in the foundation!"

Faithful to his oath, young Goiko whisper'd
Not a breath to warn his lovely consort.

When the morning dawn'd upon the morrow,
All the brothers roused them at the day-break,
And each sped, as wont, to the Bojana.

Now, behold! two young and noble women;
They—half-sisters—they, the eldest sisters—
One is bringing up her snow-bleach'd linen,
Yet once more in summer sun to bleach it.
See! she comes on to the bleaching meadows;
There she stops—she comes not one step farther.
Lo! the second, with a red-clay pitcher;
Lo! she comes—she fills it at the streamlet;
There she talks with other women—lingers—
Yes! she lingers—comes not one step farther.

Goïko's youthful wife at home is tarrying,
For she has an infant in the cradle
Not a full moon old; the little nursling:
But the moment of repast approaches;
And her aged mother then bestirs her;
Fain would call the serving maid, and bid her
Take the noon-tide meal to the Bojana.
"Nay, not so!" said the young wife of Goiko;
"Stay, sit down in peace, I pray thee, mother!
Rock the little infant in his cradle:
I myself will bear the food to Scadra.
In the sight of God it were a scandal,
An affront and shame among all people,
If, of three, no one were found to bear it."

So she staid at home, the aged mother,
And she rock'd the nursling in the cradle.
Then arose the youthful wife of Goiko;
Gave them the repast, and bade them forward.
Call'd around her all the serving maidens;
When they reach'd Bojana's flowing river,
They were seen by Mrljavchevich Goiko,
On his youthful wife, heart-rent, he threw him;
Flung his strong right arm around her body;
Kiss'd a thousand times her snowy forehead:
Burning tears stream'd swiftly from his eyelids,
And he spoke in melancholy language:

"O my wife, my own! my full heart's-sorrow!
Didst thou never dream that thou must perish?
Why hast thou our little one abandoned?
Who will bathe our little one, thou absent?
Who will bare the breast to feed the nursling?"
More, and more, and more, he fain would utter;

But the king allow'd it not. Vukashin,
By her white hand seizes her, and summons
Master Rado,—he the master-builder;
And he summons his three hundred workmen.

But the young espoused one smiles, and dreams it
All a laughing jest,—no fear o'ercame her.
Gathering round her, the three hundred workmen
Pile the stones and pile the beams about her.
They have now immured her to the girdle.

Higher rose the walls and beams, and higher;
Then the wretch first saw the fate prepared her,
And she shriek'd aloud in her despairing;
In her woe implored her husband's brothers:

"Can ye think of God?—have ye no pity?
Can ye thus immure me, young and healthful?"
But in vain, in vain were her entreaties;
And her brothers left her thus imploring.

Shame and fear succeeded then to censure,
And she piteously invoked her husband:
"Can it, can it be, my lord and husband,
That so young, thou, reckless, would'st immure me?
Let us go and seek my aged mother:
Let us go—my mother she is wealthy:
She will buy a slave,—a man or woman,
To be buried in the wall's foundations."

When the mother-wife—the wife and mother,
Found her earnest plaints and prayers neglected,
She address'd herself to Neimar Rado:
"In God's name, my brother, Neimar Rado,
Leave a window for this snowy bosom,

Let this snowy bosom heave it freely;
When my voiceless Jovo shall come near me,
When he comes, O let him drain my bosom!"
Rado bade the workmen all obey her,
Leave a window for that snowy bosom,
Let that snowy bosom heave it freely
When her voiceless Jovo shall come near her,
When he comes, he'll drink from out her bosom.

Once again she cried to Neimar Rado,
"Neimar Rado! In God's name, my brother!
Leave for these mine eyes a little window,
That these eyes may see our own white dwelling,
When my Jovo shall be brought towards me,
When my Jovo shall be carried homeward."
Rado bade the workmen all obey her,
Leave for those bright eyes a little window,
That her eyes may see her own white dwelling,
When they bring her infant Jovo to her,
When they take the infant Jovo homeward.

So they built the heavy wall about her,
And then brought the infant in his cradle,
Which a long, long while his mother suckled.
Then her voice grew feeble—then was silent:
Still the stream flow'd forth and nursed the infant:
Full a year he hung upon her bosom;
Still the stream flow'd forth—and still it floweth.
Women, when the life-stream dries within them,
Thither come—the place retains its virtue—
Thither come, to still their crying infants (Bowring, 64-75).

***

A small stream of liquid carbonate of lime is shown on the walls of Scutari as evidence of the truth of this story (Bowring, 75, note 1).

Tales of Treasure Hunting

The following tales come from *Twelve Years' Study of the Eastern Question in Bulgaria*, written by two Englishmen, S.G.B. St. Clair and Charles A. Brophy, and published in 1877. At this time, Bulgaria was still a part of the Ottoman empire. In the preface, the authors—in addition to their "impression" of the Bulgarian people—make mention of a Bulgarian uprising in 1876 (April to May).

> We have in this book depicted the Bulgarian as he is, and not as he may appear to the superficial glance of a passing traveller, or the interested imagination of the missionary resident. We have shown him to be a lazy drunkard and a fanatical fetishist. We have roughly sketched the outline of foreign intrigue, and painted the Secret-society agent from life. How can anyone, if he can realise the true Bulgarian as we have drawn him, be at all astonished at what happened in May last? (St. Clair, vi)

The brutality the Ottoman Army used to suppress the rebels created a public outcry in Europe. Support grew for the Bulgarians, and as a result, in 1878 the country was freed of Ottoman rule.

Ottoman infantry. October 1863. Photograph by Josef Székely [Public domain].

What's important to this book is the authors described Bulgarians as fanciful people, believing in charms and spells—especially in rural areas.

> The Bulgarians … will confront all kinds of supernatural dangers on the chance of discovering a treasure; … he will dig for three or four consecutive nights with his hair standing on end, and the cold sweat of terror on his brow, in the hope of finding some treasure supposed to have been buried by Delhi Marco or Alexander the Great (St. Clair, 34-35).

Even today, many Bulgarians still believe treasures are guarded by such Talasumi. Here are a few of these treasure hunts for your enjoyment.

Winds and a Giant

We have been lately invited (probably because it is thought that two Englishmen must be more than a match for all the Spirits of Darkness in Bulgaria) to assist in digging up a famous treasure which is buried somewhere near the river Kamchyk, and guarded sometimes by a sudden and violent storm of thunder, wind, and rain, sometimes by a gigantic and frightful negro, whose head reaches to the clouds, and whose lower lip hangs down to earth. The man who requested our presence and assistance had tried six weeks before to unearth this treasure, but at the first blow of the pick the storm made its appearance, and as on the second night the negro showed himself, everybody was frightened, and judged it better to give up the undertaking for the present, in consideration of the supernatural obstacles encountered.

Besides the well-known method of discovering treasures on the Eve of St. John, a curious rite is practised here to propitiate the guardian Spirits. When the precise locality has been found, some of the ashes thrown out into the Harman during the Kulada are spread at night over the place. The footmark which is seen imprinted next morning is that of the animal which the genius requires as a propitiatory offering.

In the case of one treasure of which we have been told, the footprint seen the next day was that of a man, showing that a human victim was required before the money could be dug up; for the present this spot has been abandoned, and it is to be hoped that no Bulgarian will be tempted to make his fortune by a preliminary murder.

An hour's journey from Alaja Monastir (a Greek monastery), in the neighbourhood of Baltchik, is a rocky valley called Kourou Dere, in which is a cavern with an iron door, always ajar, through which may be seen an inner cave filled with gold and silver. A Bulgarian Choban entered one day, filled his belt and his pockets with coin, and turned to go out; to his dismay he found the door closed and a hideous negro, armed with pistols and sword, guarding the exit.

The Choban threw away all his gold, but the door remained shut, and the negro drew his sword; then he noticed that a piece of money had stuck in his *charrek* (sandal), and on flinging this away he was allowed to escape, very glad to have come off so well.

Strip Poker with a Spirit

Another time a Turkish Hodja resolved to possess himself of the treasures enclosed in the same enchanted cavern, and set out for Kourou Dere armed with an ancient book of necromancy, and accompanied by seven Bulgarians to carry the spoil and three Turks to guard it. He entered the ante-chamber and, having strictly forbidden his followers to utter a word whatever they might see or hear, commenced reading aloud from his magic volume. As he read, a side door opened in the rock, disclosing a motionless lady of marvellous beauty. The Hodja continued reading, and the damsel took off her headdress and laid it upon the ground; the Hodja, without ceasing his reading, removed his turban and laid it on the top of the headdress: presently the lady took off her jacket and the Hodja his, observing the same ceremony of superimposition, and so it went on till lady and schoolmaster (the latter still reading) appeared in the costume of Adam and Eve before the fall. Then a young Turk forgot the injunction given, and called out, "I say Hodja, what are you doing?" At these words a sudden blast of wind transported the treasure-seeker and his companions to a spot just outside the walls of Alaja Monastir. What became of the Hodja's garments our informant was unable to tell us.

Scared to Death

At Pietrych Kaleh, near Gebidjie, the villagers of Evren found a great treasure, but four men (they were Bulgarians) died of terror in digging it up.

Rising from the Dead

Between our village and Varna there is an old choked-up well which the country people say is Genoese.* Nicolaki went there with others to search for treasure, and after a whole day's hard work they found a dead squirrel, which they threw out on the ground. Nicolaki said, "Why, I think it's a squirrel!" and the little animal jumped up and climbed on to a tree. When they had dug to a depth of twenty feet they saw a big snake, also dead, and pitched him out too. Next day they resumed their labour, and, to their horror, saw the same snake alive in the same hole. This was too much for their nerves, fear conquered cupidity, and they left the place; but in the course of their excavations they sounded a hole beneath them of about sixty feet, so that they would have had three days' good work to arrive at the bottom of the well, even supposing that they were not impeded by any further supernatural manifestations.

*Footnote in original text: "In Bulgaria, almost all antiquities are attributed (both by Turks and Rayahs) to the Genoese; at Karamanja, in Roumelia, there are some very perfect remains of Hadrian's Wall, in which may still be traced the gate and flanking towers; these are termed Genoese by the people of the neighbourhood, as are also some ruins in the same vicinity, which, judging from the fragments of pottery and sculptured stone which we saw, appear to belong to the old Macedonian empire."

Beware the Turks

The same Nicolaki was also engaged at night in looking for another supposed treasure not far from this well. The workers heard mysterious voices from the depths of the lake, enjoining them to desist; but though they were in a terrible fright they kept on until all at once day broke, and they saw a squadron of Turkish cavalry charging at them through the cover. Then the Bulgarians took to their heels and never ceased running till they got to their own village, where, to their astonishment, they found it still black night, and that the earliest cock had not yet crowed! (St. Clair, 35-37. The subheaders included with the stories are mine.)

Smok. Illustration by Anna Błaszczyk (Evelinea Erato). © Bendideia Publishing.

Smok (Смок)

It's not so easy to make a snake show you its legs.

> **Smok** (singular); **Smotzi** (plural)
> **Other names**: tsmok,[109] cmok, zmek.[110]

Snakes are creatures that are both feared and revered. In Christian belief, they have been forever cursed since the day Satan in the form of one of the beasts deceived Eve in the Garden of Eden.

Their further evil intent is shown in Bulgarian folklore, which tells how snakes make a nest in the bones of the dead and drink from their eyes. You must not speak the creature's name, for then it will appear and bite you on the heel. Call the cold-blooded creature a devil, evil, or beast, if you will instead.

However, these creatures that slither from beneath the ground in the spring and warm themselves on top of stones have a dual nature. Not all are bad as you'll discover. Some guard, protect, and heal. And folklore tells how snakes are useful in other ways:

- When snakes creep out of their dens in the spring, sick people and childless women leave their clothes in a field, hoping snakes crawl over them, imbuing them with health and fertility.
- Women place a "grass-snake belt" (a snake skin wrapped in cloth) around their waists to help them conceive, and they continue to wear it until they give birth.
- Planting a snake's head along with seeds ensures a good harvest.
- Bullets cannot harm a person carrying serpent's eggs with him.

Origins

In some regions, a snake in a family's home symbolizes the soul of their ancestors. The one called Tsmok, for example, is the personification of the Domovoi. And, like the other ancestors, he desires respect and nourishment before he'll bring prosperity to the household.

Various explanations exist regarding the origins of snakes:

- A horse's hair that falls into water turns into a snake.
- If a severed lizard head gets stuck on a domestic animal's horn, the lizard head will become a snake.
- A rope used to bury treasure turns into a snake if the person burying the treasure says a proper incantation.

Appearance

The guardian spirit appears most often in the form of a non-poisonous snake or a hedgehog. It's not a wonder that people revered the spirit in the former guise. Not only does the snake spirit protect the home and occupants, it also rids the house of rats and mice.

People have related stories of huge snakes with a head like a catfish and hair like a buffalo. Depending on their country of origin, the guardian snakes have different attributes:

- Blind (Bulgaria)
- Shines like gold (Czech)
- Colorful or red or with white ears (Serbia)
- Gray (southern Russia)
- White (Serbia, Croatia, Bosnia, Slovakia)
- Cross on the forehead or wears a golden crown (Slovakia)

A guardian spirit called *smok sinurlija* protects entire villages. He appears as a giant snake with wings and feet, and flies over houses like a big ball of fire. You might consider him a dragon. (This topic is better suited for a future book on dragons.)

You can also see him as a demon incarnation, where he flies from Hell as a black-winged snake.

Getting to Know the Smok

Smok, like the Domovoi and Stopan, symbolizes the souls of deceased relatives, and is a guardian of the home (also of any family property, vineyards, and places where treasure has been buried). A house without the spirit is considered unhappy.

Did you know?

If you're experiencing domestic unhappiness, you may have a frog buried under your threshold ("Old World Building Customs," 201).

Keep him satisfied, and he'll warn you of danger and be concerned about the happiness of all who live in the house. You can expect to live a long, healthy life and have plenty of children (if this is your desire). And he'll supply you with an abundance of everything you need to survive (be it a plentiful harvest or a multitude of livestock).

The snake in your home is your protector. He curls up beneath the stove, the right side of the hearth, or under the threshold, where he comes and goes through the chimney. If not in those places, he could be hiding in the basement, under the table, below the stairs, or in the walls. When not inside the home, he's likely to be in the backyard or barns near cattle.

Not all snakes are guardians, however. Others you find around the home—especially those you chase away on March 25 (Blagovets)—are a menace. The head of any of those other snakes killed on this day holds great healing and magical powers.[111]

Sometimes, one snake lives alone; other times, you'll find both a male and female living with the family. And where that's the situation, you're certain to have plenty of tiny creatures slithering around your house as well.

Your guardian snake likes omelets. Don't be so surprised. Snakes like eggs, so why not cook them for the creatures now and again? Or after you've celebrated a ritual meal, leave a glass of wine, a piece of bread, and a cup of boiled wheat for your guardian snake on a small table in the corner of your house or near the fireplace. You can even put his meal on the roof of your house, or on the threshing floor if you have one. You'll know when to leave him food: when he's hungry, he'll tap the ceiling or whisper to you in a dream.

The spirit is fond of milk. The idea possibly comes from ancient times when people believed grass snakes sucked milk from the clouds, which were considered "heavenly cows," since the food of the gods was milk and honey. In later ages, this idea transformed to snakes drinking milk from cows.[112]

Snakes and Milk

The Smok is especially protective of the family's children. He plays with them, sleeps with them, and eats and drinks from the same dishes with them—just like a family pet. When the adults leave for work, he watches them and guards the livestock as well, as told in the following story:

> There once was a farmwife who had small children. She had to work in a field and had to leave her children at home. She poured them milk in a bowl so she wouldn't leave them hungry while she was gone. They never left anything in the bowl, thus their mother always praised them for being such obedient children.
>
> But the children claimed: "But we never eat alone; a beautiful birdie comes and eats with us."
>
> The mother thought that a cat might come and join her children while they ate, but she found it strange that they were talking about a white bird. She wanted to make sure which animal the children were talking about. Therefore, she hid in the house behind the doorway after giving the children milk.
>
> Soon, a white snake with a beautiful crown slithered from under the table straight into the lap of the youngest. The mother was paralyzed by fear. But the children caressed and stroked this beautiful "birdie."
>
> When the snake filled up on milk, she shook the beautiful little crown off her head and again found her way into the hole. As soon as the snake was gone, the mother jumped from behind the doorway, grabbed the children, and took them to a safe place.
>
> Of course, she didn't forget to take the crown as well and put it into the wooden chest where they kept yarn. The grandfather had to spin the yarn all winter long, but still he couldn't spin it all.
>
> The woman thought to herself: "What could this be? Does the crown have power?"
>
> Thus, she removed the crown, and the yarn was soon threaded. They put the crown in with the grain, and they had to measure it over and over again, but still they never ran out of it. They also added the little crown to other things, and shortly the house became the richest in the village. They kept the little crown as long as lived this generation of people who treated the snake with such kindness and affection.[113]

As the story above demonstrates, if you treat the guardian snake well, he'll provide for you. If you don't want the snake interacting with your children in this way, be sure to set out a bowl of milk for him near where he lives. He'll remain there and not come near your children.

Be careful. Stories tell how some snakes drink milk from an infant's bottle or even from the nursing mother herself. To keep the creature away, women may smear themselves and other objects with garlic and an herb called *pulchets*. Garlic is especially potent against snakes if the woman has taken it to church for the priest to bless on Todorovden (St. Theodore's Day, the first Saturday of Lent).[114]

Did you know?

The snake in the Garden of Eden was actually a dragon. When God cursed him, he lost his wings and legs (Bethedi).

Other versions of the snake and milk story start off the same with the parents leaving the children home alone. To keep a child out of trouble while they're gone, they give him something to eat: broth, milk, and other items. After a while, the child says or does strange things, so one of the parents pretends to leave, but stays hidden to watch. The parent feels various emotions when discovering a snake is "entertaining" her child. From there, the stories vary.

Another example of a happy ending like the story above is the following tale:

When this boy was bigger, they used to leave him alone at home; every morning they put milk on the stove and went to work. When the boy woke up, he knew where his milk was. He went to the stove, picked up the milk, and took it down. And always, as soon as he sat on the ground, a huge snake slithered toward him. They sat together like best friends. Janko ate with a spoon and fed the snake. When they were full, the snake talked with the boy, played with him, and then said goodbye and left.

A rock in front of the door had a hole under it. There the snake had its lair.

The parents were worried:

—What can it be?

The father said to his wife:

—My old one, what's happened to make our son so skinny?

—Indeed, you're right, my old one. With the amount of milk he drinks, he should look much better. We need to pay attention to what the boy does with the milk.

And they paid attention. After a long time, a huge snake slithered toward the boy. And since the parents saw that they were playing nicely, they didn't kill him. So, little Janko lived with the snake for twelve years.

Once they were playing and when the snake was about to leave, it said to the boy:

—My dear friend, I have to go but let me tell you something. Once I die, roll this rock away, and there is a hole in the rock. Go inside and look around carefully. You'll find a hat and a whistle there.[115]

And the snake proceeded to tell him how to find the treasure.

The following account of an encounter with a snake is milder. No one receives riches, but nobody dies or gets hurt either.

And she was there, they were there ... such an old grandma. She always left the child at home. And they cooked a mash. Such a mash! Such a milled rye and buns made of it. That's what they did, and they gave her milk too. Because what was she eating at first? Only that.

And the snake, it was a grass snake. A huge snake, terrible. And it always ate the milk, drank it. The snake drank it. And now the child saw him. But did she know what it was?!

It drank the milk, and she was hungry. The mom came there. She thought: "She drank the milk, at least she did. It will keep her on her feet at least."

> And once somebody went around, and the child was talking to the snake. "And how about you?"
>
> They were listening there behind the door. And the child had a spoon in her hand and threw it after the snake: "Eat buns too, not only milk!"
>
> The snake was smart enough to eat the buns too, not only the milk. But the snake was just doing its business. Maybe it curled up a little when she threw the spoon at it.
>
> But it was such a snake. I was eleven years I believe. And there were so many people around the snake! It was a huge snake. It grew so big from all the milk it ate. It was a huge snake. There were so many men. They couldn't kill it.[116]

Other accounts are less optimistic. The parents either deter the snake from coming, try to kill it but fail, or kill the snake. Even if the snake dies in this version of the tales, disaster doesn't overcome the family.

> My mom told me they had a dependent child. They went into the field in the morning and prepared some milk, some wafer, some noodles, or pastry for her. She took it and ate it when she was hungry. But the child was losing weight day by day, and she was always hungry, hungry, hungry; she was a hungry girl.
>
> "We have to wait to see why you're still hungry; it should be enough."
>
> And they went away and left the window open. After a while, they watched the window. A huge snake came and drank all the milk.
>
> And the girl said: "Eat bread too, not just milk."
>
> The parents didn't know what to do. One morning they poisoned the milk and put it far away from the child so that the snake would die. And it never came back anymore. It drank it and never came back anymore ...
>
> They said different things: that snakes were under each ... stove ... because when they demolished the cottages, they found holes down there ... but they aren't there anymore.[117]

All variations of the snake drinking milk story do not have such a happy ending. The following one is disastrous because of the actions of the parents.

> And that girl, she was always squabbling. When they gave her oats, goat milk ... And she was always squabbling in the yard. When they gave her the meal, she threw a spoon at it ... at the bowl. "Don't just drink milk, eat oats too!"
>
> One day her parents got mad: "Who are you talking to?"
>
> They thought she was talking to a cat or a dog. And then they saw a snake. So they killed him.
>
> And it's said that the child died within a year. That such a snake shouldn't be killed because it causes no harm. It happened here somewhere, but not during my life, nor during yours, but there were all sorts of events that happened.[118]

On the Dark Side
The families above would have been spared all their troubles if they followed traditional beliefs: A snake in the home is sacred and must not be killed. Causing him any harm will destroy the happiness and well-being of the family. At minimum, if you kill a snake, your hair will fall out.

The following describe a few other beliefs about snakes:

Farmer and Snake.
Artist: Wenceslas Hollar, 1673.
British Museum [Public domain], via Wikimedia Commons.

- If the snake dies, the master of the house is destined to follow him. Or, if not him, then the person he cares about the most.
- Another portent of death is seeing the guardian snake in the garden.
- On Blagovets (March 25), the home guardian makes his appearance, even if you don't see him. He slithers around, counting the people living in the house. If he misses anyone, that person will die within the year.

If you accidentally kill a guardian snake, you have a few options to ward off disaster. You can wrap the dead snake in linen and bury it under a thorn bush, covering the gravesite with a piece of white cloth. Depending on what region or country you're from, after you bury the snake, you'll want to light a candle over its grave for the next 40 days. If you killed the snake with a stick, toss the weapon into water right away. This will prevent your cattle from dying.

Relationship to St. Petka

Snakes also have a connection to St. Petka, one of the most beloved female saints among the Orthodox. She's the patron of women's activities, such as spinning and weaving. But, like many saints, she derives characteristics from a pagan personage: the female mistress of Friday, who is a deity of the underworld. This connects her with the spirits of the dead, and as such, she becomes a guardian of the home altar—the hearth. (See "Threshold: The Home Altar" for more details.)

Her holiday on October 14, Petkovden, marks the approach of winter and harsher conditions for those who live off the land. It's a time when they fear wild forest animals even more. These colder, darker months see an increase in rituals and feast days that not only ward off these creatures, but also honor the ancestors—and the saints.

Long before Christianity became the official religion, after the harvest, communities honored both nature and the *saybia*, the protector of households and livestock. This person was often an influential family member, a priest, or a well-known member of the community. After he died, his spirit remained to guard families and their possessions. People even believed he entered the dreams of the eldest living male to give warnings of danger or misfortune. Once a year, the family gathered to honor the *saybia* with a special meal. With the arrival of Christianity, instead of expressing gratitude to a *saybia* on a single day, people dedicated numerous days to honor many saints.[119]

Petkovden is a day when no more sowing of the fields takes place. To do so causes the saint's wrath, and she may appear as a snake as the following shows:

THRESHOLD CUSTOMS

The following are customs that take place at the threshold besides the ones you've already learned about (such as washing an ill child over it so the guardian spirit will drive evil from the home, burying stillborn children beneath it, and holding a recently baptized child over it).

- When an honored guest arrives at the threshold, he receives bread and salt, which are symbolic of the flesh and blood sacrifices of ancient times.
- A cross drawn on the threshold keeps away the evil Mara, who causes nightmares.
- Because the threshold is sacred, people cross themselves before stepping over it, and they won't sit on the threshold.
- A horseshoe on the threshold brings good luck.
- Burying a bat (animal, not the wooden club) and gold coin below the threshold will also bring good luck.
- Before a bride can cross a threshold, the groom's friends who have come to collect her must "cleanse the threshold" by placing coins in a bowl and offering them to the family.

Speaks the fierce snake,
Fierce snake, viper:
I am not a fierce snake,
I am Saint Petka,
Why do you plough on Petkovden
Why do you plough to finish your work?[120]

In St. Petka's honor, women also don't perform spinning or weaving on Fridays or on the saint's day. She doesn't always appear as a snake when someone breaks her rules. In a Russian tale, when a woman was spinning on a day she wasn't supposed to, the saint appeared to her as "an ugly and terrifying hag all in rags and covered with mud." But that's not all. She told the woman that because she toiled, she had destroyed the saint's beauty and radiance. The saint punished her by jabbing her with a knitting needle.[121] Other punishments included turning a woman into a frog, causing eye diseases, and inflicting infections on the offender's fingers.

Wealth of Snakes

From the home, you'll now journey to where other snakes from folklore live. Many tales tell of the wealth and unusual powers of snakes. (See the "Language of Animals" story at the end.) They guard treasure, but not in the same way that a Talasum does. This is their own wealth in their own kingdom. An ancient Snake King or Snake Queen rules them. The monarch has wings, much like a dragon, and sits on a golden throne, decorated with gems. Grass snakes are the ruler's princes and nobles. Under the monarch's tongue lays a magical ring that provides him with all his desires.

Snakes with gems in their mouths are also present in literature. For example, in one of the stories about Marko Kraljevic (a king about whom many folk tales are told: c. 1335 – 1395), a princess begs the hero to defeat the Black Arab in battle so she wouldn't have to marry him. One of the rewards she offers Marco is a salver, a serving tray:

THRESHOLD: THE HOME ALTAR

Throughout the ages in many cultures, snakes have been seen as wise and are associated with healing, often adorning a physician's staff. They are also part of the Tree of Life or World Tree.

Ancient civilizations considered nature sacred, and they deeply venerated the World Tree as a force of strength and protection. The three parts of the tree symbolize the nature of the universe. Branches represent the heavens where divine spirits reside. The trunk signifies Earth, which is the home of men and preternatural creatures like nymphs and fairies. And roots represent the underworld and the dead who dwell there. Like nature itself, all these creatures live in harmony with one another (Aveela, 9).

World Tree. Illustration by Nelinda. © Bendideia Publishing.

The snake curls around the base of this sacred tree's trunk. His presence there connects him with the land of the living. Since he burrows his way into the soil, he's also connected with the underworld, the land of the dead. His easy passage from one realm to the other is shown also in the home, where he can cross boundaries between the living and the dead.

Before families worshiped in churches, they performed sacrifices in the home to appease divine beings. The hearth, which you've learned about in other chapters, is an important "altar" to the household spirits, but it's not the only sacred place in the home. The threshold also acts as a boundary between the living and dead, divine and human. This primitive altar is where many sacrifices took place, with the head of household acting as the priest (Trumbull, 3). It's also the place where the guardian snake often resides.

You've learned about customs related to building a home, where the family sprinkled the blood of animals on the threshold. This was an essential element in maintaining a covenant with the spirit or deity of the place. Stepping over the blood, without touching the threshold, showed your acceptance of the covenant between you and the deity. To step directly on the threshold displayed contempt for the guardian spirit (Trumbull, 9-10).

> And I shall give thee a golden salver.
> Whereon a twisted snake
> Lifteth up his head on high.
> Holding in his teeth a precious stone.
> That shineth so as ye may sup by night
> As it were by the light of day.[122]

When snakes rise from their dens on Blagovets (March 25) to enjoy the sun after long winters, they are so happy they bring some of their wealth to the surface with them. If you want to take advantage of their friendliness on this day—since they don't bite people—you'll have to roam meadows and mountains, looking for the queen. If she favors you, she might give you some of the precious gems she hides beneath her tongue.

Other times when snakes are on good terms with people is when a human helps out one of their children who's in danger. In one story a poor shepherd saved a snake princess trapped in a burning house. The boy returned her safely home. When the king told the boy he could have anything in the kingdom, he of course chose the ring. Why have one object when you can have your heart's desire at any time?

Snakes in these kingdoms have not only wealth, but also wonderful powers. If you ever discover such a lair, you must never reveal the secrets you've found, and most definitely don't go back to try to steal the wealth. The snakes will take revenge upon you. Or, as the story at the end about the language of animals demonstrates, you might get to have your own revenge.

Fact or Fiction?

Tales about the belief of the powers of snakes are peppered among stories and forums around the internet. Here's a modern one you may find interesting.

> I know from the old people that a snake should not be killed! They'll curse their murderers. My grandmother told me that she knew many who after the murder immediately fell ill and died! My aunt, around Christmas, found a Smok in the house crawling up the door hinges. She closed the door tightly and pressed it hard until the creature died. Not long after that, she died from a stroke. She didn't listen to the stories that said snakes are the "guardians of the house."[123]

Smok in Literature

Stories about animals often have a moral or lesson for the listeners. These two tales about snakes are no exception.

- "Language of Animals," translated by Woislav M. Petrovitch, published in 1915.
- "The White Snake" by Karel Jaromír Erben, date unknown.

Language of Animals

This story comes from a collection of Serbian songs, folklore, and hero tales Woislav M. Petrovitch (1885 – 1934) translated into English and published in 1915. They are not sung by educated poets, but rather by the common people.

A wealthy peasant had a shepherd, who served him for a great number of years most honestly and faithfully. One day, as he drove his sheep through a forest to the pasture, he heard a hissing sound, and wondered what it could be. Listening carefully he went nearer and nearer to the spot whence the sound came, and he saw that the forest was on fire and that the hissing proceeded from a snake that was surrounded by flames. The shepherd watched to see what the poor creature would do in its trouble: and when the snake saw the shepherd, it exclaimed from the midst of the flames: "O shepherd, I pray of you, save me from this fire!" Then the shepherd reached out his crook and the snake entwined itself swiftly round the stick, round his arm, on to his shoulders and round his neck.

When the shepherd realized what was happening he was seized with horror, and cried out: "What are you about to do, ungrateful creature! Did I save your life only to lose my own?"

And the snake answered him: "Have no fear, my saviour! But take me to my father's house! My father is the king of the snake-world."

The shepherd endeavoured to move the snake to pity and prayed it to excuse him, for he could not leave his sheep. Thereupon the snake said to him: "Be comforted, my friend! Do not trouble about your sheep; nothing amiss will happen to them, but now do hasten to my father's house!"

So the shepherd went with the snake round his neck through the forest, till he came at length to a doorway constructed entirely of serpents. When they came near the gate, the shepherd's guide hissed to its servants, whereupon all the snakes instantly untwined themselves, leaving a way open for the shepherd, who passed through unmolested.

Then the snake said to its preserver: "When we come before my father he will surely give you, as reward for your kindness to me, whatever you may wish: gold, silver and precious stones; but you should not accept anything of that kind. I would advise you to ask for the language of animals. He will undoubtedly be opposed to your wish, but finally he will yield."

They now entered the apartments of the king, who, with evident relief, inquired: "My son, where have you been all this time?"

The reptile then told all about the fire in the forest and of the kindness of the shepherd, who had saved his life.

At this the snake-king turned with emotion to the shepherd: "What reward can I give you for having saved the life of my son?" he said.

The shepherd answered: "I desire nothing but the power of understanding and speaking the language of animals."

But the monarch said: "That is not for you, for if I give you that power, and you should impart the secret to another, you will instantly die. Therefore choose some other gift."

But the shepherd insisted: "If you wish to reward me, give me the language of animals: if you do not care to gratify my wish, no more need be said; I bid you farewell!"

And indeed he turned to go, but the king, seeing his determination, stopped him, exclaiming: "Come here, my friend! Since you so strongly desire the language of animals, the gift shall not be withheld; open your mouth!"

The shepherd obeyed, and the snake-king blew into his mouth, and said: "Now, blow into my mouth!"

The shepherd did as he was told, and the snake-king blew a second time in the shepherd's mouth, and then said: "Now you have the language of animals. Go in peace; but be sure not to impart your secret to another, else you will die that very moment!"

The shepherd took leave of his friends and as he returned through the woods he heard and understood everything the birds, plants and other living creatures were saying to each other. When he reached his flock and found all his sheep safe as had been promised, he lay on the grass to rest.

The Buried Treasure

Hardly had he settled himself, than two ravens alighted on a tree near by and began to converse: "If this shepherd knew what is under the spot where that black lamb is lying, he would surely dig in the earth; he would discover a cave full of silver and gold."

The shepherd at once went to his master and told him of the buried treasure. The latter drove a cart to the place indicated, dug deeply in the earth and lo! he found a cave full of silver and gold, the contents of which he placed in his cart and carried home.

This master was an honest and generous man, and he gave the entire treasure to his shepherd, saying: "Take this, my son; it was to you that God gave it! I would advise you to build a house, to marry and start some good business with this gold."

The shepherd did as his kindly master advised him, and, little by little he multiplied his wealth and became the richest man, not only in his village, but in the whole district. He now hired his own shepherds, cattle-drivers and swineherds to keep his great property in good order.

One day, just before Christmas, he said to his wife: "Prepare wine and food, for to-morrow we will go to our farms and feast our servants."

His wife did as he bade, and the next morning they went to their farms, and the master said to his men: "Now come one and all, eat and drink together; as for the sheep I will myself watch them to-night."

So the kind man went to guard his sheep. About midnight, wolves began to howl and his dogs barked a defiance. Said the wolves in their own language to the dogs: "Can we come and kill the sheep? There will be enough for you also."

Thereupon the dogs answered in their own tongue: "O come by all means, we also would like to have a feast!"

But amongst the dogs there was a very old one who had only two teeth left. That faithful animal barked furiously at the wolves: "To the devil with you all! So long as I have these two teeth, you shall not touch my master's sheep!"

And the master heard and understood every word they uttered. Next morning he ordered his servants to kill all his dogs, except the old one.

The servants began to implore their master, saying: "Dear master, it is a pity to kill them!"

But the master would not suffer any remonstrance, and sternly ordered: "Do as I bid you!"

Then he and his wife mounted their horses and started for home, he on a horse and she on a mare. As they journeyed, the horse left the mare a little behind and he neighed, saying: "Hurry up, why do you dawdle behind?"

And the mare answered: "Eh, it is not hard for you—you are carrying only your master, and I am carrying a despotic woman whose rules are a burden to the whole household."

The Importunate Wife

Hearing this, the master turned his head and burst into laughter. His wife noticing his sudden mirth, spurred on her mare, and when she reached her husband she asked him why he had laughed.

He answered: "There is no reason, I just laughed."

But the woman was not satisfied with this reply and would not give her husband any peace.

He endeavoured in vain to excuse himself, saying: "Don't keep on asking me; if I tell you the true reason why I laughed, I shall instantly die!"

But she did not believe her husband, and the more he refused to tell her, the more she insisted that he should do so, until at last the poor man was worn out by her persistence.

Directly they arrived home, therefore, the man ordered a coffin to be made, and, when it was ready and he had it placed in front of the house-door, he said to his wife: "I shall lie down in this coffin, for the moment I tell you why I laughed, I shall die."

So he laid himself in the coffin, and as he took a last look around, he saw his faithful old dog, coming from the fields. The poor animal approached his master's coffin and sat near his head howling with grief. When the master saw this, he requested his wife to give it food. The woman brought bread and gave it to the dog, who would not even look at it, still less eat it.

The piece of bread attracted a cock, which came forward and began to peck at it; the dog reproached him saying: "You insatiable creature! You think of nothing but food, and you fail to see that our dear master is about to die!"

To this reprimand the cock retorted: "Let him die, since he is such a foolish man! I have a hundred wives, and I gather them all round a grain of corn, which I happen to find; and then, when they have all assembled, I swallow it myself! If any of them should protest, I just peck at them; but he, the fool, is not able to rule a single wife."

At this the man jumped out of the coffin, took a stick and called to his wife: "Come in the house, wife, and I shall tell you why I laughed!"

Seeing the obvious intention of her husband, the woman begged him to desist, and promised that nevermore would she be curious, or try to pry into his affairs (Petrovitch, 230-235).

The White Snake

Snakes in folklore are sometimes not protectors, but instead are a menace— especially when they swarm across the land, destroying the livelihood of the peasants. And even more terrifying when they're led by a huge white snake, which was considered the queen among them.

How do you get rid of them? The following tale, originally from Karel Jaromír Erben's (1811 – 1870) "A Hundred Genuine Popular Slavonic Fairy Stories in the Original Dialects" (translated by W.W. Strickland), provides one method to banish the snake.

Karel Jaromír Erben

nce the snakes multiplied about Osojan to such an extent that everything swarmed with them. Gruelly did they torment the peasants in these districts. They crept into their churches, their rooms, and milk chests. There was no peace even at table, for the hungry serpents slipped into the dishes. But a terrible big white serpent caused them the greatest fear, which they had frequently seen to fall upon the Osojan flocks of sheep. The peasants knew not how to help themselves: they got up processions and went on pilgrimages, that God might be pleased to avert this dreadful punishment. But even this was of no avail.

When the poor people were in such great distress and did not know what to do to free themselves from this infliction, came one day into this same district an unknown man, who promised them to make an end of all the snakes at once if they could certainly assure him that they had not seen a great white snake. "We have never seen one," answered some of the multitude that had collected round the stranger.

Snake in Flames.

Now he bade them prepare a large heap of firewood round a tall pine, and when he had climbed to the top of the pine, ordered them to kindle the heap from all sides and then quickly to disperse themselves.

When the flames lashed against the tall pine from all sides, the unknown man takes a bone fife from his pack and begins to whistle so loud upon it that every one's ears tingled. Quickly writhe and wriggle from all sides a tremendous quantity of snakes, adders, and vipers to the wood heap, and, urged by some mysterious impulse, leap into the fire and perish there. But all at once is to be heard from Ososhtsic a still louder piping, which fills all present with fear and horror. The man on the pine tree hearing it, turns deadly pale: "Woe's me! now there is no more help for me!" so he shrieks. " 'Tis the white serpent; I heard it hiss. Why have you thus deluded me? At least be so far pitiful and do not forget every year, on this day, to distribute alms for the soul of me, ill-fated one!"

Scarcely had the unhappy man uttered these words when a terrible serpent, with a loud clattering like a stream in flood, rolled over a perpendicular precipice and flung itself into the lake, so that the foam flew aloft. In a short time it had swam to the other side of the lake, and, full of fury, writhed into the burning wood heap, towered aloft, and pressed the wretch on the fir tree into the fire. Terribly did the serpent hiss and fling itself this way and that in the fire, but the intense heat little by little overpowered it.

Thus this monstrous snake, which had wrought such havoc among the flocks, perished, together with the whole tribe of serpents. Again the peasants could attend to their work without fear, and the shepherds on Ososhtsits (the Alps belonging to the common of Osojan) pasture their flocks without apprehension. Grateful to their benefactor to this day, the people of Qsojan do not forget the promise of their ancestors, and every year, on the return of the day, offer rich gifts to the poor (Strickland, 46-47).

Bannik. Illustration by Anna Błaszczyk (Evelinea Erato). © Bendideia Publishing.

Bannik (Банник)

To carry fire in one hand and water in the other.

> **Bannik** (singular); **Banniki** (plural)
>
> **Other Russian names:** baennik,[124] bayennik, bainnik, baynushko, bannyy, baynik,[125] bayennik, bayennyy, baynushko, bannoy, bannyy bes, bannyy pastyr', bannyy khozyain, banshchik, bayannik, bes bannyy, pastyr' bannyy, khozyain bannyy.[126]
>
> **Belarusian:** laziennik, laznik,[127] lazenník (from *laznya* for "bathhouse").[128]
>
> **Polish:** łaziebnik, łaźnik.[129]
>
> **Feminine:** baennitsa, bannaia babushka,[130] bannaia, bainikha,[131] bannikha, baynitsa, bayennaya matushka, obderikha, Shishiga.[132]
>
> **Slang:** Anyone who is annoyingly persistent about a matter is said to be "sticky as a banya leaf."[133]

The Bannik brings to mind the opening words of a popular song from 1958. Bobby Darin belts out that he was splishing and splashing while taking a bath.[134] The singer of the song was fortunate that only a party was going on while he was in his tub. Imagine how different it would have been if he had run into a Bannik instead. Rather than putting on his shoes to join the dance, he would have found himself screaming and running.

As you read about this spirit, you'll understand why he could put such fear into a person. This goes well beyond modesty.

Origins

You may recall the story in the Domovoi chapter about the creatures tossed from heaven. In one version, all the creatures start out as *domovye*. This includes the Bannik (and Dvorovoi and Ovinnik, whom you'll meet in the following chapters. Each group of spirits takes on the name of the place where they fell.)

Various beliefs also say the Bannik, Dvorovoi, and Ovinnik are ancestral spirits like the Domovoi. Some sources say they are all the same spirit—except the Domovoi's name changes with where you'll find him on your property. Other people maintain each one is a unique spirit.

Appearance

The Bannik lives in the *banya*—a Russian steam bath (see sidebar "About a Banya" for more details), but he doesn't inhabit a new building until after a woman gives birth and washes herself there. Although seldom seen, from time to time he does crawl out from his hiding places and sit in the steam with people while they swat themselves with leafy twigs to open their pores. He has a bit of a perverse nature, as you'll soon

Etymology

Bannik comes from the word *banya*, for "bath."

discover. He may sit close, his smiling face inches from yours. Can you see the glimmer in his eyes? What's crossing his mind as the two of you sit alone? Nothing good, I can tell you.

Sometimes, he shape-shifts into a boar, a cat, a frog, or a white rabbit—but never a dog. Although he's friends with your pet cat, he despises dogs. If you see a strange animal in the banya, it should be a giveaway that it's the Bannik. Instead of a male spirit, a female demon, called a bannikha, may occupy your banya. She's often described as having one eye.

Most often, however, the Bannik appears as a short, wrinkled old man with long, white hair and beard. And, yes, he's naked. This is a bathhouse after all. He may even appear as your best pal or a close relative. In such a steamy room, it'll be difficult for you to realize it's not your friend, but instead is the bathhouse demon.

If he happens to scoot over to you and lay his hands on your back as if to help you beat yourself, move away as fast as you can. That old man has the longest claws you've ever seen—or felt. If you've ever experienced that, and you're not speechless right now, you're probably saying something profane. You have that right. He's *not* your buddy.

Another clue to his true identity is the hissing manner in which he speaks. You may think at first that it's water sizzling on the hot stones. But if it's the banya demon, you'll catch a hint of giggling in his voice as well. Yup, he's one crazy dude you should avoid.

If he happens to be bathing when you enter the banya, you may startle him. He'll rapidly change from a humanlike appearance to a creature still in the form of a person, but one made out of birch twigs. It's your own fault. You shouldn't have gone to the banya when it was the Bannik's turn to bathe. If you don't already know when it's safe to enter, you will by the time you've finished reading this chapter.

Getting to Know the Bannik

Are you terrified to take a steam bath yet? Just wait. Even more frightening things can happen in a banya if you don't take the proper precautions. But first, you may want to learn more about a Bannik.

First of all, he's a bath attendant, making sure the fire in the stove doesn't go out when you're bathing, and keeping the birch sticks the proper softness. He usually goes undetected

Bannik as Twig Man. Illustration by Nelinda.
© Bendideia Publishing.

since he hides after he has everything in running order. You can find him under the benches or behind the stove. He especially likes to spy on women who bathe alone. That's rather creepy, knowing he's there, even if he doesn't make an appearance. But, taking a steam bath is normally a communal activity, so knowing the Bannik's hiding doesn't seem to bother anyone. He's just one more presence in an already crowded bathhouse.

A warning sign isn't posted at a banya, but perhaps it should be. It would tell you activities you should avoid while you're in the banya—all of which annoy the Bannik.

- Whistling (a sign of disrespect; it isn't even proper to whistle in the presence of ikons inside your home).
- Getting rough (beyond what's needed as you beat yourself with the birch twigs).
- Lying.
- Boasting.
- Wearing any Christian symbols (he's a demon, after all).
- Making out (he might be a voyeur, but even he doesn't want to witness that behavior in his home).

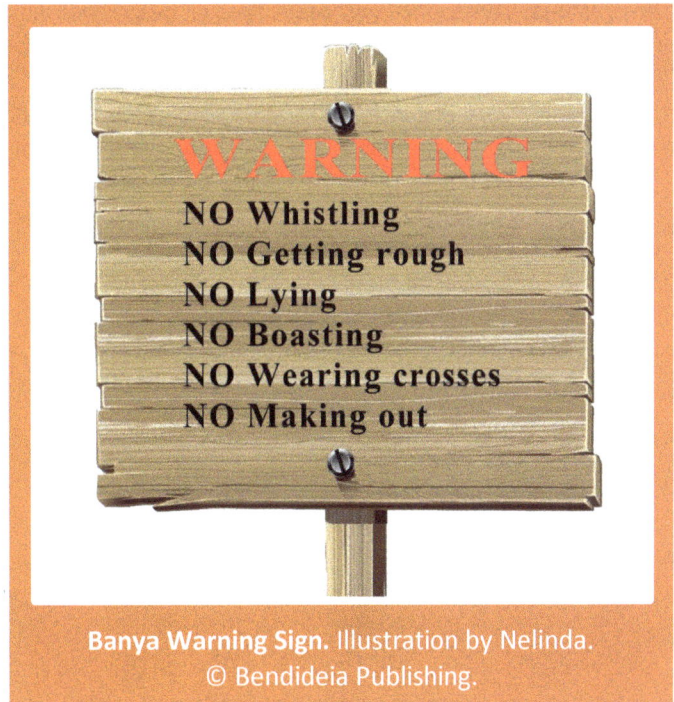

WARNING

NO Whistling
NO Getting rough
NO Lying
NO Boasting
NO Wearing crosses
NO Making out

Banya Warning Sign. Illustration by Nelinda. © Bendideia Publishing.

A Gathering for Life Events

People use the banya for more than bathing. It can be a place where they go for privacy. You may joke about sitting on the "throne" when you occupy the bathroom, spending hours in there—to have peace away from yelling children, a scolding spouse, and clucking chickens (well, maybe you don't have chickens, but plenty of people living in rural areas do). Every now and then you need time to read the newspaper! You can imagine it's the same situation when someone escapes to the banya.

Even today, people use the banya to perform rituals, have therapeutic treatments, and simply organize social get-togethers. In the past, it served other purposes as well: childbirth, pre-wedding ceremonies, rituals for the dead, fortune-telling, and casting spells. It's likely some of these activities still take place in rural areas. You can find out more about these activities in the sections that follow.

Childbirth

On the practical side, a woman gives birth in the banya not so much for privacy or cleanliness, but because hot water is readily available. She is also considered unclean and should remove herself from the presence of others, allowing only a midwife to be in attendance. During the woman's labor and after delivery, the midwife administers a steam bath. This includes the customary beating with the *venik* (plural, *veniki*; a bundle of switches made from birch twigs), even around the woman's abdomen to speed up the birth. Overly difficult or prolonged births receive even harsher treatment: the midwife shakes the woman, hangs her upside down, rubs her abdomen, or gives her vomit-inducing drinks. Even after the birth, the steam bath continues for both mother and infant. She places the child on the upper shelf—which receives the most steam and heat—and beats the child with the *venik*.

A woman also gives birth in the banya because she's susceptible to mistreatment from evil spirits and becoming ill from curses from those who dislike her. In the banya, the Bannik protects her. This is his home, and other demons are powerless in his domain when he's there. Even so, demons hover above the banya during an infant's delivery. One legend tells how a youth summoned Saint Petka to act as midwife. When she arrived, devils swarmed on all the banya benches around the girl who was in labor. Although terrified, the saint stayed, believing the devils could eat her only if God allowed it. She delivered the infant and silently prayed over him as she washed him in water. As soon as she hung a cross around his neck, a whirlwind arose in the bathhouse, taking the devils and mother with it. The child, however, remained safe in the arms of the saint.[135]

Even if the Bannik is there to chase away other demons, it's important that someone always stays with the woman. The spirit doesn't like women in labor, perhaps because he despises loud noises in his bathhouse. The midwife's responsibility is to keep the Bannik and devils away from the mother while she's delivering. She'll dip stones in water and toss them into corners of the room. This distracts the Bannik from the mother.

When the infant is born, the midwife tries even harder to keep the Bannik away. She strips off all her clothing and chants to the Morning Star while she carries the infant around the banya to keep the child from crying. Although the Bannik protects the woman and infant from other evil spirits, he also feels a fondness toward children born in his place, and he tries to steal them away from the mother before they can be baptized. If the Bannik is particularly evil, though, he'll eat the infant or beat him with birch branches until the skin peels away.

Inside a Banya. Illustration by Dmitry Yakhovsky. © Bendideia Publishing.

ABOUT A BANYA

A banya is a steam bath, like a sauna. It's not taken in a tub like a water bath, but happens in a room or building especially made for that purpose. You first enter a changing room, where people also socialize when they take breaks from the intensity of the heat in the steam-filled room—which can reach upwards of 100 degrees F.

From the changing room, you have to stoop to enter the banya through a small door. Inside, you'll find a cobblestone stove in one corner, with gaps between the stones. Next to it, wide benches, stacked like stadium seats, allow many people to sit or lie down. The higher you go, the more intense the heat. Another smaller, single-level bench lines the opposite wall.

Scraps of wood burn inside the stove. Older buildings may lack a chimney, and the smoke from the burning wood has no place to escape, except through cracks between the stones in the stove. These are called "black banyas" because soot darkens the interior. "White" banyas are more modern and have chimneys that allow the smoke to go outside. Often in the black banya, a small hole in one of the walls enables some of the smoke to escape the room.

Taking a steam bath usually requires assistance. The bather lies on the upper bench to get the full effect of the steam, and he uses the lower one when he's ready to wash. When the stove's stones reach a high temperature, the assistant pours water onto them, creating steam. He heats additional water for washing by dropping cobblestones into a large wooden vat.

Once steam fills the room, the assistant prepares a *venik*, which you may recall is a bundle of twigs used to beat the bather. Most often they are birch, which helps ease muscle ache and joint strain.

Other varieties of *veniki* and their remedies include:

- **Oak**: to soften dry oily skin.
- **Lime**: to relieve headaches.
- **Alder**: to cure colds.
- **Fir**: to increase blood circulation.
- **Eucalyptus**: to relieve sore throats.

After the assistant bundles together the *venik*, he lets it first seep in a bucket of cold water. Afterwards, he puts it onto the stove so the heat softens the leaves. When it's ready, the assistant beats both sides of the bather's body with the *venik*, helping to open his pores, cleansing his body.

When the bather has been beaten enough—usually after being in the steam for five to ten minutes, which probably feels much longer—he can cool off by dumping cold water over himself. If the building is near a river or lake (which many are), he can run outside and dive into the water. In the winter, people often roll around in the snow.

Bathers are likely to repeat this process several times.

In the stories in "Hot, Steamy Bathing" at the end of this chapter, you can read a few banya experiences.

Horrible, for certain, but you were warned he did terrible things. This belief about how the Bannik treats infants possibly became popular because of mishaps when newborns were overly beaten by their mothers.

Pre-wedding Ceremonies

The night before a wedding, a bride takes a purification steam bath. Before she can do that, she has to make sure the Bannik won't interfere. The evening is his time to use the banya after all. The guests attempt to scare him away by throwing rocks and pottery against the walls outside. With the spirit safely out of the way, the bride can take a steam bath in peace.

From that point onward, the woman's friends take over her prenuptial steam bath. The washing represents the woman's separation from her family and also the loss of her *volia*, her freedom. Her friends unbraid her hair, then re-braid it for the last time in the single plait of an unmarried woman. When she's married, she'll plait her hair into the customary two braids. In some places, the friends beat her with the *veniki* until she mentions the name of the man she's about to marry. The longer she can withhold speaking, the more respect she garners from her friends. Her friends also try to keep the fire quiet by not disturbing the brands. This ensures the woman's husband won't beat her, as was typical in most families, especially when the husband was drunk.

A *koldun* (sorcerer) may also be in charge of the woman's ritual bathing. He wears a fishnet around his waist as he leads her into the banya. As he beats her with the twigs, he recites a spell:

> On this birch besom the leaves will never go away. The same will happen to God's servant [the bride's name], the husband will never go away from her. Amen.[136]

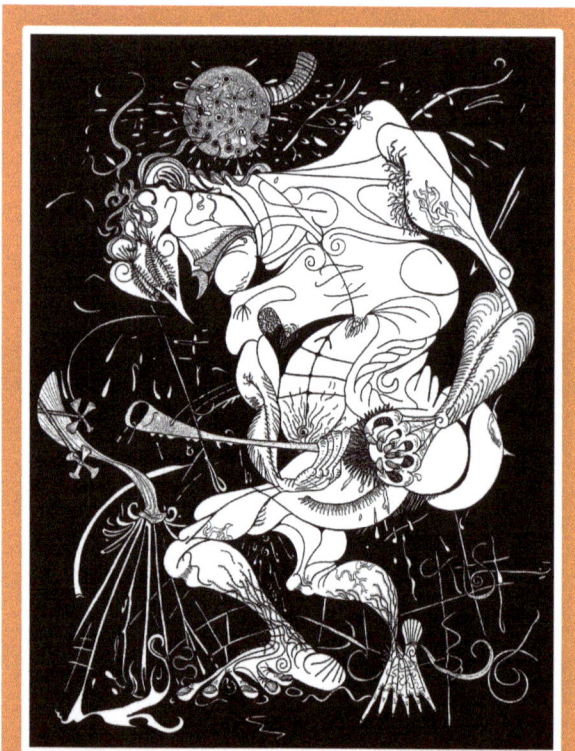

Bannik by Marek Hapon, 2012.
[CC BY-SA 4.0 (https://creativecommons.org/ licenses/by-sa/4.0)], from Wikimedia Commons.

When the bride finishes her bathing, the *koldun* wipes away her sweat with a whole raw fish. The bride takes the fish and cooks it for her groom. Both fish and sweat have magical, sexual connotations.

Rituals for the Dead

It isn't necessary to drive the Bannik away when the banya is used for rites for the deceased. The spirit is probably happy to have another person join the ranks of the dead, perhaps someone to chat with before the soul leaves for the afterworld.

You've learned a little about ancestral beliefs in the previous chapters. It's interesting to note that the soul is perceived as being visible, often taking the form of a butterfly or bird (or even a fly or moth) after it leaves the body. Before the soul can reach its final destination, it undertakes a journey to every place special to the person during his lifetime. For 40 days, the soul wanders about, reliving both good and bad times.

While the soul is traveling the world, the grieving family prepares the deceased's body. The customs vary by country. In Russia, a family puts a glass of vodka on the windowsill, and they set aside a bowl of water and a towel for his washing in the banya. On the final day, they invite the soul home from its travels, where the banya is heated and ready for the soul to take its final steam bath in this world.

Fortune Telling

A popular activity among girls during the Yuletide season is to perform a divination ceremony at the banya. While standing at the entrance at midnight, each girl, one at a time, pulls her skirts over her head, her bare backside jutting into the steam room. The Bannik, rather perverse as he is, can't resist that temptation. He sneaks over to touch her buttocks. And you thought it was creepy when the Domovoi rubbed the faces of his family while they slept.

Depending on the Bannik's mood, his touch varies. If it's rough, and he scratches the girl's backside with those long claws, or if his caress is cold, misfortune is coming her way. A wet slap means she'll marry a drunkard. If, however, he's gentle and gives her a warm pat, her year ahead will be happy. If his hand feels shaggy, she'll marry a rich man. As you can well imagine, youth often used this opportunity to pursue their own perverse actions.

The Bannik might even be generous and place a ring on the girl's finger, if she has her hand stretched out behind her. This jewelry is a symbol of good fortune. One story, however, tells about a girl who thought the Bannik had given her a ring. When she looked, she nearly died of fright. The spiteful spirit had encased all her fingers in hideous iron links.[137]

If the spirit doesn't respond by touching the girl, he may leave something on the stove for her instead. If the item is smooth, it means her future husband will be handsome.

Divination was popular in Russian literature as well. In Leo Tolstoy's (1828 – 1910) *War and Peace* (translation published in 1889), an old lady tells a tale of a young woman who once went into the banya at night for such a purpose:

> …The guests were invited into the drawing-room, and refreshments were provided in the ballroom for the serfs.
> "No, but what a terrible thing to read your fortune in a bath!" exclaimed an old maid, who lived with the Melyukofs.
> "Why so?" asked the oldest daughter of the family.
> They were now sitting down at supper.
> "No, don't think of doing such a thing, it requires so much courage."
> "I would just as lief," said Sonya.
> "Tell us what happened to that young lady," asked the second Melyukova girl.
> "Well, this was the way of it: a certain báruishnya," said the old maid, "took a cock, two plates, knives, and forks, as the way is, and went and sat down. She sat there and sat there, and suddenly she hears some one coming — a sledge drives up, with harness bells jingling; she listens, some one is coming! Some one comes in, absolutely in human form, just like an officer, and sits down with her where the second plate is set."
> "Oh! oh!" screamed Natasha, rolling her eyes in horror.
> "And how was it — how did he speak to her?"
> "Yes, just like a man, everything was just as it should have been; and he began to talk with her, and all she needed to do was to keep him talking till the cock crowed, but she got frightened; as soon as she got frightened, and hid her face in her hands, then he clasped her in his arms. Luckily, just then, some maids came running in."[138]

The tale, however, didn't deter the young ladies who listened to it. Immediately after that they set off to do their own divination in the granary (another place where predictions were sought, which you'll learn more about in the Ovinnik chapter).

Keeper of Secrets

Since the banya is a place where people perform communal bathing, they tend to talk a lot, sharing secrets or making plans. Of course, the Bannik hears it all. Some people say the Bannik uses magic to loosen the tongues of bathers: he wants to know what's going on outside his abode. If you can grab hold of the Bannik while he's unaware of your presence, you can force him to spill the secrets he's heard. One way to get him to appear is to remove a baptismal crucifix from around your neck (something many Russians commonly wear) and put it under your left heel. As you'll learn later, it isn't wise to wear a cross or utter religious prayers in the banya.

Making the Bannik appear when you want him to may be difficult to do, however. You have a better chance of finding out what secrets the spirit knows simply by asking him questions while you're taking your steam bath. A soft touch on your back signifies a positive answer. But watch out if the answer isn't what you're looking for. You'll know he's displeased if he flays your back with his claws.

Bannik. Figure by Ivan Bilibin, 1934.
[Public domain], via Wikimedia Commons.

Your future isn't looking too bright from that point forward. It might be better to take life as it comes instead of trying to weasel information out of the Bannik.

You'll have better luck getting on his good side if you first pour vodka onto the hot stones. He's likely to do more than have physical contact. He'll whisper or even screech a few words, telling you more about what you want to know.

Casting Spells

The banya is also a place where a *koldun* (wizard or sorcerer) or *ved'ma* (witch) goes to cast spells and perform healing rituals. Sorcerers patronize the steamy room during times reserved for the Bannik: after midnight, in particular. Also, anyone who goes to the banya during Mass (another time when the Bannik and demons congregate) *has* to be up to something sacrilegious. It's here a sorcerer meets with the demon and pledges that he'll perform all manner of blasphemous activities. In return, through the demon's support, the sorcerer becomes powerful and influential. The initiation is not an easy task. One story tells of a woman who went to the banya to become a *ved'ma*. First she had to pass through the jaws of a gigantic frog three times.

The following is one spell you may hear if you dare to approach and spy on bathhouse proceedings:

The dark blue black smoke goes out by the steam from the bottom of a bath. The motley cat dances on an apple mountain. Run on valleys of valleys, on mountains of mountains.[139]

124

It sounds like an incantation to call the demon forth. The "cat" could refer to the Bannik, who can shape-shift into a feline; "motley" most likely refers to the smoke or steam filling the banya; and "dancing" brings forth an image of flames flickering within the stove.

Sorcerers use the banya as a meeting place because whenever the powers of elements intermingle, it's certain to create a threshold from which they can communicate with spirits and other creatures. In the banya, the two powerful elements of fire and water abound, making it suitable for magic to reign.

Certain days are auspicious for performing magic. In particular, sorcerers perform *koldovat'* (*koldovat'sya*) *dekovatsya* on Holy Thursday. The meaning of this is:

> … 'to perform some magical actions in order to harm a human or animal', 'to perform some magical actions to ensure well-being, prosperity and marriage'. The noted magical practices are divided into preventive, precautionary, cleansing, protective and others. Some general rules must be followed: All magic actions must be carried out before sunrise; magic actions must not be talked about, otherwise they will not work.[140]

The banya also serves as the place where a dying sorcerer chooses to end his earthly life. It's here that he passes on his secrets of the magical arts to an apprentice "without the 'magic' leaking and accidentally conveying their gifts to the unsuspecting."[141] It's hidden from everyone, that is, except the Bannik, who's certain to be absorbing the knowledge and storing it away for later use.

If the sorcerer fails to find a willing heir, he'll do what he can to force someone to receive the knowledge. This can easily be achieved when a person touches or accepts an item from the dying sorcerer. To die without this transfer of information puts the sorcerer at risk of becoming one of the restless dead. As he approaches death, his followers raise the roof of the banya and hold it open with a branch from an aspen tree. This enables his "sinful soul" to fly free.

Did you know?

In addition to birch, people use red rowan in the banya for its magical powers in driving away evil spirits. Satan created the tree, but God, seeing the crosses on the berries, selected the tree for his own, making it "clean" (Color-mir.com).

On the Dark Side

Since ancient times, the Bannik has haunted the banya. It is, or at least it was in the past, unsafe to take a steam bath after dark—or even walk anywhere near the banya after seven in the evening. That's the hour when the Bannik likes to bathe—either by himself, or he invites his demon friends to enjoy the heat and steam with him. A banya is a communal activity after all. You definitely don't want to be around for that demon-infested event.

The bathhouse was considered unholy or "unclean." This didn't mean dirty or even "sinful, evil, but simply less sacred, more accessible to the action of evil forces."[142] People did not bring anything that belonged in the banya back into their homes for fear one of the evil spirits or magical powers could be attached to it.

Ikons and other holy objects were once forbidden to be present in the banya because they were certain to agitate the demons, and people had to remove their crosses before entering, although today, crosses are common accessories worn in the steam bath. Even praying in the banya in the past could incite the Bannik's wrath as the following story demonstrates:

> A man stayed for the night in an abandoned banya. At midnight, the bannik came. He started to rip off the man's skin. The man prayed to God, which made the bannik pissed

off. After the man had uttered several prayers, the rooster crowed and the bannik disappeared. Instead of pieces of torn skin, the man was covered in rugs. He thanked God and went away.[143]

You can be sure that he learned his lesson and never entered a banya at night again.

To make sure the Bannik remains happy, people who bathe separately during the day leave the banya empty for about a half hour after every third or fourth steam bath. That's the Bannik's special time, in addition to his nightly escapades.

Each person provides him with gifts to use for his bath—a pail of water, soap, oils, towels, and a *venik*. Although he'll use the dirty, leftover water from your own bath, showing him respect by leaving him a clean bucket of water is highly recommended—especially when you find out what he does when he's upset. And make sure you leave the room clean for him when you're done, or he could do to you what he did to an evil spirit in the story that follows:

One day an evil spirit saw people going to the banya. He wanted to go there, too. At night he broke in, lit the stove, and began to wash himself. It was nice with the steam, and he liked the banya a lot. He left two smoking pieces of wood in the stove after he was done.

The bannik came out and saw a lot of smoke in his banya and the mess left by the spirit. He was angry and wanted to punish the evil spirit for that.

The evil spirit liked the banya so much that he decided to go there again. He went to the nearby forest to look for birch tree branches (the people usually hit themselves with small birch tree branches tied together in the banya, for massaging and cleaning their skin).

The birch tree warned the evil spirit: "Don't go to the banya!"

Then the evil spirit went to the linden tree to make a sponge. That tree also warned him about the banya.

After that the evil spirit went to the creek to get water and heard the same warning.

He ignored all that and went back to the banya. He started washing himself there, but the birch tree branches froze, and the water he brought turned into ice. He asked the bannik if that was his doing.

After that, a lot of steam came out of the stove, and the evil spirit found himself sailing in a wooden barrel in a lake of boiling water. A giant fish jumped out of the water and was going to eat him.

The evil spirit was terrified. He closed his eyes and when he opened them again, he found himself flying on a birch tree branch into a cloud of steam. He got scared and fell from the branch right into a pot of boiling water. He jumped out screaming and ran away from the banya.

When he looked back, he saw a big, dark, old man covered with long hair. His beard was made of birch tree leaves. The evil spirit was so terrified he never went to the banya again.[144]

The Bannik doesn't always do evil because he's irritable. Sometimes, the requests people make of him go against his sense of justice. The following stories mention horrifying things the Bannik does to those who displease him:

- An elderly woman was asked to tend to the needs of a visitor who was bathing in the banya. When others came to the banya later for their own steam bath, they found her strangled and peeled to death.
- Another woman wanted to get rid of her husband, so she asked the Bannik to do it for her. Instead, angry at her deceit, he peeled off her skin and thrust a bucket over her head.

Bannik. Illustration © Andy Paciorek. Used with permission of the artist.

- One old woman constantly scolded her children and told them to go to the devil. (You may recall from the Kikimora chapter that this was an open invitation to demons, who did come and claim what a parent offered them.) The Bannik got fed up with her behavior. When she went to the banya one day, he tore off her skin from head to foot.
- When angered, he may burn down the banya—preferably with the person who annoyed him inside.
- He can throw a fit—and more. Bathers have to be wary of hot bricks or stones falling on them, boiling water thrown at them, steam scalding them, and hands suffocating them or breaking their neck.

A good lesson from the above: don't bathe alone or when the Bannik tells you not to.

Even though a Bannik sometimes bathes with his demon pals (those he invites, not party-crashers like the evil spirit in the earlier story), he also protects the people in his village from his evil friends. In one tale, girls were at a party in a house by the lake. A group of young men arrived, but a young girl of five, who had come with an older girl, became uneasy because of the men's glowing eyes and teeth like iron. The two planned their escape by going to the "potty." But the demons chased them.

> She ran into the bathhouse and said, "Sir Master of the Bathhouse, protect me from a senseless death." And she hopped up onto a ledge. And so then the master of the bathhouse jumped down from a ledge to fight with the youth. They fought and fought, and then the cock crowed. Both of them disappeared, and she then got up and left for home. In the morning the peasants missed the other girls; no one was at home. They set off for the place they had gone for the evening party, and there they found only tufts of braids and hair. There was nothing more.[145]

That's a painful lesson learned too late: listen to your parents.

The Bannik was also thought to be "the guardian spirit of Russia to defend her and her people from the enemy."[146] A historical account circa 947 A.D. does not mention the Bannik himself as protecting the people, but it's possible to interpret the fatal events that occurred as having his blessing. In this story Princess Olga punishes the soldiers who murdered her husband, Prince Igor of Kiev. She wasn't about to allow the men to add her to the booty they'd already plundered. Feigning complicity to the prospect of marriage to their leader, she invited him and his soldiers to use the banya after their long journey. When they gathered inside waiting for the near-scalding steam, they got more than they expected. The princess ordered her servants to bar the doors and set the banya on fire.

Did you know?

The Bannik has a red cap that makes him invisible. Sometimes he leaves it on the stove to dry. If a person is daring enough to steal it exactly at midnight, he must hightail it to the church before the spirit catches and kills him (Russian Wikipedia, "Банник").

But what happens if you need to be protected from the Bannik himself when you upset him? Then you can call on the Domovoi, who is lord over all the spirits living on your property. Yell to him, "Dedushka, help us!" and he'll come and set the Bannik straight.

Appeasing the Bannik

You'd think with all these potential disasters, no one would venture into the banya. That's not the case, however. Like the other spirits you've learned about, the Bannik wants your respect. Follow his rules, and you should be safe—at least the majority of the time: don't bathe when you're not supposed to, don't bathe alone, leave his banya clean, leave him gifts for his own bathing, and don't ask him to perform unreasonable tasks.

You can show him your respect in other ways as well:

- When building a new banya, sacrifice a black hen and bury it, unplucked, under the threshold. Walk away backward when you're finished, making sure to bow and recite incantations to the Bannik. It's important to never turn your back on a demon, so walking backward is a way to trick him into leaving you alone.
- Toss salt onto the stove the first time you start it up in a new banya.
- Any other time you're in there, leave the spirit rye bread and salt, in addition to his bathing supplies.
- Ask his permission before you bathe by saying, "Banya grandpa, please allow me to enter," even if it's not one of his scheduled times. It's his home, and he likes people to acknowledge him before they enter.
- Men should walk into the banya with their right foot first, and women with their left foot first.
- Most important, thank him for the pleasant bath when you've finished.

Fact or Fiction?

The following are some banya customs still practiced today. Whether or not they mean people still believe in the bathhouse spirit, or they are merely fun customs to continue, is up to you to decide.

- During Yuletide, young women frequent the banya after dark to practice divination. With unbound hair, they perform the ritual with cinders, banya besoms, or mirrors and candles. Many tales tell of how girls and men alike practice divination with a mirror in the banya at midnight. They place the mirror opposite the open door. At midnight, the image of their future spouse appears in the mirror.
- People prepare baths for their ancestors on Maudy Thursday. After they make everything ready, everyone goes out and leaves the door open for the souls to enter for their steam bath.
- Other people go to the cemetery to visit with their ancestors and invite them to the banya. When they return, they light candles in the banya and leave the doors open for the deceased to enjoy their private baths.
- It's important to greet the Bannik when you take your own bath. You can ask him to help cleanse your body, soul, and mind. When you finish, pour cold water over your *venik* and sprinkle it in all four corners of the banya, beginning on your left. Say to the spirit, "Bannik, o bannik, take away the dirt of our bodies, of our souls and of our minds, take away the evil, the ailments, the sorrows and the sadness." Repeat the entire process three times. Thank the spirit as you're leaving the banya. Bow and walk backward, not turning your back on him.[147]

Banya in Literature

I was unable to find anything beyond short tales about the Bannik, but I hope you enjoy these impressions of a banya that people have written about over the ages.

Hot, Steamy Bathing

Perhaps you've never heard about a banya before you've read this chapter. If this has been your first experience, your reaction may be similar to these accounts foreigners have recorded throughout the ages.

St. Andrew among the Slavs

One of the earliest accounts of a banya was recorded in the *Russian Primary Chronicle* in the year 1113. It relates to an account of the Apostle Andrew in his missionary work in Russia.

He saw these people existing according to their customs, and, on observing how they bathed and drenched themselves, he wondered at them. He went thence among the Varangians and came to Rome, where he recounted what he had learned and observed.

"Wondrous to relate," said he, "I saw the land of the Slavs, and while I was among them, I noticed their wooden bathhouses. They warm them to extreme heat, then undress, and after anointing themselves with tallow, they take young reeds and lash their bodies. They actually lash themselves so violently that they barely escape alive. Then they drench themselves with cold water, and thus are revived. They think nothing of doing this every day, and actually inflict such voluntary torture upon themselves. They make of the act not a mere washing but a veritable torment."

Bathing vs. Cholera

Most stories about the banya, both old and recent, talk about the frequency of its use. The following one by Russian-born British novelist, historian, poet, and musician Frederick Whishaw (1854 – 1934)—published in 1895 about the 1892 cholera outbreak in Russia—gives a different perspective. It talks about a priest's attempts to get the peasants to live more sanitary lives. After some haggling about whether or not the priest would bring the ikon and a special litany to bless them, the peasants agree to "wash." Perhaps it was after such an epidemic the following statement became true; the Bannik "caused more regular attendance of the Slavs to the bath," because he "encouraged more hygienic activities." (Kośnik, 19)

The following is the author's account of the aversion of peasants to bathing in pre-cholera times.

[T]he peasants] proceeded straight to the village drinking-shop and there drank the priest's health times enough to secure his immunity from cholera anyhow, unless the fates persistently disregarded the vows of the pious intoxicated. Afterwards some of them took a bath in the streamlet which ran like a silver ribbon through the village; being but eighteen inches deep or so, this rivulet could scarcely afford scope for the malice of a *vodyannui*, or water-demon, so they were safe enough; but they did not like the feel of the water, it was unfamiliar and uncanny, and gave them the shivers. Others patronised the bath-house and employed hot steam to take off as much of the outer coating of griminess as each considered safe or desirable; for there is nothing so certain to give one cold as the sudden leaving off of clothes or other coverings to which the body has become accustomed (Whishaw, 277).

Intoxicated with Exuberance

Howard Percy Kennard's (d. 1915) book *The Russian Peasant* (published in 1908) has been described as reflecting "his deep sympathies for the Russian peasantry among whom he had lived in many parts of European Russia since the time of the Russo-Japanese war" (Cross, *In the Land of the Romanovs*).

The first part of the book describes village life, with a focus on customs, beliefs, family relationships, and ceremonies. Within this section, his rendering of the communal banya is quite comical as you will see from the excerpt below. He compares the Russian peasant's style of bathing to that of the English, saying they are "cleaner in body" and "superior in cleanliness" to their own English agricultural laborer—quite the contrast to the opinion of cleanliness in the example you read above.

The peasants love their vapour bath as a fish loves water, and not content with turning their izbas into ovens filled with steam, in order to indulge in their favourite relaxation, they are in the habit of frequenting *en masse* the village vapour bath once a week, or, at any rate, once a fortnight. It is a quaint sight! Round the walls of the public perspiratory establishment are broad shelves in tiers one above the other; wooden tables lie here and there, on which are emblems of castigation, in the shape of bundles of twigs. A huge stove, from which protrudes a chimney, is seen in one corner of the room, and from this emerge volumes of steam, filling the room with a moist heat, which would seem to those unaccustomed to it absolutely unbearable.

In the villages where the bath is of a less up-to-date quality, the steam is produced by means of heating bricks to a red heat, and then pouring cold water over them, the water being contained in an immense tub standing by the stove. The steam thus produced rises in thick volumes, and fills the bathroom. But be the steam produced how it may, the actions of our friend the peasant remain the same from one end of Russia to the other. Old and young assemble on bath-night, and, naked as their mothers bore them, stand, sit, and lie full length in every conceivable attitude on bench, table, and even floor. Enthusiasm waxes fierce, their faces reflect the keen delight of anticipation which fills their souls, and as the heat of the room gets greater and greater, and the vapour rises and falls in great thick rolls, their spirits rise with it. They dance and sing in the exuberance of their enjoyment, for it would seem that as the pores of their skins are opened by the artificial heat, and provide an exit for all the excrementitious material collected during the past week or fortnight in their bodies, there enters through those same pores a stream of life-giving ether which, coursing through their veins and reaching the heart's core, engenders a sense of wild exultation, and raises them from their usually melancholy mood to heights of delirious joy, such as one would never dream the solid, apparently inert, passionless muzhik capable of.

The twigs are seized, and with shouts of mad glee the peasants — debauched, intoxicated with the superabundance of spirits permeating their whole organism — beat each other mercilessly on head, back, front, and legs. All is chaos — a shouting, revelling mass of human beings, apparently deprived of reason

— surging this way, that way; leaping on bench and table, performing the most ludicrous and almost impossible antics — one standing on his head, and shouting at the top of his voice, while others beat him with an energy which one would imagine would be productive of the most intense pain and produce weals that would last for weeks; but no — the scene goes on: this one full length on the floor, while those actually stand upon his prostrate figure and dance a sort of Highland jig; another may be seen running madly against the wall of the bathroom, and butting it with his back, and then rushing again to the centre of the room and executing a feverish war dance — arms, legs, head, body, moving in every conceivable direction at one and the same time, till finally he falls exhausted, and lies a panting, perspiring, speechless mass on the floor of the reeking bathroom. To this stage all the partakers in this orgy eventually arrive, but only for a few moments are their limbs and lungs deprived of power to act. The final scene is yet to come. Rising *en masse*, with blood-curdling yells they run to the door of the bathroom, fling it wide ajar, and with shouts and screams redoubled, roll in the fallen snow. A minute thus, and with bodies glowing with the exercise, and the blood coursing wildly through their veins, they rush pell-mell back to the heated bathroom, where they sit subdued and rub each other down, *and then again don their discarded, filthy sheep-skins, their vermin-infested shirts, their parastically-peopled vestments* of whatsoever kind they may be in the habit of wearing (Kennard, 75-78).

No Place for Privacy

The account below comes from *Undiscovered Russia* (published in 1912), written by British journalist Stephen Graham (1884 – 1975) about his travels in pre-revolutionary Russia. It details more of the communal aspect of the banya. As the author learns, you can't get privacy when there are naked bodies walking all around you.

The village did not sleep. Smoke issued from many of the outhouse baths. There are several bath houses in the village, and every two or three families use one in common. The old and the sick were steaming in these frantically hot bath rooms. I saw one man come out naked, and go in again probably the smoke in his eyes had driven him out. Does the reader know what a black banya is? He is happier in his ignorance. But the moujik would tell him that it was better than all physic to stew for an hour in his little inferno of smoke and steam, and to hold the twelve weeds on the head with one hand, while with the other he poured hot water over them in order that the precious influence might rain down.

…

I left her and went to find the banya. Very few houses indeed in Russia are fitted with a bathroom. Every one goes out to the banya. Every town has its banya: Moscow and Petersburg have hundreds of them; the villages have their little banyas. There are general bath-houses, and family bath-houses. The general is divided into men's department and women's department, and the family ones are large bathrooms to which one may take one's whole family. A Russian in the town often takes his wife and children to one of the latter, and they do the whole business of washing themselves simultaneously.

The Russians are singularly lacking in shame, especially with regard to the naked body. In the wash-halls of Moscow one may frequently see a hundred people all naked at the same time, and all strenuously washing themselves, all strangers to one another, and perfectly unselfconscious. It is probably because the people are almost all of peasant origin. The bath, moreover, is a religious function. The banyas have their Ikons, and the people, though naked, all wear their baptismal crosses round their necks. Washing is akin to praying, and one must certainly wash before going to Church Service: it is enjoined by the priests. Cleanliness is certainly *next* to Godliness in Russia.

"How much does your banya cost?" I asked the man at the door. He seemed rather flurried, as if at an unexpected question.

"They are different," he replied. "Some cost a penny, some twopence, some threepence; there is that which we reserve for generals, and that is sevenpence."

"What! Isn't there a place where all can bathe together?"

"There is, but it is not very proper except for moujiks. It is very crowded, because to-night is the feast of the Transfiguration, and everybody wants to wash before going to church. There are men there and women and children."

"What! you don't mean to say men and women are bathing in the same room!"

"Yes," he answered with an apologetic smile.

"How Lacedaemonic!" I thought. "Well, put me in the generals' apartment," I said aloud. "I suppose you can do that."

I paid him sevenpence and he led me to a cell, gave me a bundle of oak twigs with which to beat myself, and a handful of loofah-like fibre for soaping purposes. He opened the door and I walked in.

The first thing I did was to exclaim in Russian, "*O Gospody, Bozhe moi!*" [Oh my God!]

It was so hot, so dark. Even in the place where I was supposed to undress the heat was atrocious. My clothes were soaked with steam and perspiration even before I could get them off. I stripped in double quick time, climbed to one of the heating shelves, lay down and gasped.

Perhaps it was hotter than other compartments, just because it was dearest, and was reserved for generals. I couldn't stand the heat, simply because I was a parvenu.

How the place burned! It was so hot on the stone floor that I feared my skin would come off. Then, when I climbed up to the shelf the wood was scorching. The idea of beating myself with oak twigs in that heat!

When I got over the heat, there was a greater astonishment in store for me. From where I lay on top of my steaming shelf, I could see right over the top of the partition which separated me from the next cell. What was my astonishment to see two people come into view holding buckets of soapsuds and great handfuls of loofah. I heard a noise of children somewhere: it was evidently a family party. I climbed down from my point of vantage.

Hardly had I done so when there was a knock at my door, and a man came in and said,

"Hail brother! would you be so kind as to do me a service? I am a stout man and cannot easily wash myself behind. If I kneel down, will you scrub my back ... I don't mind doing the same for you."

We did make the exchange, he purveying the lather—the hottest and most abundant lather I have ever seen. When the wash was over he wished me many good things and congratulated me on the Transfiguration.

I hastened to complete my ablutions, pouring bucketful after bucketful of water over my head. There was no shower bath.

Whilst I was doing this, the door opened again—it would not lock—and in came three children, two boys and a sort of Little Red-riding-hood girl with a red cape on. Behind them were the father and mother and the bath-man. There was such a mist of steam they didn't see me at first, but the little girl called out in a squawky voice.

"Oh-h, there's a man in here," and they all scuttled out. I barricaded the door and then took my towels and tried to dry myself. Drying was in vain. I put a few things on hurriedly. My clothes simply wouldn't go on me; they were soaked with the steam of the room. I took my coat and waistcoat on my arm and evacuated the position. Then I chaffed the bath-man. I told him I had found that the generals' compartment overlooked the neighbouring cell, and that, though both were sold as private rooms, the occupants were visible to one another.

"That's nothing," said he, and waved his hand.

"A special privilege of generals, eh?" I asked.

He grinned, and said it was nothing compared to the five copeck division. There they had curtains.

Russians in some respects are not out of Eden (Graham, 35-36, 213-217).

A Pleasurable Beating

Your final example of a banya (although you can find many more if you search the internet) is a modern one. This excerpt comes from a blog post where the author wrote about his first banya in the coldest habitable place on the planet, a place known as the "Pole of Cold."

During the first phase, the leaves are dragged along the back and legs, stroking and scraping and dredging, producing a not unpleasant ticklish sensation, though with the occasional feeling of piercing hot needles pressed against the skin. Then the lashing commences, gently at first but soon building to a barrage of whipping, thrashing, lacerating. Best — or worst — of all is that the leaves of the Veniki seem to trap the heat and then apply it directly to the skin, amplifying and channeling into a direct, searing temperature onslaught. Then Alexei raised my feet and proceeded to flail my soles; truly the most extraordinary feeling of pleasure, seasoned with pain.

After that, it was a full-on Banya assault, pummeling my body, whacking the Veniki against my back, buttocks and legs, beating the breath and desire out of me until I felt like a chunk of meat on a slab. When it was done, he fetched a bucket of snow and smeared it all over my quivering skin. "Refreshed?" he asked, with a wide satisfied grin, "Obnovalis?" Yes, I was definitely refreshed, more refreshed than I had ever been in my life before (Excerpt comes from O'Mahony).

Ovinnik. Illustration by Anna Błaszczyk (Evelinea Erato). © Bendideia Publishing.

Ovinnik (Овинник)

A little spark may cause a big fire.

> **Ovinnik** (singular); **Ovinniki** (plural)
>
> **Other names**: gumennik, podovinnik, ovinnyy, zhikhar', ovinnyy dedushko, podovinushko, ovinnyy batyushka, ovinnushko, tsar' ovinnyy,[148] yevnik, asetnik, oŭník, osetnik,[149] joŭnik or jownik.[150]

The life of a peasant was and is hard. This chapter shows that sentiment more than the others have. It touches briefly on the topic of threshing, the final stage of the harvest. Peasants depend on nature cooperating in order to survive, especially in the harsher lands where winter reigns for much of the year. It's no wonder they have a spirit to blame for the loss of their grain that they worked long and hard for.

Origins

Some researchers believe that the Ovinnik, the spirit of the threshing floor, was originally associated with the solar cult. One example cited for this revolves around two stone circles located on the Devica mountain in Serbia.

A local legend says the circle is called Bogovo Gumno (which means "God's threshing floor") because "god came from heaven with his horses and he threshed grain there."[151] More than a legend and a name are at play, however. How does a sun circle, that's used to determine the summer solstice, have any relevance to a threshing floor? And how is a sun circle created?

> In order to determine the beginning of the year, you need to determine the day of the solstice. To do that you need a sun circle, a large circle which is permanently marked on the ground. How can you permanently mark a circle on the ground? You start by marking the centre of the circle by either a stake or a standing stone. You then draw a circle on the ground using a rope and a stick. To mark the circle edge permanently, you can build a henge if the soil is soft and easy to dig deep. But if the place therein is rocky, if the soil is hard stony and unsuitable for deep digging, or if there are a lot of boulders lying around, then it is much easier to just use stones, place them along the line that defines the circle and create a permanent marking by making a circular wall.[152]

Next, a threshing floor requires a smooth, flat surface where oxen or horses can trod upon the sheaves to separate the grain from the chaff. Often animals are tied to a pole in the center of the area, and they walk around it in a circular motion. A location with a good wind is important when the farmers begin winnowing the grain (to blow away the chaff) after the stalks have been separated and carted off. Therefore, they often selected hills. A threshing floor has a wall along the exterior to prevent the grain from being blown away.

Etymology

Ovinnik comes from the Russian word *ovin* for "barn."

The construction of both the sun circle and threshing floor are identical: a flat, shallow, pan-like circle with a pole in the center, and the perimeter surrounded by a boundary. In fact, threshing floors were once used for both purposes: threshing and a "solar observatory"—the observation being made that the sun pivots around the central pole daily and yearly the way animals do during threshing. Even without calendars and clocks, peasants could tell the date by the position of the shadow in the circle at sunrise, and tell the time by how long the shadow was throughout the day.

So how does this all play into the worship, or at the minimum, honoring of spirits such as the Ovinnik who frequented the threshing floor?

Before Christianity reached the Slavic people, they worshiped pagan gods. Marking the year out with the solar circles let them know when it was time to propitiate the deity.

> Being the solar observatory designed to determine and mark the summer solstice, the big stone circle in Bogovo Gumno was also dedicated to the Sun, also known in Serbia as Višnji bog (the high god), Vid. In Serbian tradition, Sun, the "Višnji Bog", the High God, is perceived as a living being, which is born every year in the winter on New Year's day, winter solstice. He then grows into a young man Jarilo on the 6th of May the day of the strongest vegetative, reproductive power of the sun. This day marks the beginning of the heating of the world, the beginning of summer. Then he becomes the powerful ruler Vid at the summer solstice, 21st of June the longest day of the year. He then becomes the terrible warrior Perun on the 2nd of August the hottest day of the year. This day marks the beginning of the cooling of the world.[153]

These solar circles/threshing floors were sacred places where villagers gathered to perform celebrations and ceremonies. After they were Christianized, the old gods became demoted to demons or were replaced by the saints, but other spirits—such as the Ovinnik—still retained their popularity, especially among the rural peasants. Many of the rites and traditions they formerly celebrated for their ancient gods are reminiscent of those performed for these lesser beings that the Church was unable to eradicate.

Appearance

As with other spirits, the Ovinnik doesn't make himself visible to people often. If you're fortunate—or unfortunate as the case may be—you may catch a glimpse of him in a garden or pea field at noon. Or perhaps you'll see him during Mass on certain holidays, in particular on Easter. When he appears in the barn, you'll find it difficult to distinguish his shape because he lurks in the shadows, hiding behind cobwebs. He often appears as sparkles among the dust motes and soot floating in the barn—especially near the threshing floor, where he likes to keep an eye on the threshing process. You'll get a better look at him if he comes near the window to cough up soot and dust. He'll have chaff in his hair and dried grass florets stuck in his paws.

When he does appear, he may materialize as a stocky black cat the size of a large dog. More than his size tells you he's not an ordinary cat, though. His eyes burn like embers, and he barks like a dog, and sometimes even laughs like a human—a crazy one. In some places, he takes on the shape of a ram, a dog, or a bear. From time to time, he appears in human form as well. He resembles the owner of the house or one of the family members, or even someone you know who's died. Or he may appear as an old man, or a tall, hairy man. His hair is long, disheveled, and smoky colored. But you can tell he's not human because he'll have hairy goat's feet.

In all cases, he'll be black or covered with soot due to the smoke from the stove or fire pit he lives near—and sometimes inside of. The blackness can also come from the banya smoke if the bathhouse is attached to the barn. The smoke often seeps through the cracks in the wall to cover him, making him look like what has been described as "a big shapeless lump of bran with small short legs."[154]

Getting to Know the Ovinnik

The Ovinnik lives in the *ovin*, or barn. Specifically, he lurks in the darkest corner of the barn, or in a fire pit. (See the sidebar, "The Threshing Process" for more details.) Some people say he hides because he's a coward and cowers when people come into the barn. Others say he hides after picking a fight with a human or with his friend, the Bannik from the bathhouse. He usually loses the battle and runs away to lick his wounds—possibly even literally. Or he withdraws from people because he gets surly when they let the grain drying on the open fire burn—which happens frequently.

Busy at Work

The spirit symbolizes "diligence, order, rationality, practicality, and economics,"[155] so it's no wonder when no one is around, he keeps busy ensuring the drying and threshing of the grain are done properly. He maintains the fire in the oven to keep it properly heated. That's one reason he's always covered with soot. He checks the sheaves to be sure they dry evenly before they're threshed. He might even drop by to visit the Bannik to check on sheaves that are drying in the banya. He can't tolerate the stench when they're soaked or stale. Perhaps the fights between the two of them are due to the Bannik not taking care of the sheaves properly because he's spending too much time spying on bathing women.

Ovinnik. Figure by Ivan Bilibin, 1934.
[Public domain], via Wikimedia Commons.

139

Ovin and Fire Pit. Illustration by Dmitry Yakhovsky. © Bendideia Publishing.

Once the workers have begun the threshing, the Ovinnik wanders around the threshing floor—invisible to everyone—to see how well the workers have threshed the sheaves. If they're slacking in their responsibilities, he'll frighten them—by appearing suddenly and glaring at them with glowing eyes, by knocking on the barn, by clapping near them, or by chortling with an eerie laughter.

When the sheaves have been threshed, he'll direct or deflect the wind so the chaff is blown away during the winnowing process. The spirit even helps grind the grain while everyone's asleep, and he makes sure everything that's stored in the barn stays dry and free of rodents.

He'll tidy up his home by sweeping the floor of any messes he's made and any you and your workers have left. All he asks for his services is clean water to wash away the dirt and grime—even though he seldom remains clean for long.

Tending to the Family

The Ovinnik not only takes care of the barn and the grain, but he'll also protect you from other spirits passing through your property. Like the Domovoi who fights with the neighbor's household spirit, the Ovinnik battles ghouls and devils trespassing on his territory. One tale tells of an Ovinnik who protected a child by battling an old woman demon until the crowing of a rooster at dawn, when she disappeared.

If you have to work late or spend the entire night in the barn (which isn't advised; it's as dangerous being there as it is going to the banya at night), you can ask for the spirit's help by saying, "Father Ovinnik, take care of me, protect me from all evil, from every adversary of the servant of God."[156] Make sure you really need his help. If you call on him, especially at night, in some kind of prank, he'll end up scaring and harming you instead of protecting you.

THE THRESHING PROCESS

The harvest ends with the threshing of the grain. Although many threshing floors are outside, it can also be inside. A threshing barn is a two-story, open-air wooden structure, which allows for a draft to blow through. The farmers dig a pit in the ground on the first floor and install a stove there. They use the second floor for drying the grain after it's been threshed.

A fire blazes in the stove, which is about three to five feet deep. Six to ten poles line the hole, with their upper ends touching. To dry the sheaves, the workers lay them over the poles. Some pits have a raised platform above them, with a part left open so the entire pit isn't covered. This allows smoke and heat to exit the pit and go into the barn.

During the initial threshing process, farmers beat the bound sheaves with a pitchfork or stick, causing the highest quality grain to fall to the ground. They often use these seeds for the next year's planting. Next, they lay out the sheaves on the threshing floor, thrash them twice, turn them over, then thrash them again twice. It's important to turn over the grain sheaves so all of them are thrashed. When done, farmers remove the straw for cattle fodder. Workers have to perform the threshing quickly to avoid the dried-out chaffs from catching fire. This is especially important when they do the threshing inside the barn.

Farmers perform winnowing next. They toss the grain into the wind with a wooden shovel or winnowing forks, or by pouring the grain and chaff into a winnowing basket. This process removes the inedible chaff from the outside of the seeds. They then shake the grain in a sieve to remove the remaining debris. Work alternates between the two until all that is left is the grain. Women perform the final stage of cleaning the grain by pouring it onto a large sheet, which they sift through, removing the non-edible portions.

However, if you're not feeling well, you can go to the barn and request his healing. The spirit will doctor your fever, inflammation, and other aches and pains. The power of the Ovinnik works best in a heated barn. In particular, if you have lower back pain, rub that area on a corner of the barn saying, "Father Ovinnik, cure my back so it won't hurt, so it won't ache, so it feels good." Or you can say, "Father Ovinnik, release my lower back pain." If you have aching arms, tie them with a stiff string, which you'll later throw into the barn while repeating three times, "Ovin, Ovin, take my pain."[157]

Sometimes you might want to bewitch someone, and you'll go to the barn spirit to ask for his help. As long as it's not a member of your family, the Ovinnik will help. To accomplish this, take the person's "footprints" by gathering soil he or she has stepped on. Hang it in a bag in the barn at the same time that person is drying sheaves. As the soil dries, it will inflict agonizing pain on your enemy. He'll dry up, wither away, and die.

Fortune-Telling

You can seek predictions about your fortune from the Ovinnik on New Year's Eve between midnight and three in the morning. Much divination occurs between Christmas and the Epiphany (January 6), a time when evil spirits are most active and play mischievous tricks. You can ask questions for predictions about the harvest. A warm, soft touch means good times are ahead. A cold, prickly hand caressing yours will give you shivers from more than his contact: ill fortune awaits you during the year.

Girls also seek information about what kind of person their future husband will be. At night, they thrust their hand through an open barn window into the drying room. If the Ovinnik doesn't touch her, she won't marry that year. But if he does stroke her hand and his fingers are smooth, she'll marry a poor man. If his touch is rough or hairy, she's certain to marry someone rich. More daring girls pull their skirts over their heads and put their bare bottoms in front of the window, much like they do when seeking predictions from the Bannik in the bathhouse. However, in this case, they make "indelicate suggestions inviting the sprite to fondle their bare buttocks."[158] This ritual may have been related to fertility magic rites.

In a variation of this divination, each girl pulls grass flowers from the sheaves with her teeth. If she pulls out one that's full, she'll have a rich life. If it's skinny and dried up, her life will be lived in poverty. If the spikelet has lots of spikes, she'll marry a young man. One with no spikes means she'll marry a widower.

On the Dark Side

Although the Ovinnik fights ghouls and demons to protect you, your family, and your harvest, he gets along with the other spirits residing in the same homestead: the Bannik (most of the time), the Domovoi, and the Dvorovoi (yard spirit). He visits the Bannik in the bathhouse, but the Domovoi refuses to let the Ovinnik into the house because he's likely to strangle a family member if one of them has irritated him.

The home is the Domovoi's domain, and he'll share it only with his human family—and spirit wife and children if he has them. If anyone is going to play tricks on the people, it will be the Domovoi himself.

Even though the house spirit is unsociable to the barn spirit, the Ovinnik may entice him to leave the house when he throws a party on the threshing floor at night. He even invites mermaids (Rusalki), unclean dead (those who have died an unnatural death), and others to join in the fun. They dance the night away and make plans about what kind of mischief they can get into. Witches and demons may crash the party as well.

The Ovinnik, being a moody spirit, also does even worse things than throwing parties. Or at least people blame all misfortunes that happen in the barn on him. This irritates him. It would annoy you, too, wouldn't it to be blamed for things that someone else might have done?

Granted, if you go to work in your barn in the morning and find a stranger strangled among the corn cobs, it has to have been the work of the barn spirit, doesn't it? He likes to chase away people who don't belong in the barn during the threshing process, or those who come intending to cause mischief. The Ovinnik follows them everywhere they go, frightening them until they leave. He doesn't stop there. Even though the Domovoi prevents him from coming into the house, the Ovinnik gets his revenge if the person happens to fall asleep in the barn. The spirit will disturb his sleep, either by blowing smoke his way or by choking the person.

If the Ovinnik is in a particularly bad mood, he's apt to burn down the barn with the person slumbering inside. He'll do the same thing to you, the owner, if you get on his bad side. He'll even try to push his master into the stove. One story tells how a man outwitted the spirit and threw him into the fire instead. Of course, it didn't kill the spirit, but it made him vengeful. Years later, the Ovinnik got his revenge. He burned the threshing barn when the man's son was working inside. In another story, he burned a woman who was beating flax on a day when it was prohibited to do so.

You can't attribute all barn fires to your own Ovinnik, however. If a mellow spirit lives in your barn, it's likely another family's Ovinnik has set your property ablaze. Your barn spirit takes a burning barn in stride though—whether it's his fault or not. He calmly stands on the sidelines, watching the building burn while your family and friends frantically run around trying to save it. If the barn burns to the ground, he's still not worried. He'll crawl back into the stove and live on the charred logs until you rebuild the place.

Fire can't hurt him because he can't burn. On the other hand, give him a good old thunder-and-lightning storm, and he'll behave like your household dog, cowering in his dark corner. He'd rather stay inside the burning building than venture outside. One strike from a lightning bolt ends his existence. He vanishes completely, not even a pile of dust is left to be swept away.

Ovinnik. Illustration © Andy Paciorek. Used with permission of the artist.

No longer having an Ovinnik in your barn may or may not be good news for you depending on how your spirit had behaved. If lightning burned both your barn and the spirit, no other Ovinnik will make his home in the new barn if you rebuild it on the same spot. To them, the place is cursed, and they're not willing to sacrifice their existence to keep your grain safe.

Appeasing the Ovinnik

You can avoid problems with the Ovinnik if you follow his rules. He forbids you from lighting a fire in the barn on saints' days and festival days (such as September 14, The Exaltation of the Holy Cross; September 24, the day of Fekla Zarevnitsa; and October 1, The Feast of the Intercession of the Blessed Virgin Mary).[159] You should be off paying homage to the saints instead. He also gets angry if you light fires in the barn when the wind is too strong. You should know it's likely to set your barn on fire, and then you'll blame him for burning it down.

Statistics even show it's your fault the barn burned and not his. In 1914, vodka prohibition went into effect in Russia. As a result, disastrous fires went down by almost half (47 percent in the first three months of prohibition). A commentary about the Ovinnik says, "… since August, 1914, he [the Ovinnik] has shown a marvelously restrained temper."[160] Restrained, indeed. Alcohol and fire don't make good companions.

When you're done blaming him for your own carelessness, you can offer him sacrifices to appease his anger and request his help in multiplying your harvest. First, sweep the barn and spread the smoke of incense around.

During the threshing process, you ask him to do plenty for you to make sure everything goes right and is successful. Do you remember to thank him for all his faithful service? You should. Every day. You can at least light a new fire in the oven at the beginning and ending of the threshing period. Make sure all your family and neighbors participate in the ceremony. Be solemn and bow toward the fire to show your respect for the spirit.

The beginning of the threshing period in September is also a special day for the Ovinnik. It's his name day. This is a day celebrated like a birthday, and is often called a "half-birthday," but it's done in honor of your name. Names in ancient times held power like an amulet; they were magic words. Knowing someone's name gave you control over that person—or spirit, as the case may be. Everyone has a special name day, so make sure you celebrate the Ovinnik's the way he requests.

Ovinnik Busy at Work in the Field and in the Ovin.
By Natalia.sk [CC BY-SA 4.0 (https://creativecommons.org/licenses/by-sa/4.0)], from Wikimedia Commons, 2016.

First, offer him the blood sacrifice of a rooster on both September 4 and November 1 by cutting off the fowl's head and feet over the barn's threshold. Sprinkle the blood in the corners of the barn and around the stove to get on the spirit's good side.

At the beginning of the threshing period, sprinkle the stove with holy water and toss salt onto it. If you put a stone inside, you'll add more protection against loss and misfortune.

Then you can start the celebration of the Ovinnik's name day.

> On the preceding evening he [the farmer] begins to heat the *ovin*, and next morning he calls together the threshers, and regales them with *kasha* [a favorite Russian dish made of stewed grain]. After the meal they stick a few ears into each corner of the barn or corn-kiln, in order that their labours may prove richly productive, and then they fall to work, usually commencing with the sheaf which was gathered the first at harvesttime.[161]

In addition to the stewed grain, the Ovinnik also enjoys it if you leave him *bliny* (pancakes) and pies by the fire, with beer to wash it down.

While you perform the ceremony, "pray under the ovin" or "pray to the fire under the ovin" as a show of respect for the spirit living there. Say to him, "King of the drying house, help us dry the grain and finish our threshing!"[162]

You can now light the fire for the first time in the season. Every time you're ready to throw wood into the fire, cross yourself from each of the four corners of the barn. Shout, "Go away!" to warn the Ovinnik, so you don't hit him.

Before you begin threshing, don't forget to throw into the fire the first sheaf of hay that you gathered.

You're done for now and free to go about your work. After you've cut down the sheaves and left them to dry, take off your hat, bow, and say, "Thank you, Father Ovinnik. You've served us faithfully this autumn."[163] Leave him a sheaf of rye in the barn so he has something to keep an eye on.

When the threshing season is over and you've turned off the fire in the barn because you're afraid he still might burn down the building, be nice and at least light him a fire outside where he can come out to warm himself in the cool weather.

Fact or Fiction?

The Ovinnik may not be as popular today as the Domovoi, but he has found a place for himself in our world. If you're a gamer, you're probably familiar with the Pathfinder Roleplaying Game by Paizo. This tabletop roleplaying game "puts you in the role of a brave adventurer fighting to survive in a world beset by magic and evil." One creature you can battle is the Ovinnik, who appears in Bestiary 5. He has friends to hang out with there, since the Domovoi, Kikimora, and Dvorovoi are also included in that set.[164]

Dvorovoi. Illustration by Anna Błaszczyk (Evelinea Erato). © Bendideia Publishing.

Dvorovoi (Дворовой)

There are no friends in tastes and colors.

Dvorovoi (singular); **Dvorovye** or **Dvoroviye** (plural)

Other names: domovoi dvoroff,[165] dvorovik, dvorovyy,[166] dvorovoy, hlevnik.[167]

By now, you must have noticed a pattern to how the Slavic spirits are named. They take on the designation of their location: the house spirit Domovoi (from *dom* for house), the bathhouse spirit Bannik (from *banya* for bathhouse), the barn spirit Ovinnik (from *ovin* for barn), and now Dvorovoi, the courtyard spirit (from *dvor* for yard). Many others not mentioned in this book follow the same pattern.

It could be because this relates back to the origin myth that all the spirits who fell from heaven were *domovye*. As time went on, they blended in with their environment, and became different entities, all with a common ancestor. In this way, the Dvorovoi is considered a descendant of the Domovoi, or even his younger brother or cousin. According to other sources, the Bannik, Ovinnik, and Dvorovoi are all actually the Domovoi, who is known by different names depending on where you find him when he's outside the house.

In 2005, two university students spoke with an elderly village woman about the "house spirit." Much of what the woman relates speaks more of the Dvorovoi than it does the Domovoi. In the final comments, the woman replies, "That's the same one, it's him, it's all the same: dvorovoi, domovoi and dobrokhodushka. It's the same thing."[168] (You can read more of the interview in the "Fact or Fiction?" section.)

Some people insist the Dvorovoi is insulted if you call him the Domovoi. To be on his good side, avoid that mistake. Keep to calling them all by respectful euphemisms, and you should be safe from their anger at the mistaken identity. The Domovoi doesn't seem to mind, though. It's more fame for him. Besides, the house spirit is the lord over all of the other spirits residing on the homestead, so he can make the rules.

In this chapter, you'll read stories that use the word "domovoi" instead of "dvorovoi." These stories appear here because they relate to events that occur outside the home—in the *dvor*, or yard, and are more suited to a discussion of the Dvorovoi.

Origins

The Dvorovoi is identical to the Domovoi in terms of ancestor worship, so refer to those pages for a recap.

Appearance

In looks, the Dvorovoi is exactly like the Domovoi: fur-covered with blazing eyes. Or perhaps he'll appear like the homeowner or an old man with a white beard. He may also masquerade as your family pet or one of the farm animals (as long as it's not white, a color he loathes).

Etymology

Dvorovoi comes from the Russian word *dvor* for "yard."

Since he can look like your pets, you're advised not to let them go outside at night. You don't want to accidentally bring the yard spirit inside instead of good old Fido, do you? The riddle below identifies him with a black cat as well, which sounds as if he's more related to the Ovinnik, rather than to the Domovoi:

Our dvorovoi walks with a black head. He wears a velvet coat. His eyes are fiery; he is snub-nosed; his mustache sticks up; his ears can hear everything; his legs are prickly; his claws are tenacious. During the day he sunbathes and tells a wonderful fairy-tale; at night he wanders around and goes hunting.[169]

His catlike appearance is described in an even more frightful manner below. This monster is certain to terrify you if you meet him in a dark corner of the yard:

A little bigger than a cat, and the body looks like a cat, but there is no tail. The head is like a man's. The nose is crooked and squat. The eyes are huge, red like fire, and above them the eyebrows are black. The mouth is wide, and there are two rows of black teeth. The tongue is red and roughened. The arms are like a man's, only the shoulders are curled. The whole being is covered with wool, like a gray cat, but has the feet of a man.[170]

He's even appeared as a snake with a rooster's head and crown. But, usually he's not seen. However, you can catch a glimpse of him crouching in a corner of a stall in the stable on Easter and the Thursday preceding it.

He differs at times from the Domovoi. Whereas the house spirit looks completely human, the Dvorovoi may be mostly human, with chicken, goat, or cat legs.

Unlike the Domovoi, the Dvorovoi has been compared with other spirits who roam outside. Some researchers say these are other incarnations of the spirit, so they deserve a brief mention. Vazila or Vasily is a protector of horses. The spirit walks erect like a human, but he has horse ears and hoofs. The guardian of the herds is called Bagan. He lives in a hay-filled crib in the stables.

Getting to Know the Dvorovoi

As his name implies, the Dvorovoi lives outside in the yard. You may find him amid the branches of fir and pine trees. He enjoys being among the prickly needles. If you don't have any of those trees nearby, you can find branches elsewhere and hang them outside for him to nuzzle up to.

Darkness bothers the spirit. He's like a young child who needs a night light. If you see a flickering glow outside, it's only him, wandering around with a candle that he lit by striking flint against steel. He could be on his way to the barn, going to one of those dancing parties the Ovinnik throws on occasion. A good old hoedown brightens his disposition.

You're probably wondering why he's upset.

Besides being mistaken for the Domovoi, he gets tired of being second-best to the house spirit, always being respected less and feared more. You say that's because he's more hostile and vindictive than your Domovoi, and he plays even worse tricks on the family than the Domovoi does. He, in turn, says he acts that way only because of the way you treat him. It's a vicious circle.

Portent of Disaster

Like the house spirit, the yard spirit has predictive powers. He wails in the fields if war, fire, or an outbreak of a disease is imminent. Sometime, even his mere presence indicates disaster, as this story demonstrates:

> Once upon a time a servant maid awoke one morning, lighted the fire, and went for her buckets to fetch water. Not a bucket was to be seen! Of course she thought 'a neighbour has taken them.' Out she ran to the river, and there she saw the Domovoy [Dvorovoi]—a little old man in a red shirt—who was drawing water in her buckets, to give the bay mare to drink, and he glared ever so at the girl—his eyes burned just like live coals! She was terribly frightened, and ran back again. But at home there was woe! All the house was in a blaze![171]

Although the story says this is the Domovoi (you can hear the angry grunts from the Dvorovoi in the background at that comment), it really could be the yard spirit because it takes place outside. You may recall that one popular belief is that the Domovoi seldom—if ever—leaves the house except to move to a new residence. So, if a spirit appears outside, it's likely to be the Dvorovoi.

He may also howl around the village when disaster is about to strike, making the dogs dig holes in the ground. His screeches bother their sensitive ears. He can also knock on your house walls to alert you of danger, or he may ride your horses all night, completely exhausting them. (He does this when he's angry as well, as you'll discover later in this chapter.)

Upon occasion, the spirit may even speak to a person. Even this does not bode well for the unfortunate human. Illness or death will follow as this story shows:

> A woman once told me a story. A man would go for walks, and every time he came back, a Dvorovoi would meet him. He was white with yellow eyes. This man had a scarf, and whoever had a scarf at that time was considered noble. So, the Dvorovoi says,
> —Vanya, present me with the scarf.
> —Here, take it.
> —No, you should present me with it, but don't tell anyone. Then we will live well.
> Vanya's mother started questioning him about what he did with the scarf. So, he told her everything and started feeling unwell. His mother went to have her fortune read. She was told, 'Leave this house, or it will be bad'. They changed their residence and Vanya went back to feeling well.[172]

Another story tells of a disaster of a more personal nature. A village couple lived a happy, peaceful life, with an abundance of everything they needed—until one day when the husband went away for business. That evening, when the wife went into the courtyard, she saw her husband pushing around a cart. Only it wasn't her husband because he was away. It was the Dvorovoi. After that event, things fell apart in their domestic life. The husband fell in love with the woman who did chores at their house, and he threw his wife out.

A Peasant Farm. Illustration by Dmitry Yakhovsky. © Bendideia Publishing.

Animal Care

One of the Dvorovoi's favorite places to visit is the stable, where the animals don't judge him—especially dogs and goats, whom he's particularly fond of. This is one way he can distinguish himself from the Domovoi. The house spirit despises goats.

The Dvorovoi has other animals he favors as well. You may notice that your grandpa's favorite cow is treated quite well. If that's the case, there's a good chance the spirit is your deceased grandfather.

During the day, he'll supervise the workers and make sure they do everything to promote the well-being of the creatures. If they don't, he's likely to play tricks on the workers by tipping over milk pails or tripping people as they walk past him. He gets a good chuckle out of your confusion.

He keeps track of all the animals, counting each one at night. Slaughtering a chicken for your dinner, or worse, sacrificing one to another spirit makes him angry and jealous. It's bad enough he has to share the spotlight with the house spirit. Now you're honoring other spirits as well. When you decide to propitiate the Vodyanoi (the water spirit) with a goose, for example, you'll want to hide the deed from the Dvorovoi as long as you can. After you cut off the fowl's head, hang it up in the yard where the other geese and chickens run around. The Dvorovoi will be easily deceived as he counts that one along with the others in his nightly security rounds.

His other duties include chasing away forest spirits, keeping them from playing pranks in your garden. He also makes sure any local witches won't injure your cows by draining their milk.

ABOUT THE FARMSTEAD

A peasant farmstead consists of multiple buildings, the *dom* (home), *ovin* (threshing barn), and *banya* (bathhouse), which you've learned about throughout these chapters. While the bathhouse is more often a community building, it may also be attached to the barn. The *dvor* (courtyard) is at the front of the property and is closest to the street. This is where the house and any utility buildings are located. A high-plank or log fence encloses the property to keep out the wolves.

Vegetable gardens and orchards, called the *harman*, are farther from the street. This is the area where the threshing floor stood up until the mid-twentieth century. The *ovin* is positioned as far away as possible from the main dwelling to avoid it catching on fire from sparks the wind can blow from the barn furnace. The communal *banya* is situated even farther way, close to a body of water if one is nearby.

You may have noticed as you read these chapters that the farther you proceed from the home, the more vicious the spirits become. The house spirits are the kindest, playing non-life-threatening pranks. Next comes the yard spirit, who is much like the male house spirit, although he is harsher to the animals when he gets angry. The barn spirit resides a bit farther away, and he is more vicious. In the *banya*, the bathhouse spirit is the fiercest, flaying the skin off unwary bathers.

A comparison has been made by experts in the fields of mythology and folklore that this relates to the peasant's own world. Close to home, safety reigns. Father away, in the fields and forests, many dangers lurk: some known, many unknown. All these become spirits of the land, protecting or harming as they choose.

This information comes from Dushakova (26). It refers to a study of Old Believers in Moldova and Southern Ukraine, and is used as an example of how farmsteads are set up. Others throughout Eastern Europe will differ.

At night, the Dvorovoi keeps himself busy looking after the animals, making sure they're healthy, smooth, and clean: giving them food and water, grooming them, braiding the manes and tails of horses, and tying red ribbons in them. He means well. Although if he attempts hair-braiding, he usually doesn't produce nice even plaits. The poor horse will need some TLC after the yard spirit's ministrations: its hair will be twisted into knots that you'll have difficulty untangling.

He likes to ride horses at night, too. From time to time, you might even see him on the goat. He'll be mostly kind and gentle since he's fond of the critter.

Color Matters

The Dvorovoi never mistreats animals—unless, of course, he's upset or they're the wrong color. He hates—and abuses—animals with white fur or hair, although he tolerates white chickens and geese since they have the chicken god (the Kurinyi Bog you learned about in the Kikimora chapter) to protect them from beings like him. He's a night creature, and white, in his estimation, is not suitable for the night.

This is where we get into the blame game again. You say you can hardly always cater to his vanity and get the color of animal he likes; sometimes those creatures aren't healthy. He should like any of them you bring home. He, on the other hand, says it's a simple request. He doesn't care how fast they are, how strong they are, or how healthy they are. All that matters is that they are the right color. If you don't get the ones he wants, those "healthy," hated-color animals you bring home won't stay that way for long. He'll mistreat them until you wish you had listened to him in the first place.

It's not difficult to find out what color animals he prefers, although you will have to spend the night watching the Dvorovoi's activities. You'll have to wear a horse collar or harrow so you can see him. He doesn't like to be spied on any more than the Domovoi does, so wearing this item that's shaped like a cross also provides protection against anything he may try to do to you.

If you don't want to spend the night shadowing the spirit or are afraid to be out there with him, you can wait until Easter to find out what color animals he likes. Wrap a piece of cake in a rag and hang it in the stable. Check it after six weeks. "But, it will be full of maggots," you say as you shrink back. Exactly! The color of the maggots is the color of animal the Dvorovoi prefers—all animals on your homestead: dogs, goats, cattle, horses, cats (if you insist on having them, because he doesn't like cats), and even poultry if you can manage that.

Why that particular color? It's the color of his own hide, of course—when he chooses to become visible. So, yes, you're right. It is a matter of his vanity that you have to purchase the animals he wants, not the ones that would be best for your farm.

If you haven't yet determined the color he likes, but you need an animal for your farm, you can try to predict whether the Dvorovoi will accept it or not. The way to do this is to recite the following while you're bringing the animal home: "A shaggy beast for a rich farm-yard; give it drink, give it food, dear little master of the house (*khozyainushko*), and make it smooth with your little mitten."[173] If the animal isn't "smooth" by the time you reach home, you can be certain the Dvorovoi won't like it. You'll have to sell it, even if it means you lose money.

One story tells of a peasant who lost all his horses because he bought the wrong color. Another version says his horses went lame, his oxen died, and the cows produced no milk—all because the creatures were the wrong color. The man probably didn't recite the above invocation to the Dvorovoi. The story continues:

> At last the poor man, who was almost ruined, bought a miserable hack, which was of the right hue. "What a horse! There's something like a horse! Quite different from the other ones!" exclaimed the delighted Domovoy [Dvorovoi], and from that moment all went well with the peasant.[174]

I hope you've learned your lesson. Get the right color animals, and your life will be easier.

New Animals

When you buy any new animal, you'll also have to lead it to its stall to ask the Dvorovoi to welcome the creature. To have a better chance of this, get on his good side. Bring the spirit bread and salt. Bow low and turn to each corner of the building, and say, "Here is a shaggy beast for thee, Master! Love him, give him to eat and to drink!"[175] To be even more polite, add the following: "Grandfather, I bought myself a horse (or other animal). If you don't like this colour, wait until summer (or winter) and I'll sell it."[176] Next, bring the animal into the house. Lead it to the kitchen and attach its halter to the stove, so it can get the house spirit's blessing as well.

If the animal does poorly after all your rituals and placating of the spirits, it's time to trade it for another one. Don't argue with or beg the Dvorovoi. It's a battle you can't win. If, for whatever reason, you still insist on bringing home an animal in a color he despises, especially white, you'll have to be sneaky and bring it into the yard from the back gate. From there, lead it into the stables by having the creature step onto a sheepskin spread on the ground with the wool side up. Somehow this shaggy fur fools the Dvorovoi into accepting the animal.

Animal Abuse

Even if you buy animals that are the right color, you may have to worry about those born on your farm. The Dvorovoi can get rough when he's taking care of your livestock. He likes to tease the creatures—all in fun, he'll tell you. You'll have to take newborn lambs, calves, and foals into your house until they're strong enough to take care of themselves. If they're born the wrong color, sell them!

Sometimes, it's not even the color of the animal that bothers the Dvorovoi. It's you. You're not paying attention to him, or you're paying too much attention to the Domovoi, and the yard spirit gets worked up. To relieve his frustration, he'll take it out on your animals. When he rides your horses, it's not a gentle trot. If he's excessively angry, he'll gallop them all night until they're foaming and exhausted. He'll tie their tails to the manger, throw food and manure around the stalls, and tease the animals so much that they stomp the ground all night. It may be difficult to tell if it's the Dvorovoi tormenting your animals, or if it's the Ovinnik hosting a wild party for his demon friends.

If you've seriously disturbed him, he'll torment your animals even worse. Torture is more like it. He'll withhold food from the cows and horses until they get thin and weak. On top of that, he'll find a way to make you think your groom has been selling your corn and hay, so you won't blame it on the spirit. He can get even more vindictive and mutilate your horses and cattle by cutting off their tails, or by sticking burrs all over them, or even by making the wool fall off your sheep. Peasants recall one story where the Dvorovoi got so mad at the home owner that instead of taking care of the animals, he strangled them all.

Is it worth all this to have your way about the color of the new animals you bring home? I think not.

> **Did you know?**
>
> In the cold northern climates, a "shaggy" coat protects animals against harsh weather. This may be one reason why so many of the spirits—especially ancestral ones, whose souls people of old said could inhabit animals—take on the form of shaggy animals (Diechkoff, 238).

Beware the Jealous Neighbor

Sometimes you might cause trouble for your Dvorovoi because of advice from a jealous neighbor. He's not happy that your yard spirit cares for your animals, while his—if he has one—abuses them. Your neighbor will try his best to trick you, so be careful you don't fall for his deceit the way the farmer below did.

> One [peasant] owned horses that were well fed and well groomed, whereas the neighbor's horses were sickly and thin. Wishing to find out why his horses were so much finer than those of his neighbor, the peasant hid at night and caught the domovoi [dvorovoi] grooming, feeding, and watering his horses from the large water cask in the yard. The following day, not wanting his drinking water supply to be contaminated by an ugly spirit, he asked his neighbor what he should do. The neighbor knew that a domovoi [dvorovoi] was surely helping this lucky fellow, and keen to see him reduced to the same terms as himself, he suggested that the man drill a large hole in the cask. He could then plug the hole during the day but let all the water out at night. The man foolishly followed his advice, and when the domovoi [dvorovoi] came to water the horses he found the cask empty. Enraged, he smashed the stable to pieces and killed all the horses.[177]

An alternate ending to this tale says that the distraught Dvorovoi "clung to the bottom lip of a horse like an icicle in the form of a little man in wool."[178] And you can be sure that he raced the horse around all night until it was foaming.

Keeping the Dvorovoi Happy

If you take care of your yard spirit, he'll more likely be kind to you in return. Everything you do will be successful: you'll buy cheap and sell at a profit, you'll have better crops than your neighbors, hail will never destroy what you've planted, your cows will give plenty of milk, and diseases won't kill your animals. If any of those outcomes fail, the Dvorovoi won't hesitate to steal what you need from others: oats, hay, livestock, you name it. He and the Domovoi probably join forces to check out the neighborhood to see what you might need the most. It'll create quite the ruckus when they meet up with their neighbor's yard and house guardians out on the prowl with the same intention. Four spirits fighting to get supplies for their homeowners!

So, what do you have to do to stay on his good side?

He wants harmony among the family members and quiet in the barn—at least what he can get with all the noises the animals make. Like the house spirit and banya spirit, the yard spirit has a list of things you shouldn't do:

- Don't swear when you're outside.
- Don't let rubbish pile up.
- Don't work outside or in the barn at night and disturb him.

What's really important, though, is to give him food. All spirits enjoy a good meal—especially carbs to keep them going and salt to go along with it. Wrap a hunk of bread in a white cloth and place it in the courtyard—where you've seen his candle flickering at night is a good spot. Don't be stingy and give him moldy bread while you give a fresh piece to the Domovoi. You've learned what he can do when he's angry. Bow in all four directions, begging him to stop being angry. Make everyone in your family join in the entreaties.

Leave the Dvorovoi sauces of oil in the stable, too. It's possible he likes to dip his bread into it European-style. Put the saucers around an object you want to protect, and the spirit won't touch it. You can read an example of this in the excerpt from "Casuals in the Caucasus" later in this chapter.

Blood sacrifices are another way to reconcile with him. Kill a rooster at midnight. If it's a white one, the spirit will probably be thrilled. Since you're sacrificing the fowl to him, he'll know what happened to it and can cross it off his list of creatures to check up on as he does his nightly security check. Sprinkle the bird's blood around the courtyard. That's all there is to that ritual. You can go back into the house and rest soundly, knowing the spirit should be satisfied.

If for some reason you've upset the yard spirit, and he's neglecting your farm animals, you can bribe him to take care of them by performing a ceremony called "giving to the Dvorovoi." Gather up the following "gifts" for him: colorful scraps of paper or cloth, sheep wool, shiny trinkets, a penny with a horse on it, and the heel of a previously uncut loaf of bread. Bring them to the barn and recite the following prayer: "King of the yard, master, spirit, good-natured neighbor! I gift you these items and thank you: take care of the cattle, give them water and feed them."[179]

Old boots are among his favorite presents, so all you have to do is hang a pair—or several—in the yard for his entertainment. This gift makes him so agreeable that he won't even pester your chickens.

When the threshing is done and you cozy up inside for the winter, don't forget about your yard spirit. Although an outside fire is enough to keep the Ovinnik happy when you're work is done, the Dvorovoi wants more. If you want to keep him around after the harvest, you must perform a special ceremony on Mikhailov's Day, or Michaelmas (November 8, or November 21 in the Julian calendar, and September 29 for Slavonic Catholics).

Even before dawn, the oldest woman in the family brought out a cup of beer mash to the yard. And before noon the owner rode around the yard on the dvorovoi's favorite horse. At

154

> this time, the landlady, waving a broom said, "My dear dvorovoi, don't go away! Don't ruin the yard, don't kill the cattle! Don't show the Devil the way here!"[180]

Showing him a little respect goes a long way for your yard spirit.

Controlling a Misbehaving Dvorovoi

If bribery doesn't work to get your Dvorovoi to behave, you'll have to resort to punishment. These methods also work to rid your property of a neighbor's yard spirit. The easiest way to get either one to behave is to hang a dead magpie on the fence. Both the Domovoi and Dvorovoi detest the bird (even though it's not white). The spirit will behave just so you take the bird away.

The next step, if that doesn't work, is to get a load of manure on your pitchfork and poke it at the bottom of the logs on your fence where he's likely to be standing. You'll pin him there, and the yard spirit will be disgusted. Messy, messy, and he hates things out of order. He'll start behaving rather quickly.

If he's still obstinate, this calls for even more drastic measures. Take the shovel you use to remove ash from the stove and dip it in tar. Next, climb on your horse and race around the courtyard waving the shovel. Yell at the spirit to behave himself and keep the law of God. As soon as you hit the spirit with the sticky tar, he'll be so disgusted he'll leave. If you don't have tar, you can strike everywhere the spirit may be outside with a plant called *tshertcgon* or "devil-chaser."[181]

Another method for beating the misbehaving or unwanted yard spirit is to take three threads from the shroud of a dead person. (Don't dig up anyone. You can be proactive and save threads when you have a funeral, in case you need them for such a time as this.) Dip the threads in wax and attach them to a stick. At midnight, set fire to the threads and whip them around the yard, then go inside the cattle shed and beat the air some more. He often hides so make sure you thrash the threads around all four corners to beat the bad spirit.

On the Dark Side

As if all that you've learned about the Dvorovoi wasn't bad enough, the yard spirit has an even darker side when it comes to people who've angered him.

Like the Domovoi, the Dvorovoi can also have a family. His wife can be a Kikimora, too. Not the same one who's married to the house spirit, of course. A different one. Plenty of the spirits roam the forest for him to choose for a bride. Their male children are all born *dvorovye*, while female offspring are all *kikimori*.

However, the real problem is when a Dvorovoi loves a human female. If the woman is a witch from his household, it's not so bad. She has her own ways of keeping the spirit under control. A regular human poses another problem. He's possessive of her.

In one well-known story, a Dvorovoi becomes enamored with a pretty peasant girl named Katya. He doesn't appear to her as an old man; to impress her, he takes the form of a handsome youth. You can read their sad tale below:

> A beautiful peasant girl had been orphaned and had inherited her parents' house. Over time she grew conscious of the fact that she was being helped around the house by a dvorovoi. As the years passed, she was able to see him clearly, a handsome youth who had obviously fallen in love with her. Katya invited the spirit to live with her. He plaited her hair and made her promise never to undo his handiwork.
>
> Some years later Katya realized that her lover was incapable of physical affection.

Dvorovoi. Illustration © Andy Paciorek. Used with permission of the artist.

Yearning for human love and affection, she met and became engaged to Stefan. The night before her wedding, after she had bathed, Katya undid her hair, which had grown very long, and brushed it thoroughly before retiring. The following morning the neighbors broke into her house when their knocks went unanswered and found her still in bed. Her long hair had been twisted and knotted around her neck. She had fallen victim to her jealous dvorovoi lover, who had strangled her with her own hair.[182]

Fact or Fiction?

In 2005, two students (Dar'ia Tuminas and Iuliia Marinicheva) from St. Petersburg University interviewed Vera Ignat'evna, an elderly Russian woman, about house spirits. When they asked her who the house spirit was, Vera didn't respond directly. Instead she talked about a day when people brought cattle into the courtyard at the end of the harvest season and gave them hay from the last harvesting—"to keep them well fed and healthy throughout the winter."[183] Their conversation follows:

VI: I haven't seen the dobrokhodushka, so I can't say. But it exists, people have seen it, [when] they have overfed [their cattle]. When I had cattle, the dobrokhodushka gave it hay. But I didn't see it. But it's like if we ask an angel [for something], [in the same way] we ask the dobrokhodushka.

IM: Is that so?

VI: Yes, when people overfeed the cattle on Pokrov, on Pokrov day, during Pokrov week, they ask the dobrokhodushka and the dobrokhodnitsa [to look after the cattle].

[. . .]

IM: So, how do you ask?

VI: How do people ask?

"Father Dobrokhodushka

And Mother Dobrokhodnitsa,

Go water, feed

Mother Cattle,

Calm her, stroke her,

So we can let her out.

Don't rely on me, the provider."

That's it. Bow to all three corners. And then the cattle, if there's none around, now you don't have to overfeed [them], you don't have to do anything.

IM: What do they overfeed them with? Do they give them something, some kind of food?

VI: Yes, they do. They give them [food], you see, and after that they take a piece of bread, salt it, and say words over it and give a little bit to everyone, and then they give the cattle their feed, you see. And they overfeed them. They give them more feed than they need on this day, so that they are satisfied [over the winter].

IM: Does the dobrokhodushka only belong to good people, to good families?

VI: Well, it doesn't matter, wherever there's cattle, they say, in every home, they say, there's a dobrokhodushka, yes. A domovoi [house spirit], you could say, a domovoi, domovoi.

IM: A domovoi?

VI: Yes, yes, a domovoi. In every home, they say, there is one . . .

IM: It doesn't belong to a person, but to a home, is that correct?

VI: Who knows! No one sees him, he just lives. And if they do see him, in our village, people say, if they caught him, they saw him.

IM: Did they catch him?

VI: Yes.

IM: How?

VI: Well, they'd meet him, he'd be giving the cattle [feed]. They saw him, but I didn't see, and I'm not going to lie. But he exists, people say they've seen him, he's like the owner of the house. Looks completely like him.

IM: In appearance?

VI: Yes, in appearance and everything else. He gives [feed].

IM: In terms of his character?

VI: [Explaining that the domovoi is dressed just as the homeowner]: Yes, it used to be, you see, there were old folks, in the village there didn't used to be cloth made out of . . . that stuff, everything was handwoven, underwear, I mean long white underpants, made out of canvas, and shirts. So they would see him in all white, if they saw him, and he'd look just like the homeowner, and he'd be giving the cattle [feed]. But I don't know, I haven't seen it. But they say it exists, they have seen it.

[. . .]

VI: If you go to visit someone in the city, invite the dobrokhodushka with you.

IM: How?

VI: Like this: "Father Dobrokhodushka, I have set off, now you come with me."

[. . .]

DAR'IA TUMINAS [DT]: Even if you're going for a visit?

VI: Yes, for a visit. You'll be less unloved (*tebe men'she napostynet*), he'll give you space (*on mesto tebe dast*). When you leave, call him with you again.

IM: That is, wherever I go, I should always call the dobrokhodushka with me?

VI: Yes, yes, yes, yes.

IM: So it works out that he is with you all the time.

VI: Yes.

[. . .]

DT: Does he protect you somehow?

VI: Yes.

DT: And is there some kind of dvorovoi [yard-spirit]?

VI: That's the same one, it's him, it's all the same: dvorovoi, domovoi and dobrokhodushka. It's the same thing.

IM: So outside, on the street, is there some kind of master as well?

VI: Even on the street, it's still you, and everyone has his own protector, a guardian angel, [unclear] and the angel will go with you. Everyone has one, when a person is born he is given an angel, they say everyone has one. You go, and he goes alongside you, you don't see him.

Dvorovoi in Literature

The Dvorovoi, like the Domovoi, appears frequently in literature. Here are a couple for your enjoyment.

- *Casuals in the Caucasus* by Agnes Herbert, published in 1912.
- *The White Slave* by C. F. Henningsen, published in 1845.

Casuals in the Caucasus by Agnes Herbert

Agnes Elsie Diana Herbert (late 1870s – 1960) was an Englishwoman who traveled with her cousin Cecily on three major hunting expeditions to Somaliland, Alaska, and Caucasus, writing about her adventures. *Casuals in the Caucasus*, published in 1912, tells of her adventures in the Caucasus, a place located at the border of Eastern Europe and Western Asia, between the Black Sea and Caspian Sea, and occupied by Russia, Georgia, Azerbaijan, and Armenia. About this place, she says:

> At the gate of Europe is an alluring, beckoning, magical country, where the centuries mingle in confused contrast, and Nature plays protagonist to herself.
>
> The Caucasus.
>
> Does not the very name breathe the weird suggestive mystery of a primitive environment, the rough-hewn fascination of barbaric peoples?
>
> Nowhere else in all the world can be found so myriad-minded and romantic a land, so many-sided, so rich in colours and fertile in forms (Herbert, 3).

The excerpt that follows talks about the Domovoi, but as the activities take place in the barn, they more accurately reflect the Dvorovoi.

A heavy snowstorm drove us to the Castle again. It came quite unexpectedly, and covered the forest in a thick white pall. Unfortunately this did not last, or it would have been of great assistance in our stalks abroad.

The first thing I did on getting back was to visit the tumble-down outbuilding called a stable in order to satisfy myself that our few trophies, particularly the head-skin of my ollen, had been looked to in our absence. In doing so, I unearthed the prettiest fancy. My treasure, securely pinned to a board, was surrounded with small saucers brimful of oil, six or eight of them. I could not understand their meaning, or guess what new system of local taxidermy was this. Then Keebeet came, and Cecily, and we unravelled the mystery.

The Castle had a titular domestic spirit, as have all properly conducted houses in the Caucasus, a tiny little thing, called the "domovoi." His proper place is behind the big kitchen stove, but at night he roams about singing for his supper. It is his business to make the round of the stables at midnight in order to satisfy himself that the cattle are safe, and there he expects to find sundry cups of oil, any kind, the "domovoi" is not particular as to brand.

Certain dates in the year, as, for instance, the Feast of the Epiphany, January 18th, and odd days in October, have a disastrous effect on the spirit's temper, and though the family prepare for the nerve-storms by boiling millet, which the soul of the "domovoi" loveth, and providing the most potent variety of vodka, that made from potatoes, nothing stems the torrent of carefully-thought-out malignancy. Sometimes, too, at these seasons, a strange "domovoi" blows in, and then the two vexed spirits, acting in concert, need some pacifying.

Only once in a great while can you see a "domovoi," a very small immortal, a sort of miniature Father Christmas, with long white beard, long hair, and brilliant eyes.

As the dies irae of the household spirit was at hand the castle baboushka feared for the safety of our trophies. What if the "domovoi" took exception to them! So the saucers were placed about, a charm no gourmand "domovoi" could resist.

I believe he came to the Caucasus with the moujik—there's something very like him in Russian folk-lore. Only the Karbardans would none of it. Other brands of "domovoi" there may be, but their own has frequented Karbarda since Karbarda was.

Even His Highness was singularly uninterested in the folk-tales and proverbial sayings which must have been familiar to him all his life. I did wish he would have added to our meagre store, for in the folk-tales and the proverbs of a country we often find the key to the locked heart of things. A land so romantic, so wild, so untutored as the Caucasus must have a vast storehouse of mysterious tales and wise sayings hidden away. But the treasure lies very deep (Herbert, 305-306).

The White Slave by C. F. Henningsen

Charles Frederick Henningsen (1815 – 1877), born in Brussels, Belgium, has been described as a writer, mercenary, filibuster, and munitions expert. He fought in civil wars and independence movements in Spain, Nicaragua, Hungary, and the United States, but failed to win any of those causes. About "The White Slave," published in 1845, he says in the preface that besides amusing and moving his readers, his desire in writing the book was "to popularize some knowledge of the condition of the Russian Serf" (Henningsen, v).

Charles Frederick Henningsen

In the following excerpt that brings up the topic of a spirit and his activities in a stable, an English servant gives an account of what caused his own earlier altercation with Billy, a Russian stable hand.

Now, as nigh as I could make him out, Billy takes it into his head that the stable is haunted by what he calls a Domovoi, a sort of Robin Goodfellow or Brownie, which eats up the corn and turns the horses' coats; and yesterday he calls me into his stable, to show me the tails of his horses, which the Domovoi had plaited together in the night, but which in my opinion had got entangled by their whisking 'em about.

Now Billy declares that sometimes the Domovoi takes a dislike to black horses, and sometimes to roan, and sometimes to grey, and that nothing would go right till he went and fetched the Pope to drive him out with holy water. So I told him by all means to do so, because I happened to know that the Pope was at Rome in Italy, where I see him with my own eyes.

But what do ye think, Sir, last night in he brings this gentleman with the knob stick, (pointing to Father Basil) saying he was the Pope, which I knowed of course to be a flam, the Pope (though a papist) being a different character altogether, and a great deal more respectable.

Well, in he goes to Billy's stable, and, after he had mountebanked enough, he says he has driven the Domovoi out and that he will never return again, which I expect was the only true part of the story. For, though I am rising five and thirty, I never see any spirits, excepting them as people keep in bottles.

Then, Sir, he wants to go into Lucifer's [the speaker's horse] box, but I said no, no; no tricks upon travellers there; the Domovoi won't plait his tail or meddle with him, I know, any more than any other foreigner that ever I saw. And when he found it wouldn't do, he asks for one of them blue five rouble notes for his trouble; Billy declaring that it was customary.

'Well,' says I, 'I'll ask my master to-morrow; and if he sees proper to encourage your tomfoolery, you shall have it, so come again and see.'

'Then,' says Billy, 'will you give him some brandy and he will give you his blessing.'

'Here's the brandy,' said I, for the bottle was on the top of my chest of drawers, and I couldn't do less; 'but he may keep the blessing for them as wants it.'

So down he sat and made hisself jolly, and out he pulls a pack of cards and wants to play with us (Henningsen, 49-51).

Hovanets. Illustration by Anna Błaszczyk (Evelinea Erato). © Bendideia Publishing.

Hovanets (Хованец)

The devil always takes back his gifts.

> **Hovanets** (singular); **Hovanetsi** (plural)
>
> **Other names**: khovanets', chowaniec, chowany, hodowany, utrzymywany, wychowywany, antipko, vikhovanets', vykhovanets, godovanets', dítko.[184]
>
> **Related spirits (Polish)**: klobuk (клобук), kołbuk, kłobuk, lubberkin (from the game "The Witcher: Wild Hunt").[185]
>
> **Related spirit (Slovenian)**: blagonič.[186]

Greed has been—and will continue to be—the downfall of many people. In the world of fantasy, you can see this with Gollum (Sméagol) from *The Hobbit* and *The Lord of the Rings* series. He becomes corrupted by a ring of invisibility and kills Déagol, who refuses to give him the ring for a birthday present. From that point on, the ring consumes not only his life but his appearance. Greed will also destroy you if you resort to conjuring a Hovanets in order to gain wealth. You may think you can escape the "cost" of this magic, but more than likely, its corruption will destroy you instead.

Origins

Some say the Hovanets has its origins in ancestor worship the way the Domovoi does, except that you have to "create" this Ukrainian household spirit in order for it to become a giver of wealth. The Polish Kłobuks is similar in many respects, as is the Slovenian Blagonič.

You can conjure the spirits in several ways.

Purchase from a Sorcerer

One method, perhaps the easiest, is to "buy" one from a "person with knowledge," which refers to a sorcerer, witch, or anyone who possesses supernatural powers. Those who have created the spirit say you can purchase one at a certain stall in the Ukrainian town of Lviv. There you'll see two crosses on the wall: one real and the other painted. Hit the real one and kiss the painted one. This means of mocking the cross is a way of renouncing Christ and the Holy Mother. It also tells the shopkeeper what you're there for, and he'll give you a Hovanets in exchange for whatever price he's set for the demon. Beware: although you're buying this demon, you're also selling your soul to the devil, and he'll make sure he collects when you die.

Egg Ritual

The most common method to create a Hovanets involves placing an egg in your left armpit and keeping it warm there for nine days (or even nine weeks) until it hatches. It has to remain there the full time, or the

Etymology

Hovanets may come from the Ukrainian word *vikhovuvati* which means "to raise" or "to educate." It indicates the way the spirit is created, in that you bring up the Hovanets and teach him what it is you desire him to do for you. He is often called "foster child," "ours," or "pet."[1] The Polish Chowaniec comes from the word *chowaniec*, which means "adopted child."[1]

An alternative thought is that it's derived from *khovatisya*, which means "to hide," indicating that either the spirit hides from people, or that those who "own" the spirit hide him from strangers.[1] Or it possibly could refer to the fact that when women had a miscarriage or aborted child, they often hid the deceased infant by burying it beneath the house.

ritual will be incomplete. Some people say you can perform the ritual any time; other say it must be completed on Easter.

Not any egg will do. It should be a deformed, malformed, or immature egg called a cock's egg or *znoska*. Several possibilities will work. It can be the first egg a young hen lays, the last egg an old hen lays, or an egg that a rooster or black hen has struck in some manner. It works best if the egg is from a black hen. That should be simple enough to find. Other possibilities are more difficult to determine. You can use an egg that has no yolk, is all yolk, or has a double yolk. If you go this route, you'll likely have to attempt this ritual many times before you find one that meets that criteria. If you get an egg from a hen that crows like a rooster, you'll have no trouble since a *chort* (devil) possesses those kinds of birds. Perhaps this is why it's so difficult to create this being.

Before you incubate the egg under your armpit, you should smear it with human ashes and wrap it in a piece of cloth. While you have the egg snug in your armpit, you have to follow several restrictions in order for the ritual to be successful. You can't be baptized, pray, go to church, or even look at ikons. That should be obvious since you're hatching a devil. Praying is certain to counteract the evil growing inside the egg. You can't bathe or cut your fingernails or toenails. You can't even talk, walk, or scratch. Your little demon must not be disturbed in any manner while he's incubating.

Nine days pass, and the happy event takes place. If you followed the belief that you have to hatch this monster on Easter, then the final day is the time to go to church. When the priest says, "Christ is risen!" you have to quietly say three times, "and mine is resurrected!"

At that moment, the Hovanets will crawl out of the egg. Congratulations! You have a new bundle of joy who's going to make you rich.

You might find a wealth-bringing Hovanets that's already been hatched if you're fortunate. It'll appear in the form of a wet chicken or chick after a heavy rain shower.

You create a Blagonič in a slightly different manner. Place a black rooster under a cup used for measuring wheat. You'll have to keep it there for seven years. At the end of this time, you'll discover an egg the rooster laid. The Blagonič will hatch from this egg.

Create from a Stillborn Child

You can also create a Hovanets from a stillborn or aborted infant, or from a child who was murdered or died before being baptized. It was a common belief that the souls of these children became dangerous demons. Such children turned into an evil being because they were unable to cross over to the spirit realm because they were "impure" or "unholy," and so they continued to roam the earthly realm.

Besides being buried under the house as you've learned was a common practice, murdered, unbaptized children were buried at boundary lines or at crossroads—both unholy places. Unholy dead children were also buried under the roots of a tree or within a tree's hollow. There's a saying that if lightning strikes a dead tree, a dead baby is certain to be buried beneath the tree.

It was believed that the spirit of these children did not want to become a guardian of their own home, and so they were buried away from the house. A magical ritual using an abnormal egg (the same type of egg used in creating a Hovanets) was performed when burying one of these children. A non-family member would carry an egg under his left arm when he went to the edge of the village. Once there, he would cut a *sverbus* (a bush), wrap the egg up with it, and set it on fire under the dead tree where the child was buried.

Creating a Hovanets from a stillborn or other "unholy" dead child takes several years—seven in fact, although in some regions, the time to wait could be as little as seven days or seven months. For this method to work, however, no one can know about the deceased infant except the mother. Since the child was not born alive, you can't baptize him. The unholy dead is ripe for you to make him into your wealth-bringing servant. Bury the poor soul under the threshold of your home or dig a hole in the basement. When seven years pass, the infant's spirit will ask you, his mother, to baptize him. If you have compassion, you will. If, however, greed takes over, you'll say, "No. You'll be a Hovanets." Your dead child now must serve you until you die.

Did you know?

The soul of an unbaptized child becomes a demon for seven years. To keep it occupied, families give the demon child a chain, a brush, and a rake (Levkovych, 247).

Although this is quite a different method from conjuring a spirit from an egg, a parallel exists: in Slavic mythology, a woman giving birth is associated with a hen and her newborn with an egg. In another respect, colored Easter eggs show similarities to eggs used to create a Hovanets. They are colored at night in silence, they should be from a hen that has just started laying eggs, and eggs from black hens are easiest to color. While an egg used to create a Hovanets is sinister, the first Easter egg is colored red and is regarded as a house guardian. On the Friday or Saturday after Easter, women bring additional Easter eggs to the church: one white egg for each older family member who died during the year and one red egg for each child who died.

Appearance

Your Hovanets servant may take on a variety of appearances. In addition to looking like the present or former homeowner, he may look like a small man with a gray beard and hair, or even a boy who's wearing red pants and a horned hat and smoking a cigar. From time to time, he appears as a shepherd with a whip. When in human form, he often takes on the circumstances of the family who brings him into existence, dressing like a rich person when a wealthy family creates him. At other times, he wears old clothes, or even appears naked when a poor man hatches him.

He may appear as a sorcerer's animal familiar: a cat, dog, frog, black snake, or chicken. Upon occasion, he's looked like a cow. Other animals he appears as are a bear, ram, or weasel. At other times, he doesn't have any visible form.

The following have all been used to describe the presence of the demon:[187]

- Something white and thin as death.
- Someone dark and fuzzy.
- A bag of bread.
- A scary noise, weeping, or other obscure sounds.
- Something knocking, crawling, or pushing.

165

Getting to Know the Hovanets

In many ways, the Hovanets—especially the Polish version—is like your Domovoi and Dvorovoi. In addition to bringing you wealth, he acts like your ancestors, or sometimes, even like the snake Smok by predicting the future or warning you about misfortune. The Ukrainian spirit is more like a demon, who will do you harm.

When you perform your ritual to create a Hovanets, you may actually be calling the founder of your property, or the spirit dwelling there, whether a relative or not. That is, if the spirit is not that of the dead infant buried beneath the house.

The spirit putters around the house and yard doing small chores until you send him on wealth-seeking errands. When he has a mind to, he also takes care of the cattle and other animals—unless he's out pilfering from the neighbors. You can have as many of these servants around the house as you choose: one to watch out for thieves trying to take back what your spirit stole, another to take care of bees if you have them, a third to work in the fields, and so on for as many tasks as you want them to take care of. If you loosen a board in the fence surrounding your property, they can come and go as they please.

Since you have to keep your Hovanets hidden from prying eyes, he often lives in the attic. Like the other spirits, he requires that you feed him to keep him happy so he'll bring you as much wealth as you desire. His favorite foods are milk, sugar, and *unsalted* wheat bread. This should tell you right away that he's not a friendly sort of spirit. For the most part, the others you've learned about like their bread and food salted. Demons, however, are adverse to salt.

The food should be cooked well. A story tells about how one of these creatures reacted to an unsatisfactory meal his owner gave him.

> It so happened that the master of a household cooked beans for a Blagonič, but undercooked them so they were hard; meanwhile he prepared sausages for himself. The Blagonič became very angry. He went into the barn and hung the best ox on the door by its tail. The Blagonič started running around the house yelling, "Beans hard; ox hanging by its tail." There was never any good fortune at that house.[188]

It's easy to tell the households that have a Hovanets. Everything prospers for them. Their homes are bigger, their animals increase, their crops—if they're farmers—are plentiful. To get one to bring you money, you place a gold coin on the windowsill. The creature will take it and return with a bag full of more coins, which he'll dump into the house. Don't try to trick him and leave something else like a thorn, stone, or dead cat. Whatever you leave for him is what he'll bring back more of in a bag. If you give him something bad to find, he's likely to cause you physical harm.

Did you know?

The souls of dead children return to earth as plants so they can live again (Levkovych, 247).

Where he differs from the Domovoi is that he's not doing it because he loves you or your family, nor is he concerned about your welfare. You created him for a purpose—to make you rich in whatever way he can. Mostly he'll do it through stealing, but magic may be involved as well. Rumors circulate about owners of a Hovanets possessing a black book of spells.

You've probably heard the saying that all magic comes with a cost. In this case, it's true. You may not like that cost, though.

166

On the Dark Side

If you do something to displease the Hovanets, he's much more destructive than the Domovoi. One thing that sets him on a rampage is if you give him salt. He'll smash the dishes and bend all your silverware. He'll punch you in the eyes. If you're lucky, the demon will leave. But even this is not a blessing because he'll take all your happiness with him, and your wealth will disappear. Money's not everything, but you were greedy enough in the first place to create this monster, so it'll be devastating for you.

A common belief even to this day is that when someone loses their wealth, the owner is soon to die. If you're that owner, even more terrible than death will be the manner in which you die. The Hovanets will cause you so much torment—and torture you in a way that only a demon can—that you're likely to hang yourself. The demon may even do the deed on his own, making every breath you take as terrible as possible.

That's not the end to your misery, though. The eldest Hovanets that you've created will drag you off to Hell. Your soul is payment for all the wealth he brought you in your lifetime. In Hell, he'll stuff you into an egg, and you'll become an even more evil being than the one you called forth in the first place. Now someone else can "hatch" you under his armpit so you'll be a money-grubbing thief like the one you created.

Remember what they say about karma… I'd think twice before trying to bring one of these nasty spirits into this world.

How to Get Rid of the Hovanets

Of course, if you've found this out too late, you'll want to find a way to get rid of the Hovanets, without losing any of the wonderful things he's brought you. You can attempt this yourself by hitting him in the face with the back of your hand. It'll kill him instantly.

Two caveats here. First, it'll be tough to sneak up on him; he's likely to do more harm to you than you can do to him. Second, if anyone hits him on the head with a beech stick, he'll revive and be certain to torture you.

You're probably better off to get a priest to come and consecrate your home. He'll have to make the rounds three times. After that, you'll be able to get rid of the Hovanets by transferring him out of your house through the roof. Make sure to do it through the ninth rafter, though, or it will all have been in vain.

If the priest refuses (since you haven't been attending church), you can hope for a thunderstorm. Send the Hovanets out on a mission to steal something. If you're lucky, lightning will strike him. A highly charged electrical volt will kill the demon in the same way that it does an Ovinnik.

All those methods have failed? Sorry, the Hovanets is waiting in glee to give you what he thinks you deserve.

Fact or Fiction?

Scour the internet for Eastern European forums where people discuss folklore and mythology, and you'll find that belief in spirits and creatures thrives—much the same way as belief in ghosts and spirits is alive in the western world. One commentator in such a place talks about the Hovanets, saying her neighbors and many other people in the vicinity have a demon, and all the families live in two- or three-story houses with many rooms, because that's what the Hovanets provides for them. They are rich by rural standards.

The grandmother is the eldest in one such family, and so controls the demon. She attends church only on major holidays, but the younger generations go to service faithfully. This is something the Hovanets despises, and in retaliation, he hurts them and brings sickness to the family.

In another family, the wife conjured the demon. She and her husband have a huge house and money that no one knows where it came from. Their children do not live with them, but it's interesting to note that the curse of having a Hovanets filters down to them as well. They suffer even though they attend church and pray. The price they pay is that the daughters suffer a genetic disease, and the son has a weak heart that required surgery when he was an infant.

A house of former residents who had a demon helper now stands empty. They can't live there, and for years, no one has even considered buying it. People who have been inside to clean have come out injured. One man broke his leg after he slipped on the second floor. The only cure, people whisper, is to destroy such a house.

Perhaps all these misfortunes are circumstantial, but to many people they are not. Demons and spirits are quite real and cause misfortune and death.

DEMON CHILDREN

In the late nineteenth century when many beliefs about spirits were popular among rural people, danger from demon abduction threatened children (Information from Levkovych). Some women chose to end their child's life, often believing the infant was not their own. They believed children with overly big skulls, deformed faces, and other physical defects were the offspring of female demons, who had carried off the human child. Or the deformed child may have been human, but a female demon suckled it, causing the abnormalities.

Young, unmarried girls who conceived a child from an adulterous affair often killed the infant, or as villagers described it: "drove out" the baby and tossed it away, befouling the land. Such children, however, were welcome in the community. A common belief among some groups was that "if a bastard is born, it's a sign that farming will go well, and wheat harvest will be bountiful." When the infant was murdered, however, disaster would strike the village for a year. In particular, hail would destroy everything along any road the woman who killed her child had walked.

Women and girls who killed their babies often committed suicide as they were unable to bear community judgment for their actions. This gave rise to the notion that perhaps the infant was demonic, exchanged for the human child at birth.

Preventive Measures
More often, though, women performed many colorful rituals and customs to keep infants and unbaptized children safe from both illness and being abducted or harmed by demons and other evil spirits. A few of these practices follow:

- After the birth, coat the bed with blessed chalk, and stick a knife into the door frame.
- Leave something made of metal next to the woman as she's giving birth.
- Ensure a family member guards the child the night after it's born.
- Place a poppy seed inside a cloth and lay it next to the newborn child.
- If you're the mother, don't turn your back on your child before it's baptized.
- Place a cat or chicken in the cradle first, so demons will attack it and not the infant.

DEMON CHILDREN *continued*

- Put coins covered in excrement around the infant's neck for three nights.
- Gather water from nine lakes and pour it over a yoke that was used nine times on twin, black bulls. Then bathe the infant in the water.
- If you're a woman going into labor, eat porridge made with hair from an infant's first haircut (symbolic of a person's spirit and health) and request a happy life for your baby.
- Place a weak baby inside a warm oven on Easter so that it can "rise" (get stronger).
- Avoid putting a child on a property border line because a demon could take it.
- Ensure that an invited guest takes a seat when offered one. Otherwise, an unbaptized infant becomes restless and sleepless.
- Be careful not to allow uninvited guests inside. They can jinx an unbaptized infant.
- Words of praise attract demons, so alter what you say a bit to deceive the demons.
- Secretly burn a piece of hair from either parent as protection against demons.

Even breastfeeding a child has its ritual practices. Before a child nurses, it's considered innocent and pure as it hasn't received into its body anything from this sin-tainted world. To keep the child safe during its first nursing, a woman does the following:

- Wear a string amulet on her arm.
- Hold a loaf of bread and a bit of salt under her armpit.
- Sprinkle herself and her child with holy water.
- Begin feeding the infant from the right side. To do so from the left will cause the infant to die quickly or be cursed by the evil eye.

A Way to Have Your Infant Returned
If a demon spirit has already swapped out your infant for her own, you can try the following ritual to have her return your child.

While water is boiling, poke holes into an egg with a special one-year-old branch of a hazelnut tree. Pour the water into the holes. This makes the spirit appear and ask, "What are you doing?"

Reply, "Making food."

The demon will respond, "Have you seen anyone making food inside an egg?"

Say, "Have you seen a demon taking my baby?"

The spirit will immediately return your infant.

Ways to Lift a Curse
A demon may have cursed your child instead. You have a couple ways to lift the curse:

- Pour clean water into the child's left shoe and wash the child with it.
- Take a bit of clay from 9 to 12 graves and replace it with a stone tied to garlic. While you do this say, "I'm not taking anything from you; I'm paying for it."

continues

DEMON CHILDREN *continued*

Preventive Measures for the Dead

Sometimes, even the above rituals fail, and a child dies before it can be baptized, leaving its soul in peril. When this occurs, families have additional options to prevent demons from carrying off the child's soul.

- Demons roam the forest naked, as those in this state of dress are considered wild. Instead of burying an unbaptized child naked as is customary, clothe the child to keep demons from taking its soul and making it wild and evil.
- Lay the child with "pure" ancestors who have been buried in the house. They'll guard the soul of the infant so evil forces can't steal it away.
- Place money with the child so it can "bribe" other spirits to take care of it.

Afterword

I hope you've enjoyed your journey into the world of Eastern European spirits. I've asked you throughout the book if you thought they were real since many stories exist today telling of their exploits.

Not all people hold the belief that the spirits are evil. I had a short email conversation with a shaman who corrected me, saying they are not "spirits" but rather are "souls" of the departed or "soul fragments" of living people. This was a belief I had also run across in my research when I read about Madame Blavatsky, who had a similar experience with what other people called a "Domovoi."

Another shaman said early pagan and other religions have corrupted these "ancient ones of mother earth." The superstitions about these souls are disrespectful. They are mostly benevolent, although you should not try to summon them. They will come to you on their own.

Other "religious" movements arise time and again, attempting to bring back the old pre-Christian Slavic beliefs. This proves difficult since so much of what occurred in the original rituals and customs was erased with the arrival of Christianity.

Both of these topics are dealt with in many other books. My mentioning of them here is merely to inform you that these beliefs are by no means dead.

About the Author

Ronesa Aveela is "the creative power of two." Two authors, that is. Nelly, the main force behind the work, the creative genius, was born in Bulgaria and moved to the US in the 1990s. She grew up with stories of wild Samodivi, Kikimora, the dragons Zmey and Lamia, Baba Yaga, and much more. She's a freelance artist and writer. She likes writing mystery romance inspired by legends and tales. In her free time, she paints. Her artistic interests include the female figure, Greek and Thracian mythology, folklore tales, and the natural world interpreted through her eyes. She is married and has two children.

Rebecca, her writing partner was born and raised in the New England area. She has a background in writing and editing, as well as having a love of all things from different cultures. She's learned so much about Bulgarian culture, folklore, and rituals, and writes to share that knowledge with others.

Connect with us at www.ronesaaveela.com!

Be sure to follow us on Kickstarter for extra goodies when we
launch new books: https://www.kickstarter.com/profile/ronesaaveela/.

Special Offer

Would you like to learn more about folklore and mythology? Sign up for our periodic newsletter and also get updates about book releases and promotions. As a thank you, follow this link to receive a FREE supplement to our "Spirits and Creatures" book series. From time to time, we'll change this free gift. The first installment is about a malicious water spirit: Vodyanoy or Vodnik. Discover where he comes from, how to protect yourself from him, how to make him "somewhat" happy, and more. Written in a conversational way, rather than dull academia, it will engage you, the reader. Illustrations and stories help provide you with an overall picture of this spirit.

Link to download: https://dl.bookfunnel.com/1rq3ku0fa9

Acknowledgments

So many people have contributed to this book. Some with art and entertainment, others with their words, stories, and translations. It's not only words that provide a reader with a sense of that which was unfamiliar to them: the illustrations, videos, songs, and stories all contribute toward creating the image.

First of all, I thank my ever-faithful critique group, Land of Oz. Alex and Erin, your comments, suggestions, and reader reactions are priceless.

A special thank you goes to Anna Błaszczyk (Evelinea Erato), whose illustration of the Kikimora graces the cover. I loved this image from the moment I saw it floating around the internet, and was delighted when I tracked down its creator. I was even more delighted when she allowed me to purchase it to use for the cover of this first book about Eastern European spirits and creatures, and feature her other illustrations throughout the book as well.

Another artist, whose illustrations haunt me, is Andy Paciorek. I first saw his version of the Kikimora on a Facebook forum. I bought his book called *Black Earth*, and discovered a wealth of information and often terrifying images of creatures from "the Slavonic Otherworld." With his permission, I have included the ones relevant to this book. See his ad for where you can get a copy of this fascinating book.

I cannot forget Dmitry Yakhovsky, who has provided many images that supplement the sidebar information throughout the book. This wonderful artist also created the cover illustration for *The Unborn Hero of Dragon Village*. You have not seen the last of Dmitry's work in my books.

My dear friend and fellow author/artist, Nelinda, is always there to provide for whatever artistic endeavors I need. I thank her for being there.

Nicole Lavoie did a fabulous job reworking my ghastly interior design so it looks clean and professional.

More than art has contributed to the fullness of this book. I'd like to thank Stepan Samokhin and KCHÖRTOO for the musical inspiration about the Kikimora. Thanks to Lily Goodchild and Nicola Everill for use of their fabulous video "Domovoi and Kikimora." I'm grateful to Marshall Dyer for letting me use his narration of the interactive fiction about the Domovoi.

Last, but not least, I thank Emma Woodcock for permission to reprint extracts from her blog about her book *Kikimora*, and Vicki Boykis for sharing her experience with trying to get a Domovoi to stay with her.

Artist Profiles

Anna Błaszczyk (Evelinea Erato) is a Polish artist interested in folklore and mythology. Her work is inspired by artists such as Ivan Bilibin, Arthur Rackham, John Bauer, Alphonse Mucha, and Gustav Klimt. Contact her at the places below to find out more about commissioned art.

Deviantart: https://www.deviantart.com/evelineaerato
Email: evelineaerato@gmail.com

Andy Paciorek is a graphic artist and writer, drawn mainly to the worlds of myth, folklore, symbolism, decadence, curiosa, anomaly, dark romanticism and otherworldly experience. His published books include *Black Earth: A Field Guide to the Slavic Otherworld*, *Strange Lands: A Field Guide to the Celtic Otherworld* and *The Human Chimaera: Slideshow Prodigies & Other Exceptional People*. He is also the creator of the Folk Horror Revival multimedia project.

Books available at: www.blurb.co.uk/user/andypaciorek
Email: andypaciorek@yahoo.co.uk

Dmitry Yakhovsky has received education at the Academy of Art in Minsk, Belarus. He mostly works for authors and publishers all over the world to illustrate books in both digital and traditional ways but is also regularly commissioned for smaller projects. Dmitry writes and illustrates his own books. Examples of this are the graphic novel series "The Shadow of the Cross" and two coloring books for adults which were all published by the British publisher MadeGlobal and two historical graphic novels set in medieval Netherlands published by the Dutch publisher Pear Productions. He is this year's winner of a big comic contest in the Netherlands. Dmitry is besides this specialized in portrait and landscape paintings which are usually done in oil paint or watercolor and regularly exhibited.

Facebook: https://www.facebook.com/entaroart/
DeviantArt: https://www.deviantart.com/entar0178

Nelinda is the artistic side of Ronesa. Not only does she have thousands of ideas for stories about her Bulgarian heritage, but she is a talented artist. You can see more of her work at www.nelindaart.com.

Nicole Lavoie is a graphic designer and project manager who used her creative eye to design the interior layout for *Household Spirits*. As a mom of three young children, she uses her "spare" time to continue to grow her design business so she can eventually leave the corporate world behind her.

In addition to her love of all things creative and crafty she is also an aspiring author who wants to share her family's experiences as a foster family, adoptive family and family with children who have special needs with others through children's stories to help parents and children understand and cope with whatever life throws them.

You can learn more about Nicole and her business endeavors at www.justsayingdezigns.com.

Books by Andy Paciorek

Andy Paciorek is a graphic artist and writer, drawn mainly to the worlds of myth, folklore, symbolism, decadence, curiosa, anomaly, dark romanticism and otherworldly experience.

His published books include Black Earth: A Field Guide to the Slavic Otherworld, Strange Lands: A Field Guide to the Celtic Otherworld and The Human Chimaera: Sideshow Prodigies & Other Exceptional People.

He is also the creator of the Folk Horror Revival multimedia project

www.blurb.co.uk/user/andypaciorek

email: andypaciorek@yahoo.co.uk

Bibliography

Kikimora

Ancient Origins. "She Brings Bad News: The Scary Slavic Household Spirit Called Kikimora." http://www.ancient-origins.net/myths-legends/she-brings-bad-news-scary-slavic-household-spirit-called-kikimora-006776.

B., Margie. "Polish Supernatural Spirits." 2003. http://www.webcitation.org/query?url=http://www.geocities.com/mabcosmic/polish/pspirits.html&date=2009-10-26+02:03:31.

Beaumont, Cyril W. *Children's Tales*. London: C. W. Beaumont, 1919.

Beggerow, Alan. "Liadov – Kikomora." November 21, 2013. https://muswrite.blogspot.ca/2013/11/liadov-kikomora.html.

D20pfsrd.com. "Kikimora." http://www.d20pfsrd.com/bestiary/monster-listings/fey/kikimora/.

Dixon-Kennedy, Mike. *Encyclopedia of Russian & Slavic Myth and Legend*. Oxford: ABC CLIO, 1998.

Dynda, Jiří. "The Three-Headed One at the Crossroad: A Comparative Study of the Slavic God Triglav." *Studia Mythologica Slavica* 17 (2014):57-82.

F., Lucia. "Beware of Kikimora – the scariest among Slavic nightmare creatures." http://www.slavorum.org/beware-of-kikimora-the-scariest-among-slavic-nightmare-creatures/.

Georgievtrifon. "Кикимора" ("Kikimora"). http://georgievtrifon.wixsite.com/bgmythology/kikimora.

Goodchild, Lily and Nicola Everill, Directors. "Domovoi and Kikimora." Produced at Staffordshire University, May 21, 2013. https://vimeo.com/66619155.

Henderson, Thulia Susannah, Mrs. *Olga, or Russia in the Tenth Century; an Historical Poem*. London: Hamilton, Adams & Co., etc., 1855.

Ivanichka, Georgieva. Българска Народна Митология (*Bulgarian Folk Mythology*), 2nd ed. Science and Art: Sofia, 1993.

Kamoń, Jan. "Kikimora, złośliwa zwiastunka nieszczęść" ("Kikimora, a malicious harbinger of misfortunes"). June 4, 2016. https://slowianskibestiariusz.pl/bestiariusz/demony-domowe/kikimora/.

Konakov, Nikolai. "Poltergeist in Folklore and Beliefs of the Komi People." http://www.folklore.ee/rl/pubte/ee/usund/ingl/konakov.html.

Kravchenko, Alexandra. "5 Slavic horror fairytales that shouldn't be told at night." October 31, 2017. https://www.rbth.com/arts/326565-5-slavic-horror-fairytales.

Liadov, Anatoly. *Kikimora* tone poem. https://youtu.be/4mli4z0Fuvg.

Máchal, Jan. "Slavic." In *The Mythology of All the Races*, vol. 3, edited by Herbert Louis Gray with consulting editor George Foot Moore, 217-330. Boston: Marshall Jones Company, 1918.

Montague-Nathan, M. "Notes on the Russian Music." *The Musical Times and Singing-Class Circular* 58, no. 895 (September 1917):417-418.

My-calend.ru. "Герасим Грачевник" ("Gerasim Grachevnik"). https://my-calend.ru/holidays/gerasim-grachevnik.

Planeta.by. "Кикимора - Болотная или Домашняя?" ("Kikimora – Swamp or Home?") November 2013. http://planeta.by/article/1251.

Ralston, William. T*he Songs of the Russian People, as Illustrative of Slavonic Mythology and Russian Social Life*, 2nd. ed. London: Ellis & Green, 1872.

Rose, Carol. *Spirits, Fairies, Gnomes, and Goblins: an Encyclopedia of the Little People*. Santa Barbara, California: ABC-CLIO, Inc. 1996.

Samokhin, Stepan. https://kchortoo.bandcamp.com/track/kikimora.

Secunda, Shai and Steven Fine, eds. *Shoshannat Yaakov, Jewish and Iranian Studies in Honor of Yaakov Elman*. Boston: Brill, 2012.

Slavic Folklore and World Dreaming. May 1, 2013. https://www.facebook.com/SlavicFolkloreDreams/photos/a.395983097142882.94112.303031413104718/454713621269829/?type=3&theater.

Sitwell, Edith. *Children's Tales from the Russian Ballet, Retold*. London: L. Parsons, 1920, 29-39.

Supernaturalcreatures.org. "Kikimora." http://supernaturalcreatures.org/encyclopedia/kikimora-2/.

Tooke, William. *History of Russia, from the Foundation of the Monarchy by Rurik, to the Accession of Catharine the Second*. London: T. N. Longman and O. Rees, 1800.

Vertsman, Marianna. "Kikimora, Domovoi, Baccoo, and Other Strange and Spooky Creatures." October 30, 2015. https://www.nypl.org/blog/2015/10/30/scary-creatures-world-folklore.

Wikipedia. "Anatoly Lyadov." https://en.wikipedia.org/wiki/Anatoly_Lyadov.

Wikipedia. "Ivan Turgenev." https://en.wikipedia.org/wiki/Ivan_Turgenev.

Wikipedia. "Kikimora," https://en.wikipedia.org/wiki/Kikimora.

Wikipedia. "Léonide Massine." https://en.wikipedia.org/wiki/Léonide_Massine.

Wikipedia, Russian. "Кикимора." ("Kikimora.") https://ru.wikipedia.org/wiki/Кикимора.

Woodcock, Emma. "The meandering path of Inspiration." September 22, 2017. https://emmawoodcock.wordpress.com/2017/09/22/the-meandering-path-of-inspiration/.

Zeluna.net. "Kikimora." http://zeluna.net/russian-fairy-tale-kikimora.html.

Domovoi

Alice. "Slavic Folklore II: Urban Spirits, Demons, and Creatures." June 1, 2012. http://nokkandmyling.blogspot.com/2012/06/slavic-folklore-ii-household-spirits.html.

All Top 5s. "Top 5 Slavic Folklore Creatures." January 10, 2017. https://www.youtube.com/watch?v=g-FUqFe-O80.

Baring, Maurice. *The Mainsprings of Russia*. London: T. Nelson and Sons, 1914.

Blackwood, William, ed. "In 'Holy Russia': Life in a Russian Family." *Blackwood's Edinburgh Magazine* 160, no. 923 (1896):692-702.

Bibliotecha-secteta. "Slavic Spirits." http://bibliotecha-secreta.tumblr.com/post/96185851378/slavic-spirits.

Boykis, Vicki. "Our Domovoi. Americans: He's just a short invisible bearded dude that lives in your home, no biggie." August 1, 2011. http://blog.vickiboykis.com/2011/08/our-domovoi-americans-hes-just-a-short-invisibile-bearded-dude-that-lives-in-your-home-no-biggie/.

Cournos, John. *The Mask*. London: Methuen & Co., Ltd. 1919.

Dixon-Kennedy, Mike. *Encyclopedia of Russian & Slavic Myth and Legend*. Santa Barbara, CA: ABC-CLIO, Inc., 1998.

Dushakova, Natalía S. "Specifics of the Traditional Culture of the Old Believers of Moldova and Southern Ukraine: Dwelling Practices." In *Anthropology & Archeology of Eurasia* 52, no. 1 (Summer 2013):22-38.

Dyer, Marshall. Narration of "The Domovoi." January 26, 2014. https://www.youtube.com/watch?v=liCVF8noVdA.

Esoterx. "Slavic Domovoi: The Heartbreaking History of a Household Goblin." November 27, 2012. https://esoterx.com/2012/11/27/slavic-domovoi-the-heartbreaking-history-of-a-household-goblin/.

Goscilo, Helena. "Slotting War Narratives into Culture's Readymade." https://www.academia.edu/5879556/Slotting_War_Narratives..._Helena_Goscilo.

Graham, Stephen. *Undiscovered Russia*. London: John Lane, 1912.

Harrison, William Henry. *Rifts in the Veil*. London: W. H. Harrison, 1878.

Harvey, G. Bianca. *Respice finem, or, Love in Exile*. London: J. and R. Maxwell, [1885?].

Henderson, Thulia Susannah, Mrs. *Olga, or Russia in the Tenth Century; an Historical Poem*. London: Hamilton, Adams & Co., etc., 1855.

Hoffman, Wickham. *Leisure Hours in Russia*. London: G. Bell and Sons, 1883.

Ijepojevic, George. "Slavic Religions." https://www.academia.edu/24643262/Slavic_Religions.

Ivantis, Linda J. *Russian Folk Belief*. Armonk, New York: M. E. Sharpe, Inc., 1992.

Kennan, George. "The 'Ritual Murder' Case in Kiev." In *The Outlook* 105 (1913):529-535.

Kennard, Howard Percy. *The Russian Peasant*. Philadelphia: J.B. Lippincott Company, 1908.

Kistanova, Anastasia. "Poems on the 1st of April: Reception of April Fool's Day in 18th-Century Russian Poetry." https://www.academia.edu/6174208/Reception_of_April_Fools_Day_in_18th_Century_Russian_Poetry.

Kovalevsky, Maxime. *Modern Customs and Ancient Laws of Russia*. London: D. Nutt, 1891.

Máchal, Jan. "Slavic." In *The Mythology of All the Races*, vol. 3, edited by Herbert Louis Gray with consulting editor George Foot Moore, 217-330. Boston: Marshall Jones Company, 1918.

Magnus, Leonard A. *The Heroic Ballads of Russia*. London: K. Paul, Trench, Trubner & Co., Ltd., 1921.

Mannherz, Julia. "Mysterious knocks, flying potatoes and rebellious servants: Spiritualism and social conflict in late Imperial Russia." In *Four Empires and an Enlargement: States, Societies and Individuals: Transfiguring Perspectives and Images of Central and Eastern Europe*. Edited by Daniel Brett, Claire Jarvis, and Irina Marin. School of Slavonic and East European Studies, UCL, 2008:1-15.

Manning, M. Chris. "The Material Culture of Ritual Concealments in the United States." In *Historical Archaeology* 48, no. 3 (2014):52–83.

Mansikka, V. J. "Demons and Spirits (Slavic)." In *Encyclopaedia of Religion and Ethics*, vol. IV, edited by James Hastings, 622-630. New York: Charles Scribner's Sons, 1912.

"Miscellany: Noteworthy Things Gleaned Here and There." In *Appletons' Journal: a Magazine of General Literature* 13, no. 326 (1875):798-800.

Morgan, E. Delmar, trans. "The Customs of the Ossetes, and the Light they throw on the Evolution of Law. Compiled from Professor Maxim Kovalefsky's Russian Work on 'Contemporary Custom and Ancient Law.' " In *Journal of the Royal Asiatic Society of Great Britain & Ireland* 20, ser. 2 (1888):364-412.

Nagy, Zoltán. "The Material Culture of Ritual Concealments in the United States Television and Problems of Interpreting Cultural Phenomena Among the Vasiugan [Eastern] Khanty." *Anthropology & Archeology of Eurasia* 52, no. 3 (Winter 2013–14):13–33.

The Pagan Files. "Domovoi, the Slavic Household Deity." May 21, 2007. http://alkman1.blogspot.com/2007/05/domovoi-slavic-household-deity.html

Petrovo-Solovovo, Michael. "Mr. Petrovo-Solovovo and the Evidence for Independent Slate-writing." In *Journal of the Society for Psychical Research* 9 (1899):57-60.

Ralston, William. *Krilof and His Fables*, 4th. ed. London: Cassell & Company, Ltd., 1883.

Ralston, William. *The Songs of the Russian People, as Illustrative of Slavonic Mythology and Russian Social Life*, 2nd. ed. London: Ellis & Green, 1872.

Rodakiewicz, Erla. "Notes on Foreign Holidays, Festivals and Saints' Days." In *Foreign-born; a Bulletin of International Service* 2, no. 8 (June-July 1921):234, 262-263.

"Russian Proverbs." In *The Quarterly Review* 139, no. 278 (July-October, 1875):493-524.

Ryan, W. F. *The Bathhouse at Midnight: An Historical Survey of Magic and Divination in Russia*. University Park, PA: The Pennsylvania State University Press, 1999.

Sinnett, A. P. *Incidents in the Life of Madame Blavatsky*. London: Theosophical Publishing Society, 1913.

Snow, Kevin. "The Domovoi" interactive fiction. November 29, 2014. https://bravemule.itch.io/domovoi.

The Spectator. " 'Death Week' in Rural Russia." In *Littell's Living Age* 194 (1892):766-768.

Stevens, Thomas. *Through Russia on a Mustang.* New York: Cassell Publishing Company, 1891.

Stewart, Hugh. *Provincial Russia, Painted by F. De Haenen, Described by Hugh Stewart.* London: A. and C. Black, 1913.

Temple bar 113. London: Ward and Lock, 1898.

Tiele, C. P. *Outlines of the History of Religion to the Spread of the Universal Religions.* London: Trübner, 1880.

Turgenev, Ivan Sergeevich. "Byezhin Prairie." In *A Sportsman's Sketches*, translated by Constance Garnett. 133-145. London: W. Heinemann, 1895.

Vertsman, Marianna. "Kikimora, Domovoi, Baccoo, and Other Strange and Spooky Creatures." October 30, 2015. https://www.nypl.org/blog/2015/10/30/scary-creatures-world-folklore.

Vlahović, Vlaho S. *Two Hundred 50 Million and One Slavs: an Outline of Slav History with Maps and Annotations.* New York: Slav Publications, Inc., 1945.

Wanderwelle. "The Domovoi." From *Lost In A Sea of Trees* album. July 31, 2017. http://shop.silentseason.com/track/the-domovoi.

Whishaw, Frederick. *The Romance of the Woods.* London: Longmans Green & Co., 1895.

Wikipedia. "John Cournos." https://en.wikipedia.org/wiki/John_Cournos.

Wikipedia. "Ivan Krylov." https://en.wikipedia.org/wiki/Ivan_Krylov.

Wikipedia. "Ivan Turgenev." https://en.wikipedia.org/wiki/Ivan_Turgenev.

Wood, Bernard H. "Nightmare fuel #3: The spirt of hearth and home." September 23, 2015. http://www.trans-siberian.co.uk/blog/the-domovoi/.

Woolmer, T, publ. "Ivan Serguievitch Tourgnieff." In *The London Quarterly Review* 63, vol. 3 (October 1884):38-54.

Wright, Richardson Little. *The Russians: an Interpretation.* New York: F.A. Stokes Co., 1917.

Zavalishin, Vyacheslav. *Early Soviet Writers.* New York: Praeger, 1958.

Stopan

Arnaudov, Michail. Студии Върху Българските Обреди и Легенди, Vol II (*Study of Bulgarian Rituals and Legends*). Sofia: Bulgarian Academy of Science, 1972.

Bachinovo Learning Center. "Тракийско мегалитно светилище 'Скрибина' при с. Крибул, Гоцеделчевско" ("Thracian Megalithic Sanctuary 'Skribina' near Kribul, Gotse Delchev"). http://satrae.swu.bg/projects-and-discoveries/discover7.aspx.

Douno, Master Beinsa. "X. Други формули" ("X. Other formulas"). https://triangle.bg/books/prayer-book.1995/other-formulas.html.

Emy. "Stopan and the House Serpent." May 6, 2006. https://folklore.livejournal.com/82201.html.

Ganeva, Dr. Radoslava. "Bulgarian Folk Costumes – Symbols and Traditions." *Bulgarian Diplomatic Review* 3, supplement (2003).

Guide-Bulgaria. "Sanctuary Skribina." http://visit.guide-bulgaria.com/a/1405/sanctuary_screensaver.htm.

Konstantinova, Daniela, trans. "Bread kneading, a Bulgarian tradition renewed." April 22, 2013. http://bnr.bg/en/post/100195314/bread-kneading-a-bulgarian-tradition-renewed.

Kovalevsky, Maxime. *Modern Customs and Ancient Laws of Russia.* London: D. Nutt, 1891.

Low, D.H., trans. "Marko Kraljević and the Vila." In *The Ballads of Marko Kraljević*, 21-24. Cambridge: The University Press, 1922.

MacDermott, Mercia. *Bulgarian Folk Customs.* London: Jessica Kingsley Publishers, 1988.

Máchal, Jan. "Slavic." In *The Mythology of All the Races*, vol. 3, edited by Herbert Louis Gray with consulting editor George Foot Moore, 217-330. Boston: Marshall Jones Company, 1918.

Mishev, Georgi. *Thracian Magic Past & Present.* London: BM Avalonia, 2012.

"Old World Building Customs and House Superstitions." In *Foreign-born; a bulletin of international service* 2, no. 7 (May 1921):199-201.

Paneurhythmy.us. "ABOUT Pan-Eu-Rhythmy." July 10, 2018. http://www.paneurhythmy.us/about_PanEuRhythmy.shtml.

Stamenov, Ivan. "Тракийско наследство в българския фолклор (10): Образ и същност на стопана" ("Thracian heritage in Bulgarian folklore (10): Image and nature of the stopan"). June 18, 2016. http://www.otizvora.com/2016/06/7908.

Stamenov, Ivan. "Тракийско наследство в българския фолклор (11): Образ и същност на стопана" ("Thracian heritage in Bulgarian folklore (11): Image and nature of the stopan"). June 19, 2016. http://www.otizvora.com/2016/06/7913.

Stamenov, Ivan. "Тракийско наследство в българския фолклор (12): Образ и същност на стопана" ("Thracian heritage in Bulgarian folklore (12): Image and nature of the stopan"). June 19, 2016. http://www.otizvora.com/2016/06/7917.

Tsankova, Diana. "Figures of snakes watch over newly discovered ancient sanctuary near Surnitsa." Translated by Milena Daynova. August 6, 2016. http://bnr.bg/en/post/100721913.

Wikipedia. "Genius (mythology)." https://en.wikipedia.org/wiki/Genius_(mythology).

Wikipedia. "Ottoman Bulgaria." https://en.wikipedia.org/wiki/Ottoman_Bulgaria.

Wikipedia. "Peter Deunov." https://en.wikipedia.org/wiki/Peter_Deunov.

Wikipedia. "Universal White Brotherhood." https://en.wikipedia.org/wiki/Universal_White_Brotherhood.

Wikitionary. "Стопан." https://en.wiktionary.org/wiki/стопан.

Talasum

Apostle. "Духове и привидения" ("Spirits and ghosts"). December 10, 2006. http://www.chitatel.net/forum/topic/2192-духове-и-привидения.

Arnaudov, Michail. Студии Върху Българските Обреди и Легенди, Vol II (*Study of Bulgarian Rituals and Legends*). Sofia: Bulgarian Academy of Science, 1972.

Aveela, Ronesa. *Light Love Rituals: Bulgarian Myths, Legends, and Folklore*. Bendideia Publishing, 2015.

Bowring, John, Sir, trans. "The Building of Skadra." In *Servian Popular Poetry*, 64-75. London: Printed for the author, 1827.

Dikov, Ivan. "Archaeologists Discover Grave of Medieval Bulgarian Princess 'Built into' Foundations of Stone Church near Botevgrad." June 5, 2016. http://archaeologyinbulgaria.com/2016/06/05/archaeologists-discover-grave-of-medieval-bulgarian-princess-built-into-foundations-of-stone-church-near-botevgrad/.

Gomme, Alice Bertha, ed. "London Bridge." In *The Traditional Games of England, Scotland, and Ireland, with Tunes, Singing-rhymes, and Methods of Playing According to the Variants Extant and Recorded in Different Parts of the Kingdom* 1, 333-350. London: D. Nutt, 1894.

Gomme, Alice Bertha, ed. "Memoir on the Study of Children's Games." In *The Traditional Games of England, Scotland, and Ireland, with Tunes, Singing-rhymes, and Methods of Playing According to the Variants Extant and Recorded in Different Parts of the Kingdom* 2, 458-531. London: D. Nutt, 1898.

MacDermott, Mercia. *Bulgarian Folk Customs*. London: Jessica Kingsley Publishers, 1988.

Marinova, Eli. "Таласъм" ("Talasum"). March 23, 2018. https://eli-taro.com/5872/таласъм.

Milkova, Stiliana. "Walled-in Wives, Dragon's Brides, and Wild Fairies: Women in the Bulgarian Folk Tradition." In *Forum Folkloristika* 1 (2012).

Mirela.bg. "Village of Shishentsi." https://www.mirela.bg/en/off-plan-properties/village-of-Shishenci-zxc25q2595.html.

Nicoloff, Assen. *Bulgarian Folklore: Folk Beliefs, Customs, Folk Songs, Personal Names*. Cleveland: The Author, 1975.

Nikolova, Lily. "Таласъмите съществуват и хвърлят живи жаби в огъня" ("Talasums exist and cast live frogs in the fire"). February, 6, 2014. http://po-krasivi.net/23987/talasamite-sashtestvuvat-i-hvarlyat-zhivi-zhabi-v-oganya.html.

"Old World Building Customs and House Superstitions." In *Foreign-born; a bulletin of international service* 2, no. 7 (May 1921):199-201.

Petrova, Tanya. "5 Митологични Български Същества" ("5 Mytholgical Bulgarian Beings"). May 28, 2016. https://alist-bg.com/5-mitologichni-balgarski-sashtestva/.

St. Clair, S. G. B., and Charles A. Brophy. *Twelve Years' Study of the Eastern Question in Bulgaria: Being a Revised Edition of "A Residence in Bulgaria."* London: Chapman and Hall, 1877.

"Таласъми и полтъргайсти налазиха малкото село Шишенчи - с видео" ("Talasums and poltergeists attacked the small village of Schishenci – with video"). Circa April 26, 2012. http://skandalno.net/talasami-i-poltargajsti-nalaziha-mal-21271/.

Travelfinder.bg. "Kadin Bridge." https://travelfinder.bg/places/bulgaria/kyustendil/attractions/kadin-bridge/.

Wenska, Izabella. "Sacrifices among the Slavs: Between Archeological Evidence and 19th Century Folklore." In *Analecta Archaeologica Ressoviensia* 10 (2015):271-294.

Wikipedia. "April Uprising of 1876." https://en.wikipedia.org/wiki/April_Uprising_of_1876.

Wikipedia. "Bridge of Arta." https://en.wikipedia.org/wiki/Bridge_of_Arta.

Wikipedia. "Kőműves Kelemen." https://en.wikipedia.org/wiki/Kőműves_Kelemen.

Wikipedia. "London Bridge." https://en.wikipedia.org/wiki/London_Bridge.

Wikipedia. "London Bridge Is Falling Down." https://en.wikipedia.org/wiki/London_Bridge_Is_Falling_Down.

Wikipedia. "Meșterul Manole." https://en.wikipedia.org/wiki/Meșterul_Manole.

Wikipedia, Bulgarian. "Таласъм" ("Talasum"). https://bg.wikipedia.org/wiki/Таласъм.

Smok

Adámek, Jakub. "Had a miska mlieka: Slovenské verzie príbehov ATU 285 a ATU 672 (Serpent and Bowl of Milk: Slovak Verisions of ATU 285 and ATU 672 Tales)." In *Ročník* XV, (2018):55-62.

Arnaudov, Michail. Студии Върху Българските Обреди и Легенди, Vol II. (*Study of Bulgarian Rituals and Legends*.) Sofia: Bulgarian Academy of Science, 1972.

Aveela, Roneasa. *Light Love Rituals: Bulgarian Mythos, Legends, and Folklore*. Bendideia Publishing, 2015.

Bethedi. "Образът на змията в митологията" ("The Image of the serpent in mythology"). December 29, 2009. http://www.beinsadouno.com/board/forums/topic/8219-образът-на-змията-в-митологията.

Bulgaria National Radio. "St. Petka's Day." October 14, 2009. http://bnr.bg/en/post/100096982/st-petkas-day.

Dixon-Kennedy, Mike. *Encyclopedia of Russian & Slavic Myth and Legend*. Santa Barbara, CA: ABC-CLIO, Inc., 1998.

Emy. "Stopan and the House Serpent." May 6, 2006. https://folklore.livejournal.com/82201.html.

Ganeva, Dr. Radoslava. "Bulgarian Folk Costumes – Symbols and Traditions." *Bulgarian Diplomatic Review*, Supplement to Issue 3/2003, Year 3.

Georgieva, Ivanichka. Българска Народна Митология (*Bulgarian Folk Mythology*). Sofia: Science and Art, 1993.

Georgieva, Ivanichka. *Bulgarian Mythology*. Sofia: *Svyat* Publishers, 1985.

Ivantis, Linda J. *Russian Folk Belief*. Armonk, New York: M. E. Sharpe, Inc., 1992.

Konstantinova, Daniela, trans. "The serpent in traditional culture: a lethal enemy, a magical helper." October 16, 2013. http://bnr.bg/en/post/100217201/the-serpent-in-traditional-culture-a-lethal-enemy-a-magical-helper.

Kropej, Monika. *Supernatural Beings from Slovenian Myth and Folktales*. Ljubljana: Založba ZRC/ZRC Publishing, 2012.

Low, D. H., trans. *The Ballads of Marko Kraljević*. London: Cambidge University Press, 1922.

Máchal, Jan. "Slavic." In *The Mythology of All the Races*, vol. 3, edited by Herbert Louis Gray with consulting editor George Foot Moore, 217-330. Boston: Marshall Jones Company, 1918.

Mishev, Georgi. *Thracian Magic Past & Present*. London: BM Avalonia, 2012.

"Old World Building Customs and House Superstitions." In *Foreign-born; a bulletin of international service* 2, no. 7 (May 1921):199-201.

Petcova, Rossitsa, trans. "Beliefs and rituals related to snakes and cuckoos." March 3, 2012. http://bnr.bg/en/post/100145675/beliefs-and-rituals-related-to-snakes-and-cuckoos.

Petrova-Aiaa, Sonya. "Дарът на Смока - една преживяна легенда." ("The Gift of the Smok - a legend.") January 11, 2012. http://magicktarot.blog.bg/izkustvo/2012/01/11/daryt-na-smoka-edna-prejiviana-legenda.880738

Petrovitch, Woislav M. "Animals' Language." In *Hero Tales and Legends of the Serbians*, 230-235. New York: Stokes, 1915.

Ralston, William. *The Songs of the Russian People, as Illustrative of Slavonic Mythology and Russian Social Life*, 2nd. ed. London: Ellis & Green, 1872.

Stamenov, Ivan. "Тракийско наследство в българския фолклор (11): Образ и същност на стопана" ("Thracian heritage in Bulgarian folklore (11): Image and nature of the stopan"). June 19, 2016. http://www.otizvora.com/2016/06/7913.

Strickland, W.W. "The White Snake." In *South Slavonic Folk-lore Stories*, 46-47. London: Forder, 1899.

Trumbull, H. Clay. *The Threshold Covenant; or, The Beginning of Religious Rites*. New York: Charles Scribner's Sons, c1896.

Wikipedia. "Karel Jaromír Erben." https://en.wikipedia.org/wiki/Karel_Jaromír_Erben.

Wikipedia. "Prince Marko." https://en.wikipedia.org/wiki/Prince_Marko.

Bannik

Avitohol. "Славянски митични същества" ("Slavic mythical beings"). June 9, 2007. http://bulgariancastles.com/bg/phpbbforum/viewtopic.php?f=53&t=100.

Brasier, Zachery. "10 Weird Beings From Slavic Mythology And Folklore." April 5, 2016. http://listverse.com/2016/04/05/10-weird-beings-from-slavic-mythology-and-folklore/.

Color-mir.com. "Red Rowan in Slavic mythology." https://color-mir.com/red-rowan-in-slavic-mythology/.

Cross, Anthony. *In the Land of the Romanovs*. https://books.openedition.org/obp/2366?lang=en.

Eugene Cat. "Банник" ("Bannik"). http://www.bestiary.us/bannik.

Diechkoff, Cyril H., Rev. "Mythological Beings in Gaelic Folklore." In *Transactions of the Gaelic Society of Inverness* 29, 235-258. Inverness: Northern Counties Newspaper and Printing and Publishing Co. Ltd., 1922.

Dushakova, Natalía S. "Specifics of the Traditional Culture of the Old Believers of Moldova and Southern Ukraine: Dwelling Practices." *Anthropology & Archeology of Eurasia* 52, no. 1 (Summer 2013):22-38.

Galeotti, Mark. *Mythic Russia: Heroism and Adventure in the Land of the Firebird*. Firebird Productions, 2006, 2010.

Graham, Stephen. *Undiscovered Russia*. London: John Lane, 1912.

Ivantis, Linda J. *Russian Folk Belief*. Armonk, New York: M. E. Sharpe, Inc., 1992.

Kaldera, Raven. "Fire and Water: Sauna Purification." 2005. http://www.northernshamanism.org/fire-and-water-sauna-purification.html.

Kennard, Howard Percy. *The Russian Peasant*. Philadelphia: J.B. Lippincott Company, 1908.

Kezina, Darya. "4 unusual Russian banya rites that are still practiced today." June 13, 2015. https://www.rbth.com/arts/2015/06/13/4_unusual_russian_banya_rites_that_are_still_practiced_today_46839.html.

Kośnik, Konrad. "Functional significance of the Slavic bestiary." In M. Danielewski, RT Tomczak (ed.), *Discovering Central Europe - from mythology to reality*, 13-24. Poznań: Institute of History of Adam Mickiewicz University, 2016.

Krasheninnikova, Yulia. "Magic Beliefs and Practices of Holy Thursday in the Modern Tradition of the Peasant Population of the Russian North (based on materials of the XXI century)." In *The Ritual Year 10: Magic in Rituals and Rituals in Magic*, 547-556. Edited by Tatiana Minniyakhmetova and Kamila Velkoborská, Innsbruck: Tartu, 2015.

Lopatin, Ivan A. "Origin of the Native American Steam Bath." *American Anthropologist, New Series* 62, no. 6 (1960):977-93. http://www.jstor.org/stable/667595.

Máchal, Jan. "Slavic." In *The Mythology of All the Races*, vol. 3, edited by Herbert Louis Gray with consulting editor George Foot Moore, 217-330. Boston: Marshall Jones Company, 1918.

O'Mahony, John. "The Ultimate Guide to the Russian Banya." November 25, 2016. http://news.ifmo.ru/en/features/life_in_russia/news/6232/.

Paciorek, Andrew L. *Black Earth: A Field Guide to the Slavic Otherworld*. Durham, U.K.: Blurb.com, 2017.

Rose, Carol. *Spirits, Fairies, Gnomes, and Goblins: an Encyclopedia of the Little People*. Santa Barbara, California: ABC-CLIO, Inc. 1996.

Ryan, W. F. *The Bathhouse at Midnight: An Historical Survey of Magic and Divination in Russia*. University Park, PA: The Pennsylvania State University Press, 1999.

Tolstoy, Leo. *War and Peace*. Translated by Nathan Haskell Dole. New York: T.Y. Crowell & Co., c1889.

Warner, Elizabeth. *Russian Myths*. Austin: University of Texas Press, 2002.

Whishaw, Frederick. *The Romance of the Woods*. London: Longmans Green & Co., 1895.

Wikipedia. "Fred Whishaw." https://en.wikipedia.org/wiki/Fred_Whishaw.

Wikipedia. "Olga of Kiev." https://en.wikipedia.org/wiki/Olga_of_Kiev.

Wikipedia. "Stephen Graham (author)." https://en.wikipedia.org/wiki/Stephen_Graham_(author).

Wikipedia, Russian. "Банник" ("Bannik"). https://ru.wikipedia.org/wiki/Банник.

Zavyalova, Maria. "Mythological Character in Spells: Latvian 'Saint Maidens'–Skin Sores." In *Oral Charms in Structural and Comparative Light*. Proceedings of the Conference of the International Society for Folk Narrative Research's (ISFNR) Committee on Charms, Charmers and Charming. 27–29th October 2011, Moscow. Moscow, 2011:159-165.

Ovinnik

Alice. "Slavic Folklore II: Urban Spirits, Demons, and Creatures." June 1, 2012. http://nokkandmyling.blogspot.com/2012/06/slavic-folklore-ii-household-spirits.html.

First Catholic Slovak Union. "Žatva and Dožinky – The Slovak Harvest and Harvest Festivals." September 26, 2016. https://www.fcsu.com/community/zatva-and-dozinky-the-slovak-harvest-and-harvest-festivals/.

Galeotti, Mark. *Mythic Russia: Heroism and Adventure in the Land of the Firebird*. Firebird Productions, 2006, 2010.

Gordon, Ernest B. *Russian Prohibition*. Westerville, Ohio: American Issue Pub. Co., 1916.

Green, Garry. "Slavic Pagan World." http://www.rodnovery.ru/attachments/article/526/slavic-pagan-world.pdf.

Korshunov, Gennady. "Евник" ("Yevnik"). http://www.bestiary.us/evnik.

Levkievskaya, E.E. and A. A. Plotnikova. "Овин" ("Barn"). https://sites.google.com/site/kokorinva/Home/o/ovin.

Pathfinderwiki. "Beastiary 5." https://pathfinderwiki.com/wiki/Bestiary_5.

Pathfinderwiki. "Pathfinder Roleplaying Game." https://pathfinderwiki.com/wiki/Pathfinder_Roleplaying_Game.

Ralston, William. *The Songs of the Russian People, as Illustrative of Slavonic Mythology and Russian Social Life*, 2nd. ed. London: Ellis & Green, 1872.

Ryan, W. F. *The Bathhouse at Midnight: An Historical Survey of Magic and Divination in Russia*. University Park, PA: The Pennsylvania State University Press, 1999.

Serbian Irish. "Bogovo gumno – God's threshing floor." August 12, 2014. http://oldeuropeanculture.blogspot.com/2014/08/bogovo-gumno-gods-threshing-floor.html.

Serbian Irish. "Stone circles on mountain Devica." July 18, 2014. http://oldeuropeanculture.blogspot.com/2014/07/stone-circles-on-mountain-devica.html.

Sidorenko, Tatyana. "Вьставка 'Жэвжик, Ёуник и Другие Герои Белорусских Сказок, Мифов и Легенд'. Гомель" ("The Exibition 'Zhevzhik, Eunik and Other Heroes of Belarusian Fairy Tales, Myths and Legends'. Gomel"). February 11, 2017. https://anonimusi.livejournal.com/627532.html.

Wikipedia. "Ovinnik." https://en.wikipedia.org/wiki/Ovinnik.

Wikipedia, Russian. "Ёвник" ("Yovnik"). https://ru.wikipedia.org/wiki/Ёвник.

Wikipedia, Russian. "Овинник" ("Ovinnik"). https://ru.wikipedia.org/wiki/Овинник.

Dvorovoi

Adonyeva, Svetlana, and Laura J. Olson. "Interpreting the Past, Postulating the Future: Memorate as Plot and Script among Rural Russian Women." *Journal of Folklore Research* 48, no. 2 (2011):133-166.

Alice. "Slavic Folklore II: Urban Spirits, Demons, and Creatures." June 1, 2012. http://nokkandmyling.blogspot.com/2012/06/slavic-folklore-ii-household-spirits.html.

Bestiary.us. "Дворовой" ("Dvorovoy"). http://www.bestiary.us/dvorovoy.

Diechkoff, Cyril H., Rev. "Mythological Beings in Gaelic Folklore." In *Transactions of the Gaelic Society of Inverness* 29, 235-258. Inverness: Northern Counties Newspaper and Printing and Publishing Co. Ltd., 1922.

Dixon-Kennedy, Mike. *Encyclopedia of Russian & Slavic Myth and Legend*. Santa Barbara, CA: ABC-CLIO, Inc., 1998.

Dushakova, Natalía S. "Specifics of the Traditional Culture of the Old Believers of Moldova and Southern Ukraine: Dwelling Practices." *Anthropology & Archeology of Eurasia* 52, no. 1 (Summer 2013):22-38.

Harrison, William Henry. *Rifts in the Veil*. London: W. H. Harrison, 1878.

Henningsen, C. F. *The White Slave; or, The Russian Peasant Girl*, vol. 1. London: H. Colburn, 1845.

Henningsen, C. F. *The White Slave; or, The Russian Peasant Girl*, vol. 2. London: H. Colburn, 1845.

Herbert, Agnes. *Casuals in the Caucasus; the Diary of a Sporting Holiday*. London: John Lane, 1912.

Hoffman, Wickham. *Leisure Hours in Russia*. London: G. Bell and Sons, 1883.

Kennard, Howard Percy. *The Russian Peasant*. Philadelphia: J.B. Lippincott Company, 1908.

Máchal, Jan. "Slavic." In *The Mythology of All the Races*, vol. 3, edited by Herbert Louis Gray with consulting editor George Foot Moore, 217-330. Boston: Marshall Jones Company, 1918.

Ralston, William. *The Songs of the Russian People, as Illustrative of Slavonic Mythology and Russian Social Life*, 2nd. ed. London: Ellis & Green, 1872.

Slavs. "Дворовой - брат Домового" ("Dvorovoi – Brother of the Domovoi"). July 14, 2013.
http://slavyanskaya-kultura.ru/slavic/gods/dvorovoi-brat-domovogo.html.

Stevens, Thomas. *Through Russia on a Mustang*. New York: Cassell Publishing Company, 1891.

Wikipedia. "Agnes Herbert." https://en.wikipedia.org/wiki/Agnes_Herbert.

Wikipedia. "Caucasus." https://en.wikipedia.org/wiki/Caucasus.

Wikipedia. "Charles Frederick Henningsen."
https://en.wikipedia.org/wiki/Charles_Frederick_Henningsen.

Wikipedia, Russian. "Дворовой" ("Dvorovoi"). https://ru.wikipedia.org/wiki/Дворовой.

Hovanets

Buiskyh, Julia. "Домовик у Традиційних Віруваннях Українців: Походження Образу" ("A Hovanets (House-spirit) in Traditional Beliefs of Ukrainians: The Character Origin"). *Ethnic History of European Peoples*.
http://shron1.chtyvo.org.ua/Buiskykh_Yuliia/Domovyk_u_tradytsiinykh_viruvanniakh_ukraintsiv_pokhodzhennia_obrazu.pdf.

Cat, Eugene. "Клобук" ("Klobuk"). https://www.bestiary.us/klobuk.

"Домовикъ въ галицко-русскихъ вѣрованіяхъ" ("Domovik in the Galician-Russian languages"). Copied from *The Living Antiquity* 2, year VII, 1897. Found on https://sites.google.com/site/kokorinva/Home/h/hovanec.

GhostOfCommunism. "Вкратце о домашних духах (некоторых)" ("In brief about home spirits (some)"). July 23, 2017.
https://pikabu.ru/story/vkrattse_o_domashnikh_dukhakh_nekotoryikh_5212489.

Hoffman, W.F. "Chowaniec – Penc." October 18, 2009.
http://www.polishroots.org/Resources/SurnameSearch/DNNArticleArticleView/tabid/353/smid/742/ArticleID/72/reftab/351/t/Chowaniec---Penc/Default.aspx.

Kreslav, Vitaliy. "Хованець (Домовик) в Народних Віруваннях Карпат і Підгір'я" ("Hovanets (Domovik) in the People's Beliefs of the Carpathians and Podgorie"). September 30, 2013.
https://uamodna.com/articles/hovanecj-domovyk-v-narodnyh-viruvannyah-karpat-i-pidgirya/.

Kropej, Monika. *Supernatural Beings from Slovenian Myth and Folktales*. Ljubljana: Založba ZRC/ZRC Publishing, 2012.

Ksaverov, Sergiy. "Хованец" ("Hovanets"). http://www.bestiary.us/vyhovanec/.

Levkovych, Nadiya. "ТРАДИЦІЙНІ УЯВЛЕННЯ БОЙКІВ ПРО ДУШІ ПОМЕРЛИХ ДІТЕЙ (За польовими матеріалами)" ("Traditional Images of Boikos Regarding the Souls of Dead Children (Based on field materials)"). *Ser. History* 47 (2012):236-252.

Slaskyov, V.V. "Хованец" ("Chovanets"). http://www.antmir.ru/html/h/hovanec.html.

Ukraine.com. "Proverbs From Ukraine's Language." http://www.ukraine.com/proverbs/.

Vorogeja. "Духи-деньгоносцы." ("Spirit-money-bringers.") October 19, 2016.
https://chernayamagiya.com/forum/index.php?topic=25413.0.

End Notes

_____

Kikimora

[1] Planeta.by, "Кикимора - Болотная или Домашняя?"

[2] Georgievtrifon, "Кикимора."

[3] Dixon-Kennedy, *Russian & Slavic Myth and Legend*, 73.

[4] Rose, *Spirits, Fairies, Gnomes, and Goblins*, 89.

[5] Slavic Folklore and World Dreaming, Mentioned in *The Space of Love*, Book 3, by Vladimir Megre in his "Ringing Cedars" series.

[6] Henderson, *Olga*, 91.

[7] Russian stoves are massive, and are used for cooking and heating the home. You can see one at https://ru.wikipedia.org/wiki/Русская-печь.

[8] Planeta.by, "Кикимора - Болотная или Домашняя?"

[9] Máchal, "Slavic," 228.

[10] Ralston, *Songs of the Russian People*, 133-134.

[11] Planeta.by, "Кикимора - Болотная или Домашняя?"

[12] Georgievtrifon, "Кикимора."

[13] Planeta.by, "Кикимора - Болотная или Домашняя?"

[14] Russian Wikipedia, "Kikimora."

[15] From Konakov, "Poltergeist in Folklore."

Domovoi

[16] Esoterx, "Slavic Domovoi."

[17] The Pagan Files, "Slavic Household Deity."

[18] Alice, "Slavic Folklore II."

[19] Ivantis, *Russian Folk Belief*, 52.

[20] After the Slavic people had been Christianized, the one to cast out the demons became the archangel Michael.

[21] Ralston, *Songs of the Russian People*," 119.

[22] Whishaw, *Romance of the Woods*, 188.
Footnote 7 in Ralston, *Songs of the Russian People*, p. 120, notes that the word *Roditeli* for "ancestors" comes from *rodit', razhdat'* meaning "to beget," and that the term applied to anyone in the family who had died, even their own children.

[23] Procopius's *History of the Wars* vol. 7, as quoted in Vlahović, *Two Hundred*, 36.

[24] Ivantis, *Russian Folk Belief*, 14, 15.

[25] Baring, *Mainsprings of Russia*, 54-55.

[26] Dixon-Kennedy, *Russian & Slavic Myth and Legend*, 73.

[27] Nagy, "Material Culture," 20. In 1992, the author conducted a study among the Vasiugan Khanty in Siberia. Although the people called this spirit *Kat juŋk*, the author goes on to describe how television transformed the image of the spirit into the representation of the Domovoi.

[28] Kennard, *Russian Peasant*, 62.

[29] Ivanits, *Russian Folk Belief*, 169-170.

[30] Ryan, *Bathhouse at Midnight*, 43.

[31] Kennard, *Russian Peasant*, 63-64.

[32] Video and image copyright Lily Goodchild and Nicola Everill, Directors, "Domovoi and Kikimora," produced at Staffordshire University, May 21, 2013, https://vimeo.com/66619155. (Used with permission of the creators.)

Inspired by Slavic mythology. A film about scavenger spirits and the child who spies on them.

[33] Blackwood, "Holy Russia," 696.

[34] Comment on All Top 5s, "Top 5 Slavic Folklore Creatures."

[35] Ivanits, *Russian Folk Belief*, 169.

[36] Baring, *Mainsprings of Russia*, 55.

[37] Snow, "The Domovoi."

[38] Ralston, *Songs of the Russian People*, 130.

[39] Ralston, *Songs of the Russian People*, 135.

[40] Ivanits, *Russian Folk Belief*, 170.

[41] Ijepojevic, "Slavic Religions." Note: In another chapter, you'll learn about the Dvorovoi, the courtyard spirit. Sometimes, the Domovoi and the Dvorovoi are considered the same; other times, they are said to be different entities.

[42] See "A Peasant's Home" sidebar for information about sleeping on the stove.

[43] Ralston, *Songs of the Russian People*, 124.

[44] Whishaw, on p. 195 of *Romance of the Woods*, comments: "In this ceremony there seems to occur that confusion between the *domovoy* and the spirits of the departed [*rodítyelui*]." An in-depth distinction between the two is not the focus of this book.

[45] Mansikka, "Demons and Spirits (Slavic)," 627.

[46] Stewart, *Provincial Russia*, 119.

[47] Boykis, "Our Domovoi. Americans." Reprinted with permission of the author.

[48] Kennard, *Russian Peasant*, 64.

[49] G.N. Zakharchenko, "Rodil' naia obriadnost'," *Lipovane: istoriia i kul' turarusskikh-taroobriadtsev* (Odessa, 2007, no. 4), 85, as quoted in Dushakova, "Old Believers,"34.

[50] Henderson, *Olga*, 137-138.

[51] Morgan, "Customs of the Ossetes," 390.

[52] Stevens, *Russia on a Mustang*, 294.

[53] Stevens, *Russia on a Mustang*, 295.

[54] *The Spectator*, "Death Week," 767.

[55] Ralston, *Songs of the Russian People*, 134.

[56] Kistanova, "1st of April."

[57] Hoffman, *Leisure Hours*, 19.

[58] Rodakiewicz, "Foreign Holidays," 262.

[59] Sinnett, *Life of Madame Blavatsky*, 14.

[60] Kennan, "Ritual Murder," 529-530.

[61] Kennan, "Ritual Murder," 530.

[62] Mannherz, "Mysterious knocks," 6.

[63] Quoted from *The London Daily News*, in "Miscellany," *Appletons' Journal*, 800.

[64] Sinnett, *Life of Madame Blavatsky*, 14.

[65] Sinnett, *Life of Madame Blavatsky*, 70, footnote 1.

[66] Sinnett, *Life of Madame Blavatsky*, 67-70.

[67] Mannherz, "Mysterious knocks," 1, as reported in 'Kartofel'naia kolonada,' Volzhskii vestnik, 16 December 1884: 3.

[68] Petrovo-Solovovo, *Psychical Research*, 58.

[69] Petrovo-Solovovo, *Psychical Research*, 58-60. I have taken the liberty to break long paragraphs into smaller chunks to conform to today's writing style.

[70] I have omitted a small section that talks about Christians and Jews, and, although relevant to the story, it adds nothing to the story about the Domovoi.

Stopan

71 Arnaudov, Студии Върху Българските Обреди и Легенди.

72 Stamenov, "Тракийско наследство" (11).

73 MacDermott, *Bulgarian Folk Customs*, 135.

74 Arnaudov, Студии Върху Българските Обреди и Легенди, 255.

75 Ganeva, "Bulgarian Folk Costumes," 5.

76 MacDermott, *Bulgarian Folk Customs*, 138.

77 MacDermott, *Bulgarian Folk Customs*, 137-138.

78 Details of this ceremony come from Mishev's *Thracian Magic*, 248-251, and from the original source: Arnaudov, Студии Върху Българските Обреди и Легенди.

79 Stamenov, "Тракийско наследство" (10).

80 Stamenov, "Тракийско наследство" (10).

81 References to this ceremony come from Mishev, *Thracian Magic*, 252-259.

82 Low, "Marko Kraljević," 21, note 3.

83 Mishev, *Thracian Magic*, 259.

84 Ganeva, "Bulgarian Folk Costumes," 8.

85 This is the spiritual name of Peter Deunov, a Bulgarian philosopher and spiritual teacher, who even today is fondly known as "the Master." He created the Universal White Brotherhood, which practices prayer, meditation, breathing exercises, yoga of nutrition, and paneurhythmy, which "is based on a deep knowledge of the Laws of energy, radiation, frequency and the correlation between tone, form, movement, color, geometry and an idea. Movements correspond to tones, and as we dance the concepts of giving, receiving and renewal, we allow the Earth and Cosmos to do the same." (Paneurhythmy.us, "ABOUT Pan-Eu-Rhythmy.")

86 Douno, "X. Други формули."

87 Details of the ritual come from Bachinovo Learning Center, "Тракийско мегалитно светилище."

88 From Stamenov, "Тракийско наследство" (10).

Talasum

89 Bulgarian Wikipedia, "Таласъм."

90 Wenska, "Sacrifices among the Slavs," 284-285.

91 St. Clair, *Eastern Question in Bulgaria*, 34.

92 St. Clair, *Eastern Question in Bulgaria*, 34.

93 Wenska, "Sacrifices among the Slavs," 286.

94 Dikov, "Grave of Medieval Bulgarian Princess."

95 Wikipedia, "Bridge of Arta."

96 Wenska, "Sacrifices among the Slavs," 286.

97 Wikipedia, "Meșterul Manole."

98 Wikipedia, "Kőműves Kelemen."

99 Travelfinder.bg, "Kadin Bridge."

100 Milkova, "Walled-in Wives."

101 Milkova, "Walled-in Wives."

102 Milkova, "Walled-in Wives."

103 Milkova, "Walled-in Wives."

104 You can read about many of these, as well as other Bulgarian holidays, in Aveela, *Light Love Rituals*.

105 Apostle, "Духове и привидения." Article comment.

106 Nikolova, "Таласъмите съществуват."

107 Story from "Таласъми и полтъргайсти."

108 To discover more about the village, visit this page: https://www.mirela.bg/en/off-plan-properties/village-of-Shishenci-zxc25q2595.html.

Smok

[109] Ralston, *Songs of the Russian People*, 124.

[110] Máchal, "Slavic," 247.

[111] Petcova, "Snakes and cuckoos." For more about this and other rituals practiced on Blagovets, see Aveela, *Light Love Rituals*, 58-71.

[112] Georgieva, *Bulgarian Mythology*, 69.

[113] Kropej, *Supernatural Beings*, 104-105. From Jakob Kelemina, *Bajke in pripovedke slovenskega ljudstva*. Celje: Družba sv. Mohorja, 135-136, written by Novak in 1858.

[114] Georgieva, *Bulgarian Mythology*, 50. You can read more about Todorovden in Aveela, *Light Love Rituals*, 54-57.

[115] Adámek, "Had a miska mlieka," 58.

[116] Adámek, "Had a miska mlieka," 57-58.

[117] Adámek, "Had a miska mlieka," 58.

[118] Adámek, "Had a miska mlieka," 57.

[119] Aveela, *Light Love Rituals*, 105.

[120] Mishev, *Thracian Magic*, 235, note 430.

[121] Ivanits, *Russian Folk Belief*, 34.

[122] Low, *Ballads of Marko Kraljević*, 116.

[123] Comment in Petrova-Aiaa, "Дарът на Смока."

Bannik

[124] Ryan, *Bathhouse at Midnight*, 51.

[125] Russian Wikipedia, "Банник."

[126] Eugene Cat, "Банник."

[127] Russian Wikipedia, "Банник."

[128] Eugene Cat, "Банник."

[129] Eugene Cat, "Банник."

[130] Ryan, *Bathhouse at Midnight*, 51.

[131] Rose, *Spirits, Fairies, Gnomes, and Goblins*, 32.

[132] Russian Wikipedia, "Банник."

[133] O'Mahony, "Guide to the Russian Banya."

[134] If you're not familiar with this song, you can find the lyrics here: http://www.carlinamerica.com/titles/titles.cgi?MODULE=LYRICS&ID=18&terms=splish%20splash.

[135] Ivanits, *Russian Folk Belief*, 46.

[136] Ryan, *Bathhouse at Midnight*, 75.

[137] Rose, *Spirits, Fairies, Gnomes, and Goblins*, 33.

[138] Tolstoy, *War and Peace* (IV, ch 11), 297.

[139] Zavyalova, "Mythological Character in Spells," 164.

[140] Krasheninnikova, "Holy Thursday," 549-550.

[141] Kaldera, "Sauna Purification."

[142] Eugene Cat, "Банник."

[143] Story translated and provided by Russian artist Dmitry Yakhovsky.

[144] Story translated and provided by Russian artist Dmitry Yakhovsky.

[145] Ivanits, *Russian Folk Belief*, 161.

[146] Kaldera, "Sauna Purification."

[147] Kezina, "4 unusual Russian banya rites."

Ovinnik

[148] Russian Wikipedia, "Овинник."

[149] Korshunov, "Евник."

[150] Wikipedia, "Ovinnik."

[151] Serbian Irish, "God's threshing floor."

[152] Serbian Irish, "Stone circles."

[153] Serbian Irish, "God's threshing floor."

[154] Sidorenko, "Белорусских Сказок, Мифов и Легенд."

[155] Russian Wikipedia, "Ёвник."

[156] Levkievskaya, "Овин."

[157] Levkievskaya, "Овин."

[158] Ryan, *Bathhouse at Midnight*, 105.

[159] Levkievskaya, "Овин."

[160] Gordon, *Russian Prohibition*, 29-30.

[161] Ralston, *Songs of the Russian People*, 157.

[162] Levkievskaya, "Овин."

[163] Levkievskaya, "Овин."

[164] You can find the list of creatures here: https://pathfinderwiki.com/wiki/Bestiary_5.

Dvorovoi

[165] Kennard, *The Russian Peasant*, 65.

[166] Bestiary.us, "Дворовой."

[167] Russian Wikipedia, "Дворовой."

[168] Adonyeva, "Interpreting the Past," 147.

[169] Slavs, "Дворовой - брат Домового."

[170] Slavs, "Дворовой - брат Домового."

[171] Ralston, *Songs of the Russian People*, 125.

[172] Bestiary.us, "Дворовой."

[173] Diechkoff, "Mythological Beings," 238.

[174] Ralston, *Songs of the Russian People*, 131.

[175] Ralston, *Songs of the Russian People*, 126.

[176] Ivanits, *Russian Folk Belief*, 55.

[177] Dixon-Kennedy, *Russian & Slavic Myth and Legend*, 73.

[178] Slavs, "Дворовой - брат Домового."

[179] Slavs, "Дворовой - брат Домового."

[180] Slavs, "Дворовой - брат Домового."

[181] Diechkoff, "Mythological Beings," 240.

[182] Dixon-Kennedy, *Russian & Slavic Myth and Legend*, 148.

[183] Adonyeva, "Interpreting the Past," 142-147. This interview took place in 2005. I have left out the commentary inserted in between the sections of dialog. The purpose here is to give testimony to what people believe and for you, as a reader, to become familiar with the spirits, not to analyze those beliefs. If you're interested in more, you can read the full article here: https://www.academia.edu/6922022/_Legend_Dialogue_and_Identity_The_Russian_Case.

Hovanets

[184] Ksaverov, "Хованец."

[185] Cat, "Клобук."

[186] Kropej, *Supernatural Beings*, 170.

[187] Buiskyh, "Домовик у Традиційних Віруваннях Українців."

[188] Kropej, *Supernatural Beings*, 171.

www.ingramcontent.com/pod-product-compliance
Lightning Source LLC
Chambersburg PA
CBHW042349030426
42336CB00025B/3424